Strategic Planning
and Forecasting

Strategic Planning and Forecasting

Political Risk and
Economic Opportunity

WILLIAM ASCHER

WILLIAM H. OVERHOLT

A Wiley-Interscience Publication
JOHN WILEY & SONS
New York • Chichester • Brisbane • Toronto • Singapore

Reproduction or translation of any part of this work
beyond that permitted by Section 107 or 108 of the
1976 United States Copyright Act without the permission
of the copyright owner is unlawful. Requests for
permission or further information should be addressed to
the Permissions Department, John Wiley & Sons, Inc.

This publication is designed to provide accurate and
authoritative information in regard to the subject
matter covered. It is sold with the understanding that
the publisher is not engaged in rendering legal, accounting,
or other professional service. If legal advice or other
expert assistance is required, the services of a competent
professional person should be sought. *From a Declaration
of Principles jointly adopted by a Committee of the
American Bar Association and a Committee of Publishers.*

Library of Congress Cataloging in Publication Data:

Ascher, William.
   Strategic planning and forecasting.

   "A Wiley-Interscience publication."
   Bibliography: p.
   Includes index.
   1. Forecasting.   2. Policy sciences.   3. Planning.
I. Overholt, William H.   II. Title.

H61.4.A82   1983   658.4'0355   83-10166
ISBN 0-471-87342-X

Printed in the United States of America

10 9 8 7 6 5 4 3 2 1

To
Herman Kahn
and
Harold D. Lasswell

Prefatory Note:
A Few Forecasts

We are gradually approaching, with the decadence of youth, a near proximity to a nation of madmen. By comparing the lunacy statistics of 1809 with those of 1909 . . . an insane world is looked forward to by me with a certainty in the not far distant future.

> Forbes, Winslow M.D. 1910, in Ralph L. Woods, "Prophets Can Be Right and Prophets Can Be Wrong," *American Legion'Magazine,* October 1966: 29.

In Germany, it was proven by experts that if trains went at the frightful speed of 15 miles an hour on the proposed Rothschild railroads, blood would spurt from the travelers' noses, mouths and ears, and also that the passengers would suffocate going through tunnels.

> E.C. Cirti, *Das Haus Rothschild in der Zeit seriner Blute, 1830–1871,* Leipzig, 1928. Translated by Lunn, Brian, and Beatrix as *Reign of the House of Rothschild,* New York (1928), pp. 77 and 94.

The abolishment of pain in surgery is a chimera. It is absurd to go on seeking it today. "Knife" and "pain" are two words in surgery that must forever be associated in the consciousness of the patient. To this compulsory combination we shall have to adjust ourselves.

> Alfred Velpeau, surgeon, 1839, on anesthesia, in Martin Gumpert, *Trail-Blazers on Science,* New York: Funk and Wagnalls (1936), p. 232.

That is the biggest fool thing we have ever done. . . . The bomb will never go off, and I speak as an expert in explosives.

> Statement by Admiral William Leahy when told about the atomic bomb. Harry S. Truman, *Memoirs, Vol. 1: Year of Decision,* Garden City: Doubleday (1955), p. 11.

I do not think there is the slightest chance of its [electricity] competing, in a general way, with gas. There are defects about the electric light which, unless some essential change takes place, must entirely prevent its application to ordinary lighting purposes.

> Remarks by Mr. Keates, "Minutes of Evidence Taken Before the Select Committee on Lighting and Electricity," in "Report from the Select Committee on Lighting by Electricity," London: House of Commons (1879), p. 146.

We hope that Professor Langley will not put his substantial greatness as a scientist in further peril by continuing to waste his time, and the money involved, in further airship experiments. Life is short, and he is capable of services to humanity incomparably greater than can be expected to result from trying to fly. . . . For students and investigators of the Langley type there are more useful experiments.

> *New York Times* editorial page, December 10, 1903.

The popular mind often pictures gigantic flying machines speeding across the Atlantic and carrying innumerable passengers in a way analogous to our modern steamships. . . . It seems safe to say that such ideas must be wholly visionary, and even if a machine would get across with one or two passengers the expense would be prohibitive to any but the capitalist who could own his own yacht.

> William H. Pickering (astronomer), quoted in Arthur C. Clarke, *Profiles of the Future*, New York: Harper and Row (1962), pp. 3–4.

If in thirty years we shall not have succeeded in reorganizing the world, it will inevitably relapse into barbarism.

> Alfred Nobel, inventor of dynamite, January 7, 1893.

On Statistics

The government is very keen on amassing statistics. They will collect them, add them, raise them to the nth power, take the cube root, and prepare wonderful diagrams. But you must never forget that every one of these figures comes in the first instance from the village watchman, who just puts down what he pleases.

> Sir Josiah Stamp, Inland Revenue Department, England (1896–1919).

The Law

"Persons pretending to forecast the future" shall be considered disorderly under Subdivision 3, Section 901 of the Criminal Code and liable to a fine of $250 and/or six months in prison.

Section 899, New York State Code of Criminal Procedure.

Preface

This book asks: how does one make forecasting useful? The answer requires movement beyond a tradition of studying forecasting primarily as a series of discrete mathematical methods. Forecasting must be studied not in isolation, but in the context of a policy-making process. The world's leading expert on regression analysis could, in practice, be almost useless to decision makers. Useful forecasting almost invariably involves: unholy mixes of different methods; interdisciplinary assumptions, processes, and outcomes; the need to address political phenomena, which are difficult to quantify; and coping in an organizational environment that determines what kinds of methods will be credible and acceptable.

Although study of the formal properties of individual methods is a valuable contribution to mathematics and an important discipline for any forecaster to master, it is only one facet of the job of a forecaster who hopes to influence decisions. We believe in that facet and try to summarize it and make some contributions to it. But what is important in this book is the emphasis on other facets. The theme of the book is that an exclusive emphasis on formal methods, particularly complex quantitative methods, will often prove self-defeating. The brilliantly successful student of formal methods will usually find him- or herself in the position of someone who has mastered the tongue twister "Peter Piper picked a peck of pickled peppers." The achievement is a source of great pride, but it is difficult to work it into a useful conversation.

Both of us found ourselves in this position upon completion of our formal training. Having recognized that forecasting is primarily a discipline that is intended to be useful to decision makers, we have devoted much of our intellectual efforts over the last decade to fashioning new approaches—approaches that went very much against the 1970s trend toward ever-greater emphasis on formal techniques. The present book is the third major product of these efforts. The first was William Ascher's *Forecasting: An Appraisal for Policy Makers and Planners* (Baltimore: Johns Hopkins University Press, 1978). The second was William H. Overholt's *Political Risk* (London: Euromoney Publications, 1982).

The present book is the culmination of a series of individual and collaborative efforts that developed while we worked as consultants to, or employees of, two major universities, a large number of corporations, several commercial banks, two investment firms, the World Bank, the U.S. Department of State, the Department of Defense, the Arms Control and Disarmament Agency, the National Security Council, the Council on International Economic Policy, various consulting and advisory firms, and some foreign governments. The book is intended to be useful to forecasters and planners in this whole range of organizations, and it is intended to provide a new perspective for scholars who study such organizations.

It is appropriate to locate this effort in relation to the central thrust of recent intellectual history in the social sciences: the behavioralist movement. The behavioralists taught two major lessons: first, the importance of studying actual human and institutional behavior, rather than just formal structures and legal relationships; and second, the value of formal quantitative methods of analysis. This book shows that pursuing quantification sometimes sacrifices the study of behavior. We affirm the importance of studying forecasting in the context of the actual behavior of people and institutions rather than in a formalistic fashion. In so doing, however, we show that formal quantitative methods have severe inherent limits and that an exclusive focus on formal quantitative methods has often led forecasters, and students of forecasting, to disregard the first and more important commandment of behavioralism.

To set forecasting in its own behavioral context, this book views forecasting as part of a larger decision-making process. It locates forecasting as one logical component of the decision-making or strategic-planning process. It analyzes the psychological and bureaucratic relationship between the forecaster and the decision maker. It identifies the properties of different analytic methods in the context of different purposes, resources, and organizational settings. It emphasizes the importance of political forecasting and the importance of political assumptions in nonpolitical forecasting—and shows how to interrelate political and nonpolitical factors. It offers an organizational approach to political forecasting that is systematic but nonquantitative. It recommends the use of systematic scenarios and an emphasis on forecasting as heuristics, rather than an excessive emphasis on predicting discrete outcomes. It makes recommendations for structuring the relationship between forecaster and decision maker, and for presenting the results of forecasts, in order to ensure maximum effective use of forecasting results.

Baltimore, Maryland
New York, New York   WILLIAM ASCHER
June 1983   WILLIAM H. OVERHOLT

Acknowledgments

In addition to those intellectual debts recognized in the notes, the authors want to acknowledge broader debts to the ideas of Harold D. Lasswell, Herman Kahn, and Ronald Brunner.

We are grateful for permission to use material in Chapter 4 on complex models previously published by William Ascher in *Policy Sciences* **13,** 3 (June 1981) and for material in Chapter 5 on the distinctiveness of political forecasting published in the *Journal of Forecasting* **1,** 3 (1983). A version of Chaper 8 was published by William H. Overholt in *American Behavioral Scientist* **20,** 4 (March-April 1977). Chapter 1 on forecasting and planning was originally a Hudson Institute paper by William H. Overholt. A subsequent version, with slight revisions, was printed by the military team which had originally contracted for the paper, with the team listed, military-style, as the author. Still another version was presented by Overholt as a paper for the annual meeting of the Military Operations Research Society in Monterey, California, December 1977. While the larger part of Chapter 10 draws on unpublished research by William Ascher, key sections draw on "Mexico and the Politics of Financial Collapse," *Global Political Assessment, 14* (edited by Overholt), which in turn relied heavily on ideas from Multinational Strategies, Inc., and from John Purcell.

Elaboration of some of the purposes of political forecasting, of aspects of the organizational approach to political analysis advocated here, and of many practical managerial concepts are contained in William H. Overholt, *Political Risk,* published in London by Euromoney Publications in 1982.

The authors are extremely grateful for the assistance and patience of Stephen Kippur, who served as the Wiley editor for this book. We are very grateful to Arlyne Lerner, who typed draft after draft of the book with great skill under intense pressure of time.

W.A.
W.H.O.

Contents

PART 2.   FORECASTING METHODS

Figures and Tables

Strategic Planning
and Forecasting

Introduction

When the Shah of Iran was deposed, there was an almost immediate post mortem to determine why the many intelligence operations of the United States and other Western governments had not predicted this outcome. Private corporations, many with vast holdings in Iran, were similarly shocked. Charges were leveled by practically everyone against practically everyone else (including academics) for having "missed" the political turnabout of the decade. Shortly thereafter, the Nicaraguan government under Anastasio Somoza fell, leaving American policy makers in the worst possible position: neither supporting Somoza adequately to keep him in power, nor abandoning him in time to avert the animosity of the new Sandinista government. Regardless of whether this debacle was caused by the inadequacy of predictions offered by the political analysts or the unwillingness of the policy makers to heed them, there was clearly something amiss in the interaction of analysis and decision. Not since Fidel Castro had announced his commitment to communism had the academic, intelligence, and business communities seemed so inept at predicting critical outcomes—outcomes that seemed, at least after the fact, to have been obvious.

The political analysts' obvious answer to these embarrassments is that great quantities of political analyses, projections, and dire warnings simply sit on the shelves, while corporate executives and government officials fly by the seats of their pants. This is true, but it is as much an indictment of the political forecaster's failure to communicate as it is of the policy maker's failure to make use of the forecasts. It is also true that decision makers receive numerous contradictory forecasts.

Since the developments in Iran, the level of resources devoted to political, economic, and social forecasting has risen impressively. Most major corporations have established or increased their staffs of analysts and planners. Partly because of regulations imposed by the Treasury Department, political risk operations in major U.S. banks with overseas operations became the rule. Research institutions formerly specializing in pure economic or national security research have entered the fields of political

1

and social research, attempting to focus on "policy-relevant" questions. There have been parallel developments in the U.S. government; the Departments of Defense and State and, of course, the Central Intelligence Agency have instituted both cyclical and sporadic political forecasting exercises, both in-house and contracted out.

This is not the first time that forecasting has become more popular just when it seemed to have failed most miserably. In the early and mid-1970s, when economic forecasting was extremely poor at predicting how the new, energy-expensive economic structure would behave, subscriptions to econometric forecasting services skyrocketed. For political forecasting, which is the new wave in social analysis, the same respectability that economic forecasting has gained (perhaps undeservedly) is still elusive. Formalized econometric analyses have lost much of their charisma at the top of the corporate and economic ranks, even for forecasting next quarter's economic growth. While "good" forecasting and analysis are acknowledged as vital in practically all circles, the credibility of political forecasting seems to be at an all-time low.

In part, this results from the many misconceptions about what social—and especially political—forecasting is and what it ought to be. Later in this introduction, some of these misconceptions are reviewed in an effort to clarify the appropriate goals and approaches to political forecasting. But the lack of respectability and credibility are also caused by justifiable skepticism toward some of the methods widely employed by political forecasters. This volume seeks to familiarize the reader with the techniques of social-economic-political forecasting, to steer the political forecaster into the most rewarding approaches, and to discuss the interactions between forecaster and policy maker, which ultimately determine whether forecasts are properly used.

CRITERIA OF POLITICAL FORECASTING

What is meant by calling an approach "rewarding"? This is a crucial question for the quality of the planning and policy-making process, because there are markedly different approaches that seem to maximize "scholarly" rewards but are inappropriate for enhancing the policy-making process. In university circles there has been a flowering of methodological fads that have become popular for reasons not associated with policy issues. The behavioralist movement gained broad and well-deserved influence as an effort by political scientists to understand the real behavior of individuals and institutions instead of viewing reality through the myopic lens of formal legal arrangements. Yet a subsidiary outgrowth of the behavioralist movement has been the insistence that social and political analysis must ape the quantitative techniques of economics (regression analysis, factor analysis, path analysis), usually in their most primitive forms. All too often this has meant a fixation upon some narrow quantitative indices (for example, the Gini index of inequality) and a set of reductionist propositions (for example, inequality causes frustration, which causes anger, which causes social upheaval), which are then marketed to business and government as if they constituted broad theory rather than a single interesting but narrow line of inquiry. In other words, methodological fads frequently dominate concerns about validity and breadth.

These criticisms of the methodological excesses (or distortions) of the behavioralist approach are not new; much of sociology and political science today is "post-behavioralist," rejecting "number crunching" in favor of a more balanced combination of quantification, case study research, and qualitative theory. The problem lies in the apparent time lag between this development in sociology and political science and the vogue that has stricken some practitioners of political and social forecasting, perhaps because of the popularity (though, interestingly enough, not the predictive success) of econometric forecasting. For the present, then, much of the forecasting that claims to be scientific, and which is perceived by its users as scientific, actually is unreliable and focused on the wrong issues.

On the other hand, many efforts at forecasting, especially political forecasting, which seem to offer an alternative to quantitative excess, have been distressingly ad hoc and unsystematic. "Popular" political forecasting has been an informal exercise, whether produced for entertainment (as in science fiction) or for information (as in journalism). When addressing general audiences whose specific needs are minimal, unknown, or very mixed, there is little reason to demand or expect the political forecast to be more than unsystematic speculation.

However, when the rewards of forecasting are determined by their utility to policy making—which is the criterion we apply throughout this book—neither of these approaches is adequate. Practical political and social forecasting is too important for business and government decision making to make do with political predictions that are not consciously designed for the needs of the policy maker. Fortunately, the apparent choice between scientism and off-the-cuff journalism is a false one. There is indeed a middle ground, based on the fact that one can be systematic without being narrowly quantitative. The key to sensitive analysis, and hence forecasting, is a theoretical understanding of political and social dynamics that is offered neither by quantification nor by unstructured intuition. This is elaborated in this book's chapters on methods and the case studies presented. There is also a middle ground for the focus and formatting of political forecasts, other than the stark choices between quantified results and ad hoc discursiveness. The chapters on methods and the presentation of political forecasts seek this middle ground as well.

If we are to depart from the typical focus of most books on forecasting, namely the intricacies of applying particular techniques, and instead focus on how the forecaster and the policy maker can get together, we must assess the behaviors of both. In the chapters on planning and on the needs and perspectives of policy makers, we address the characteristic needs and behaviors of the forecast producer and the forecast user.

THE SCOPE OF POLITICAL FORECASTING

As the newest wave in social forecasting, political forecasting is particularly subject to misconceptions. The image of the political forecaster as one who predicts when revolutions will occur acknowledges only a small part of the full scope of political forecasting. In most instances this is not even the most important role for the political forecaster, considering the rarity of major revolutions. As an initial step toward understanding the job of the forecaster and the relationship between forecaster and policy maker, we review here the characteristic tasks of the political forecaster.[1]

Understanding the System

At first glance, part of the demand on the political forecaster does not seem to be forecasting at all. The political forecaster or analyst is often called upon to provide an understanding of how a political system operates. Sometimes this is mundane information about the "nuts and bolts" of government operations: which ministries make particular decisions, who gives out import licenses, which individuals' opinions count on key issues, and so forth. Sometimes it concerns an understanding of the political dynamics of the country, for example, to aid a business executive or government official involved in negotiations with a particular country's officials or business people. The forecast user may benefit more from the contextual understanding of the country derived from the political forecaster's report than from the political forecasts themselves. In such cases, the political forecasting exercise and presentation are vehicles for conveying information about how the system works. This function does in fact entail actual political forecasting, insofar as the variability of government procedures requires the forecaster to state whether the political system's past behavior indicates the way it will continue to behave.

Anticipating Governments' Policy Decisions

Probably the most prevalent focus of political forecasting, for both business and government uses, is the prediction of the policies to be pursued by a given country's government. The host country's policies toward profit repatriation, taxation of multinational corporations, wages, employment of local rather than expatriate managers, local ownership participation, and expropriation are typically of crucial importance to businesses operating in other countries. To ensure that auspicious investment conditions are not likely to change after the investment has been made, top management is naturally anxious to determine the likelihood of: (1) replacement of that government with another government more hostile to foreign investment, or (2) a turnabout in the existing government's position on the terms of foreign investment. In Brazil, for example, many companies made huge and virtually irreversible investment commitments while the Brazilian government's regulations on foreign investment were quite favorable. In the late 1970s and early 1980s, however, Brazilian regulation of foreign investors (such as limits on the parent company's right to charge royalties for technology transfer) have become considerably more strict. This was a predictable policy change considering the acuteness of the sentiment against foreign investment in some Brazilian circles and the growing awareness of Brazilian leaders that many foreign investors had sunk costs so large that they could not easily withdraw.

Government policy makers are typically interested in other governments' policies in the areas of foreign affairs, defense, trade, and the treatment of foreign enterprises and foreign nationals. Again, the forecast user will be interested in assessments of policy changes brought about by regime changes, by shifts within the same regime, or by changing social pressures on the regime. Turnabouts in the regime's position are particularly complicated to forecast because the forecast user's own actions may have an influence on these changes, if the forecast user formulates his or her own nations' policies vis-à-vis the other country. This complication is most usefully handled through conditional forecasts, a format consisting of several different projections keyed to different scenarios of the policy options available to the forecaster's specific audience.

Because the choice of policies is influenced by the preferences of various domestic (and sometimes foreign) groups, even in the most apparently dictatorial regimes, the forecasting of policy choices involves an often very detailed assessment of the preferences and strengths of these groups. Because those preferences and strengths change as economic and social conditions change, the political forecaster who begins with a narrow policy interest soon is forced into examination of the broadest issues of economic situation and social structure.

Elaborating on Alternative Possible Futures

Since no analyst is omniscient, the political forecaster often ends up elaborating on several different but plausible futures, even if he cannot specify their probabilities with any degree of reliability. This function is, nevertheless, of vital importance, because as events unfold the policy maker who is sensitized to these possibilities (often with continued input from the political analyst) will be more capable of responding appropriately than will the policy maker who lacks an appreciation for the range of possibilities. The elaboration of plausible futures also gives the policy maker a chance to assess how sensitive key aspects of the circumstances or policy choices will be to the variations in outcomes.

For example, a study by this book's authors on the political future of the Philippines, and possible policy options that may be adopted by the Philippine government in future years, identified several circumstances (lack of political consensus, obstacles to decisive policy implementation) and several policy orientations (continued reliance on foreign borrowing, greater emphasis on urban-poverty problems) that are likely to prevail regardless of whether the regimes in power during the coming decade are controlled by the current political leadership, the opposition, or the military. Of course, it would have been better to be in a position to predict precisely which scenario would emerge, but in light of the irreducible uncertainty when the study was undertaken (1980), it was deemed more responsible to design several scenarios than to elaborate on only the one considered most likely.

Identifying "Trends to Watch"

This function of describing alternative futures is much enhanced if the political forecaster can specify advance indications (still in the future when the forecaster makes his presentation) that could serve as "bellwethers" to the policy maker that some of these possible futures have become more likely than the others. This function is directly parallel to the economist's use of leading indicators, although the political leading indicator may be an event (such as troop movements or a change in government rhetoric) rather than a continuous quantitative measure (such as inventory or investment levels) used for economic leading indicators. For example, it was specified in the above-mentioned Philippine study that the reimposition of martial law by President Marcos, after he had lifted martial law, would be a strong indication that his hold had slipped.

Another rationale for identifying trends to watch has been to sensitize the policy maker to just-emerging trends that may warrant serious concern if they continue in their present direction. The semiannual *Global Political Assessment* devotes a section of each issue to identifying such trends, without necessarily implying that they are, as yet, of high probability. These trends have included the organization of strong unions in Poland (predicted in 1976), the rise of Muslim fundamentalism in the Middle East, growing foreign debt problems of various capital-borrowing countries, and the increasing use by rightist Latin American governments of expeditionary forces provided by other Latin American nations ruled by sympathetic regimes.

Anticipating the Nature of Confrontation

Although it is certainly more satisfying to be able to predict who will win in any future confrontation among individuals and groups, often it is equally or even more important to predict the terms and conditions of political battles. In some cases the forecast user is relatively indifferent to the winner because the policies likely to be implemented by different contenders would not differ greatly, but the question of whether political dominance will be won through a bloody civil war or through peaceful accommodation is always important. For example, the military and civilian groups jockeying for power in Bolivia do not represent starkly different positions vis-à-vis foreign investment or U.S.-Bolivian relations, yet the potential investor or foreign policy decision maker is vitally interested in the prospects for protracted internal strife.

Projecting the Political "Climate"

By the time the events or actions of importance have occurred, it is often too late for policy action to minimize costs or to take advantage of opportunities. "Advance warning" is often crucial. Because political actions are rooted in political attitudes, characterizing the present and future political climate is a way of anticipating future events; however, it is by no means simple. Political attitudes are, by their very nature, difficult to measure, difficult to interpret, and volatile. Nevertheless, a large part of the political forecaster's role is to speculate on the trends in such intangibles as "anti-American sentiment," "belligerence," "war hysteria," "siege mentality," "tough-mindedness," and so on, among both leadership and mass groups. The political climate is largely subjective (though one could consider actions such as strikes to be indicators of the climate). Consequently, the projection of political climate requires approaches that monitor attitudes rather than events.

Assessing Governmental Strength

It is not only important to assess whether a government will survive, but also how capable it will be of carrying out its "preferred" policies. The policies to which a government commits itself fervently at one point in time can be rejected later because of the political opposition they trigger. Argentina provides an example. The prospects of the mid-1970s Argentine economic liberalization program turned not on whether the government was "committed" to its program of tariff reductions, floating exchange rates, and elimination of industrial subsidies, but instead on whether that government—even though it was a military regime—had the political strength to carry out the program. The government's support within the military itself depended on placating certain "nationalist" segments that would probably oppose the diminished role of domestic (and often military-controlled) industry. The government's need for some civilian support (or at least acquiescence) made it politically necessary to revitalize the economy (which occurred in late 1978), rather than attacking inflation wholeheartedly through the government's preferred measures of continued credit restriction, other austerity measures, and drastic reduction of the bureaucracy. Since the government was still under pressure to combat inflation, it adopted a policy of overvaluation (despite its opposition in principle to that tactic), which antagonized the powerful exporting groups. The insupportable combination of economic policies compromised by political pressures and rising political opposition caused by economic failure led to a broad political-economic collaspse in 1981–82. This instance graphically demonstrates that even a military government does not have carte blanche to implement its stated policies, and therefore the political forecaster must assess that government's current and future strength in order to judge whether its policies can be sustained.

Assessing the Probability of the Worst Case

Particularly in business, the function of the political forecaster sometimes is to assess the likelihood of catastrophic political developments where otherwise the political factors would play a very minor role. The political forecaster then "signs off" on the investment or commitment under consideration, indicating that other factors, usually considerations of economic viability, ought to be paramount because the likelihood of political changes upsetting these calculations is low. Similarly, the military usually has a vital interest in assessing the probabilities of worst-case outcomes. Virtually all Soviet and American strategic programs are designed, at a cost of hundreds of billions of dollars, to cope with a possibility, namely Soviet-American war, which neither believes to be probable but both believe to be important.

Policy Simulation

Forecasting can focus directly on the repercussions of given actions by the forecast user. The contemplated actions, either provided by the forecast user or offered by the forecaster, generally cover the most visible policy options available to the policy maker. With this format, the forecaster "simulates" the consequences of each of these options by projecting the reactions likely to occur under each of them. This function has become increasingly important in economic forecasting, often through the use of large econometric models. The importance of policy simulation in assessing the political consequences of government action has been gaining recoginition, though it still lags behind economic simulation. The systematic simulation with the longest and most successful history remains the military "war game."

Contextual Analysis

Finally, another important but often overlooked function of the political forecast is to provide a political context for the projection of other trends. Economic trends cannot be forecasted reliably without an understanding of likely political conditions. For that matter, all social forecasts are influenced by future political conditions, including the governmental-policy context, the political climate in general, and the possible occurrence of major discontinuities such as war or revolution. The political forecast is thus an adjunct to other social forecasts, and the political forecaster ought to take this need into account as well when he designs a forecast approach. Unfortunately, this interdependence between political forecasting and the forecasting of other trends (trends affected by politics but not primarily concerned with power relations) is not adequately recognized; consequently, forecasters of other social trends—particularly economists—often make ad hoc political assumptions instead of relying on systematic political analysis.

Some Lessons of this Overview

Several important points can be drawn from this review of political forecasting applications. The first is that very few of these applications require the forecaster to provide a single, definitive political prediction. It is much more common for the political forecaster to convey likelihoods, to elaborate on several different possible futures, to explain the context and pressures that affect decisions, and to provide the policy maker with information for further analysis on how the future might unfold. A direct implication of this point is that the manner of presentation of the forecast becomes an important aspect of the utility of the forecast. Chapter 12 of this volume is devoted to the problems of forecast presentation.

The second point is that "political risk assessment" is something of a misnomer, because identifying opportunities is as important as identifying risks. The political forecaster is not simply the bearer of bad news. The implication is that the forecaster is often in the thick of deliberations to take positive action.

The third point is that many of the questions addressed by the political forecaster are rather detailed, focusing on specific policies, the predilections of particular groups, and government procedures relevant to particular issues, investments, regulations, and so on. This point calls for an orientation toward the methods and formatting of political forecasts that emphasizes the capacity to convey detail, to aid the forecast user in his or her efforts to obtain further detail, and to work back and forth between broad trends and lower-level events. The use of scenarios as devices to convey (and even test) how the configuration of political trends and events holds together becomes very attractive from this perspective.

The fourth and final point is that the political forecaster who works in or for an organization is far from being an aloof ivory-tower analyst who sits in splendid isolation except when casting out his predictions. Contrary to the impression one may get from the political predictions seen in magazines or newspapers, the typical political forecaster in an organization is involved in complex interactions with his audience, discerning their needs, their own policy options, and their levels of information. This means that the good forecaster, and the good designer of political forecast methods, must understand the policy process in which political forecasters operate. Chapter 1 examines the logical relationship between forecasting and planning, and Chapter 2 analyzes the perceived needs—both constructive and destructive—of the policy maker and the forecaster. The last two chapters return to the theme of how to structure relations between analyst and decision maker. These complementary perspectives enable us to offer advice based on considerations of how forecasting ought to be used ideally and of the situations forecasters face in the real world where organizational politics and social-psychological factors are at play.

These considerations call for some understanding of the processes of decision making in which forecasts play a part. How are forecasts used? What forms of forecasts are most digestible by the policy maker? What problems can arise in the interaction between forecasters and policy makers?

When we argue that the political forecast has to provide contextual information for the policy maker, rather than concentrating on making a single, definitive prediction, this reflects our understanding of the use of the forecast as yet another piece of information at the policy maker's disposal—information that is useful and credible only if it can help the policy maker to sort out the complexity of the situations he or she faces. When we argue that the forecaster ought to project several conditional forecasts starting with different assumptions about policy makers' choices, we again are basing this advice on an understanding of the policy making process as one in which the policy maker retains discretion over final policy choices and resists forecasts that seem to impose particular policy decisions.

A PHILOSOPHY OF METHOD

These considerations set the stage for the actual generation of the forecast. Even if the forecast's format has been determined through considerations of its use, the political forecaster still faces the formidable choice of method. Economic, social, and demographic forecasting have developed a bewildering array of methods, as has the discipline of political science. How much effort should be devoted to methodological development as opposed to other pursuits, such as the exploration of individual, idiosyncratic situations? It is essential to put method in perspective, to clarify that the role of methods is to facilitate the exploration of insights into the workings of politics, rather than to provide mechanistic forecasting formulas.

The choice of forecasting methods is often viewed as an all-or-nothing issue. Supporters of one method or approach will argue that theirs is superior, only to be challenged by supporters of some other approach. In fact, the choice of method ought to depend on what is being forecast, just as the carpenter's choice of tools depends on whether he wants to drive a nail or to cut a board. The "pure" use of only one method is neither common nor advisable. In the real world, formal models are operated with a large dose of judgmental input, and forecasters using "only judgment" learn of, and are naturally influenced by, the results produced by other methods. Political forecasting generally entails combining socioeconomic forecasts, produced by a wide variety of methods, with a wide variety of political dynamics or theories. Moreover, the multiexpert approaches to political forecasting concentrate on orchestrating the opinions of several experts who, in all likelihood, use different approaches to generate their contributions to the group forecast. In short, methods are blended more often than they are used individually. This is a fortunate circumstance, considering the generally poor performance of single methods. Since political

trends are embedded in a complex matrix of social, economic, and narrowly
3 political conditions, a combination of methods that can capture more
angles is more promising than any single method.

Nevertheless, the temptation to avoid the issue entirely by "doing
everything" is not an option in the real world of scarce resources. The
forecaster must choose an approach, even if it involves a particular combination of methods, and must forego other combinations, simply because
of limitations of time and staff.

The choice of method is often determined by the forecaster's preconception of the future pattern of that particular trend. Methods have underlying assumptions that may or may not conform to what the forecaster
believes will happen. For example, extrapolation presumes either that the
dynamics of a particular situation will continue into the future or that the
forecaster does not know enough about these dynamics to presume
otherwise.

The choice of method often determines the format or content of the
forecast. For example, quantitative methods produce discrete, quantitative
projections, whereas scenario writing as a forecast method produces prose
"stories." It is, therefore, dangerous to choose a method without first
considering whether that method steers the forecaster away from the subject
that ought to be forecast or the format most conducive to policy influence.

Despite the biases that methods can impart, it is still true that any
method can express different assumptions held by the forecaster. From the
most elaborate complex model to the simplest mechanical extension of an
existing trend, the method can be viewed as no more—and no less—than
a means for expressing the forecaster's assumptions. The soundness of
these basic assumptions will make or break the forecast, and even the
most superbly applied technique cannot rescue a forecast based on faulty
assumptions.

The choice of method inevitably involves making tradeoffs. The forecaster has to balance explicitness against subtlety and comprehensiveness,
objectivity against intuition, decisiveness against an honest indication of
uncertainty.

Because no method satisfies all of these desiderata, no single method
can be imposed as the universal best choice. Nor can a method be judged
superior until the forecaster has sorted out the specific needs for that
instance of forecasting.

In light of these considerations, the second part of our approach to the
issue of methodology is to review the logic of different methods in terms
of their underlying assumptions, the levels of information needed to apply
a method successfully, and the tradeoffs involved. Chapters 3, 4, 5, and 6
in the section on "Forecasting Methods" address this need.

If all of these elements must be taken into account, our approach would seem to put very heavy intellectual demands on the forecaster. Is it worth the time and effort of the would-be political or social forecaster (or the consumer of political forecasts) to go through these complex considerations with us? Our ultimate intent is to aid the forecaster in the design of the forecasting operation, the choice of techniques, and the presentation of the forecasts. But aren't these obvious, making our efforts just another academic exercise in making the simple complicated?

Misconceptions of Political Forecasting

One way to find out is to examine whether common views of political forecasting are in accord with our philosophy and advice, in which case our approach would simply be a rehash of the conventional wisdom. It is striking how many misconceptions abound with respect to the record, uses, and approaches of political forecasting. The following list is but a sample.

Misconception 1. The record of political forecasting is horrendous. This seems obvious considering that there is always a nation or region undergoing a radical but unpredicted change; someone is always criticizing the CIA or other intelligence sources for their failure to predict some event. The Arab oil embargo, the overthrow of Somoza in Nicaragua, the fall of the Shah, and so on, seem to mock the earnest effort of the political analyst.

Certain events cannot indeed be predicted until they actually emerge. But the impression that these cases predominate arises merely from their notoriety. Nobody remembers the prediction that a stable regime will remain in power. Only moderate attention is focused on the prediction that a government will fall if that is indeed the result. By the time an event occurs, its prediction naturally seems to have been obvious, whether or not it was really so clearcut. In short, there is no post mortem, and no breast beating, when political forecasters do a reasonably good job. The failures get the attention.

Misconception 2. Political forecasting and political risk assessment are, and ought to be, focused on the prediction of major political events— revolutions, coups d'etat, pivotal elections, and so forth. Again, the journalistic prominence of predictions of such events conveys the mistaken impression that they are the essence of political forecasting. There is also an implicit assumption that, because these events are the most important occurrences for political actors in the systems under study, they are the most important aspects for foreign governments and businesses to predict. Moreover, since major events such as wars and leadership changes affect all the other political conditions of the polity involved, it appears that the focus ought to be on these major events, with the less prominent events left as unstated implications.

However, this view disregards the need of the policy maker to have information at a level of detail appropriate for the kinds of decisions he must make. An investor interested in a particular copper mine in the Philippines is likely to be more concerned with local unrest than with the fortunes of the national political leaders; and even if the latter are relevant, he cannot dispense with the detailed information. Nor can the investor necessarily infer detail from the overall trends. If the forecast user knew enough about the country under examination to be able to draw specific conclusions from general trends, he probably would not need the political analyst in the first place.

Misconception 3.   Precise predictions are the only criterion of a forecast's utility. It would seem at first glance that the forecast must be correct in order for it to be able to guide correct action; if the forecast is indeed correct, it will be used to make the correct policy decisions.

The only grain of truth in this proposition is that, over the long run, accurate analysis is certainly important. But precise predictions of events are seldom the central issue. For each particular forecast, moreover, a large part of its utility is tested before the events prove or disprove its accuracy. Have the policy makers been able to use the forecast to their advantage prior to the event? If the forecast lacks credibility or is framed in a fashion the policy maker finds unwieldy, then the decision maker's unwillingness to rely on it strips away its utility irrespective of its accuracy. If the analysis gives the policy maker a firm grasp of the political dynamics of the country, individual predictions may prove far less important.

Misconception 4.   Political forecasts ought to be as explicit as possible, and even as mathematical as possible, so that they can be entered into the formal decision-making models employed by sophisticated policy makers. The plethora of impressive cost-benefit techniques, optimization routines, and "figure of merit" algorithms seems to call for political forecasts that can be plugged into the model that will churn out optimal choices automatically.

The problem with this proposition is simply that "sophisticated" policy makers—who turn out to be politicians and managers—do not use these formal models to make the decisions for them. They do not trust these routines to produce reliable results. They do not relish the no-win position of having either a marvelous computer program that is so successful that it makes the policy maker seem superfluous, or a faulty program that makes the policy maker look bad for having commissioned it. Instead, policy makers use forecasts as background information, adding to the store of information and understanding they have of the situation under study. Consequently, the utility of the forecast is enhanced to the extent that it adds to the policy maker's information and particularly to his contextual understanding. Condensed, quantified predictions rarely can do this.

Misconception 5.   Political forecasting "methodology" is either a matter of unstructured intuition or else a rather esoteric and quantified affair. Political forecasters all seem to fall into the categories of journalist or arcane specialist, although many people are familiar only with the journalist types. This misconception has the very unfortunate consequence of implying that "judgment" is necessarily unstructured, that there is no way of being systematic and simultaneously giving rein to insightful judgment. Advocates of purely quantitative approaches frequently seek deliberately to create a false dichotomy between computer models on one hand and unsystematic cogitation on the other.

In fact, as accurate as it is to characterize much of political forecasting as either dismally unstructured or ludicrously esoteric, there are political forecasters who occupy the middle ground. Almost without exception, the most influential ones are found on this middle ground. Moreover, in practice, the application of seemingly technical methods involves a great deal of judgment. This practical wedding of technique and judgment occurs even with the econometric models applied to economic forecasting (see Chapter 4). Systematic analysis, as we shall argue at length in subsequent chapters, is not equivalent to explicitness and certainly not to mathematical esoterica. Given the nature of politics as an activity involving or touching upon all other aspects of the human situation, "systematic" turns out to mean "comprehensive" in exploring potentially relevant factors, whether through mathematics or not.

Misconception 6.   There are esoteric methods of political forecasting just waiting for the arrival of the political scientist who, unlike his colleagues, is well-trained enough to use them. This variant of the notion that the only choice is between unstructured intuition and science presumes that political forecasting is merely backward; the day will come (if enough effort is forthcoming) when political forecasting will become a serious scientific endeavor like economic forecasting and technology assessment.

We shall argue at length that the challenges confronting the political forecaster require an in-depth understanding of political dynamics that "technique," as usually defined, cannot address. The political forecaster must apply basic political analysis rather than a complicated algorithm; he must incorporate the forecasts of other social trends by evaluating how they affect political dynamics, and not by resorting to mathematical complexity.

THE NEED FOR PRACTICAL APPROACHES

This brief survey of some (but by no means all) of the fallacies surrounding political forecasting reveals the importance of developing a theory of practical political forecasting. The emphasis is on "practical" because political forecasting has an enormous potential for improving real-world policy making. Yet we can also theorize about the practical problems of forecasting and forecast use because the problems and the solutions transcend each particular practical application of political forecasting. It is useful to theorize broadly because the specific instances the political forecaster will face will not be the same as those chosen by any demonstration of "how to forecast."

   This book is designed to address the issues raised here by putting the forecasting process firmly into its policy-advising context. Standard approaches to forecasting emphasize particular methods, or comparison of methods. Such conventional approaches are useful but, in the absence of a strong sense of the policy-making context, can lead to methodological faddishness and policy irrelevance.

   Chapters 1 and 2 put forecasting into the context of the planning process, first in terms of the logic of planning and then in terms of the social and psychological pressures of planning.

   Chapters 3 through 6 appraise different forecasting methods and the special characteristics of political forecasting.

   Chapters 7 through 10 then outline one key theoretical approach to political forecasting, illustrated by theoretical analysis of regime instability and by two detailed case studies of Korea and Mexico. These chapters display the utility of thinking about political change in organizational terms. They also illustrate a way of thinking systematically but qualitatively about a major issue.

   Chapters 11 and 12 address the practical problems of making a forecasting operation useful to policy making. Chapter 11 surveys some of the ways that key problems can be ameliorated by institutional arrangements, and Chapter 12 reviews ways of presenting analysis in order to make it useful. These chapters address some implications of both the forecaster–decision-maker relationship addressed in the first group of chapters and the method issues addressed in the second group.

The integrating themes of this volume, which differentiate it from other analyses of forecasting methods, are:

Emphasis on the special problems created by the rising need for political forecasts.

Emphasis on the inherent limitations of quantitative techniques.

Related emphasis on the importance of contextual analysis and scenario analysis as opposed to precise prediction.

Highlighting of the interaction between political forecasts on one hand and economic and social forecasts on the other.

Suggestion that understanding politics as an organizational phenomenon is the most fruitful way to avoid the greatest problems of current forecasting efforts: narrow theory, silly quantification, and unsystematic analysis.

Insistence that the practical utility of forecasting hinges overwhelmingly on understanding the interactions between forecaster and decision maker, and on choosing methods, formats, and institutional arrangements that derive from such an understanding.

In presenting these themes, the authors have three audiences in mind. The book is intended to be directly useful to *businesspeople* and *government officials* who engage in forecasting and planning. And, by directing this study to the ways in which forecasts are actually used, we intend to alter, in line with the stated themes, the ways in which *scholars* analyze forecasting issues. With regard to the scholars, our research affirms one central tendency of the so-called behavioral movement, namely to emphasize the study of actual behavior rather than that of sterile formal or legal models, while rejecting the second central tendency, namely to insist that social science must be built upon explicit, quantitative models.

To serve the interests of all three audiences, we have tried to employ a diversity of examples. The national security planner will find the examples in Chapter 1 tailored to his or her interests, the government economic manager or academic futurist should find Chapter 6's analysis of the *Global 2000 Report* particularly relevant, and the international businessperson or banker should find Chapter 10's study of Mexico particularly useful. Chapter 11 on South Korea should provoke all these interests. Each example illustrates forecasting themes of interest to all forecasters, planners, and decision makers.

NOTES

1.   For another view of such tasks, focused on the needs of banks and corporations, see William H. Overholt, *Political Risk* (London: Euromoney Publications, 1982), pp. 15–24. See also, Stephen J. Kobrin, *Managing Political Risk Assessment* (Berkeley, California: University of California Press, 1982).

Part 1

The Relationship of
Forecasting to Planning

Chapter 1

Forecasting in the Planning Process

Forecasting exists to facilitate planning, particularly long-range planning. Aside from sheer intellectual titillation, forecasting has no justification outside the planning process. Any analysis of the methods and organization of forecasting must therefore begin with the planning process. Putting forecasting within the context of the planning process can help illuminate *why* forecasting is useful, *what* is worth forecasting, *how* forecasts should be used and presented, and the *limits* of forecasting.

In a world where some military equipment (such as ships) must remain useful for 30 years of rapid change, where corporate investments in mining or timber often mature only after 10 to 30 years, and where incremental decisions can lead unexpectedly to ecological disasters, long-range planning is essential. However, the standard methods employed for short-range planning cannot be adapted easily for the solution of long-range problems, and there is no generally accepted method of long-range planning. This chapter suggests a way of thinking designed to ameliorate the following critical problems of the long-range planning process:

1. *Uncertainty.*   Coping with the uncertainty resulting from inadequate knowledge and excessive complexity.
2. *Self-fulfilling and self-defeating prophecies.*   Coping with the fact that conditions are not fixed externally but are strongly affected by decisions.
3. *Fragmentation.*   Coping with the fragmentation of the policy-planning process into isolated regional and functional groups.

A STRATEGIC PLANNING MODEL

There is a standard approach employed for strategic planning. Using this method one takes a set of fixed *interests,* juxtaposes them with a fixed

21

environment (or world, or set of conditions), and then invents a *strategy* for attaining one's interests given the constraints imposed by the environment. See Figure 1.1.

In short-range strategic planning such a model is useful. For the short run one can state interests confidently and one can describe the environment with sufficient certainty to provide the foundation for sound strategy. In the longer run, however, uncertainty erodes this foundation. In order to rebuild the foundation, we must examine ways of coping with the effects of uncertainty on each of the three parts of the basic model: interests, environment, and strategy.

Interests

Describing *interests* in the face of uncertainty is the easiest part of the problem. Interests can be stated at various levels of generality. The United States can be said to have an interest in prosperity, or to have an interest in selling more widgets to Japan. If one states interests at the level of selling more widgets, then the interests change quickly over time and uncertainty becomes a problem for long-range planners. But if one states interests at a higher level of generality ("The country has an interest in prosperity"), then one encompasses the lower-generality interests and becomes confident that the interests will not change in unforeseeable ways over time. Thus, the solution to the problem of stating interests in the face of uncertainty is to *state the interests at a sufficiently high level of generality that they will not change greatly during the time period under consideration.*

For economic planning purposes, the appropriate interests might include economic growth, economic equity among groups and regions, diversification, high environmental standards, self-sufficient national security industries, and relative independence of foreign capital, energy, technology, and markets. For the national security planner, a variety of political, economic, military, psychological, and managerial interests are important, as listed in Table 1.1.[1] Multinational firms' interests include unthreatened ownership, protection of technology, managerial control, profit repatriation, pricing flexibility, and others, as noted in Table 1.2.

Figure 1.1   Simple strategic planning model

Table 1.1   U.S. National Interests

A. *Political*
    1. U.S. unity
    2. U.S. democracy and liberty
    3. Democratic institutions throughout the world
    4. Individual liberty throughout the world
B. *Economic Welfare*
    1. Of U.S. citizens
        a. access to raw materials
        b. U.S. trade
        c. U.S. investments
        d. efficient world monetary system
        e. limited harmful pollution
    2. Of other nations' citizens
C. *Military*
    1. Preventing attacks on United States
    2. Defending United States against attacks that do occur
    3. Preventing military attacks on U.S. interests, and defending those interests when other means prove inadequate
D. *Moral/Psychological/Cultural*
    1. Safety of U.S. citizens
    2. U.S. citizens' access to diverse cultures, experiences, ideas, travel
    3. Amelioration of human suffering worldwide—genocide, war, starvation, slavery, political oppression
E. *Managerial*
    1. Credibility—global reputation for sincerity and ability to fulfill commitments
    2. Intelligence—access to information affecting U.S. interests and ability to attain those interests
    3. Good morale—sense of confidence, rectitude, effectiveness
    4. Effective U.S. organization
F. *General*
    Whenever interests are being discussed on a regional or local basis, using the above list, it is always necessary to add an interest in facilitating attainment of U.S. interests elsewhere.

Table 1.2   Key Corporate Interests

A. *Overall Profitability*

B. *Assets*
    1. Equity position
    2. Rights to land, minerals, . . .

C. *Organizational*
    1. Decision-making capability
    2. Staffing capability
    3. Safety and comfort of employees

D. *Operational*
    1. Access to equipment
    2. Access to raw materials
    3. Technology
    4. Ability to import and export
    5. Ability to transfer funds

E. *Markets*
    1. Continued access to existing markets
    2. Access to new and growing markets

Listing and evaluating such interests is, of course, only the first step in an analysis for several reasons. First, while most planners will agree on the items listed, few will agree on the weight given to each. For instance, American policy makers have never been able to reach consensus on how much military or economic advantage they are willing to sacrifice in the interest of greater democracy abroad. Second, there are complicated trade-offs among the interests, which are poorly understood. For instance, most noncommunist countries have aspired to democratic institutions and economic prosperity. However, in some countries and at certain stages of development, Western democratic institutions may make the local government extremely vulnerable to pressure groups, causing inflation and disorder. Inflation and disorder then weaken the economy, often causing political instability. Thus, the analyst must; first, list the interests; second, attempt to weight those interests; third, evaluate the interests in the specific region and time period of interest; and, fourth, comprehend as well as possible the ways in which the different interests complement and contradict one another.

Such analysis of interests is the most neglected part of strategic planning. Frequently, interests are erroneously taken to be self-evident and thus are analyzed perfunctorily. Hence systematic knowledge of interests and their tradeoffs is relatively rare. Neither line executives nor planning staffs usually have strong incentives to think about such fundamental issues. Hence, one frequently encounters a group of colonels who implicitly define U.S. strategic interests in a given country as consisting primarily of maintaining a base there. Or one finds a group of mining corporation executives who spend all their time trying to avoid nationalization, although after questioning they may quickly concede that what they really fear is quite different: loss of management control. In the 1970s, the most notable area of confusion in national security policy concerned human rights. Henry Kissinger simply did not understand, before several African presidents shocked him, the costs of ignoring human rights issues in South Africa and aspirations to independence and racial equality in Angola. Conversely, Jimmy Carter, when he inaugurated his human rights policy, simply had not bothered to think through the tradeoffs between political interests and other interests. Like freshmen who forget to define their terms of reference on their exam papers, geopoliticians who neglect explicit analysis of interests invariably trip themselves up.

The lesson for the forecaster is that, if his forecasts are to be useful in long-range planning, he must ascertain that the most important interests are being projected, stated at an appropriate level of generality, and addressed with adequate attention to the ways in which key interests interact over the long run. Seldom will his guidance from the policy maker be sufficiently explicit or thoughtful to assure that the most appropriate variables are being forecast. Frequently, it will fall upon the forecaster to point out that a particular kind of forecast will be useful even if the policy maker has not thought of it; or to argue that the policy maker should have put his or her questions in different terms; or to show that complex interactions limit the utility of straightforward forecasts.

Environments

The principal task of the forecaster is to describe the future environment in terms useful to the policy maker. Describing the environment in the face of uncertainty cannot be handled quite so easily as suggested by simple quantitative forecasting methods and by the simple strategic planning model (Figure 1.1). Moreover, whereas interests can usually be stated at a high enough level of generality and also with sufficient precision for planning purposes, describing the environment by moving to higher levels of generality frequently yields a set of useless clichés and tautologies. The reason for this is that we understand enough about our interests to describe them with both considerable generality and considerable precision, but we understand so little about the trends, and interactions of trends, that shape the world over the long run, that attainment of both generality and precision is often beyond reach.

One part of the solution to this problem is forecasting as it is commonly understood—that is, reduction of the uncertainty by exploiting precise knowledge of known trends or relationships. The fisherman uncertain of the time of tomorrow's high tide can employ knowledge to eliminate his uncertainty. The economic planner concerned about Nigeria's population five years hence can eliminate much uncertainty through the use of demographic techniques. In such situations, quantitative forecasting techniques are invaluable. On the other hand, the Zambian leader or mining company president whose policies must take into account the kind of regime that will dominate Uganda five years hence faces a problem whose uncertainty cannot be largely eliminated through forecasting. Planners' requests for information will not be divided neatly into those for which uncertainty can be largely eliminated by generally accepted methods and those for which uncertainty is largely irreducible. Indeed, most important planning issues concern an environment that contains a very large irreducible minimum of uncertainty.

The forecaster usually does not have the luxury of replying that his tools are inadequate to the task and that no reply is possible. He must respond both to questions that are largely answerable and to questions that are partly unanswerable. If in this situation the forecaster confines himself to forecasting the answerable part and leaving the rest as an unexplored darkness, he will serve the policy maker's interests poorly. It is possible to explore the nature of the uncertainty, to explain what is important within the uncertainty and what is not, and to triangulate the uncertainty by dividing it into pieces.

One principal solution to irreducible uncertainty is to project several alternative possible environments. These alternative environments should be sufficiently few to be intellectually manageable, but sufficiently numerous to display most of the important alternative outcomes of the trends in the world. (Three has become a popular number, partly for good reasons and partly because it adapts so well to the use of straw men, as discussed below.) It is crucial that each of the projected alternative environments be a realistic possibility, and it is a fatal defect of most such projections that they project one environment that is desirable or likely and two that are disastrous or unlikely. Former Assistant Secretary of State Marshall Green was once heard to mutter, "They always give me alternatives A, B, and C, and I'll be damned if I've ever heard anyone recommend A or C." One group of colonels in 1972 projected three possible worlds for 1985: a world dominated by a single power, a world of multipolar competition, and a world ruled by universal law. The use of such straw men as the first and third worlds simply undermined the conclusions of their study. The principal technique for avoiding straw men is to insist that the emergence of the environments be described through *scenarios,* in which each step from the present to the future environment is plausibly described to the satisfaction of appropriate specialists.

Aside from straw men, the commonest errors in the construction of environments are irrelevance and incoherence. The criterion of relevance requires that the environments must convey trends that affect the interests previously identified. The criterion of coherence stipulates that the trends must be synthesized along the lines of some overall theme, such as cold war relations among big powers, or populist nationalism affecting business interests in Africa. It is not uncommon for military teams, assigned to analyze trends affecting, say, the Navy, to produce a thick volume listing many dozens of trends and then find themselves incapable of using the trends to draw specific conclusions. Many of the individual trends compiled by such an effort are irrelevant, and the overall result is incoherent.

The central role of the forecaster is to clarify the policy maker's thought about the future environment. Use of reliable forecasting techniques is only one component of this role. The forecaster who confines himself to that component may produce intellectually titillating insights but will be of greater use to graduate students than to policy makers. The forecaster who serves policy cannot escape from the tasks of clarifying the issues of interest and of charting the dark areas that cannot be illuminated by formal techniques.

Strategies

Thus, our solutions to the problems of projecting interests and environments in the face of uncertainty could be diagrammed as in Figure 1.2, in which highly generalized interests are denoted by *Interests*.

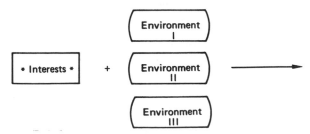

Figure 1.2   Abstract interests and multiple environments

The problem now is to get from these newly defined interests and environments to strategy. Two errors frequently intrude at this stage. First, many analyses simply forget about the alternative environments, or the detailed relations between interests and environment, and simply state a set of things that the authors think should be done, a set of things that often was in the authors' minds before they went through the mechanical process of stating interests and presenting alternative environments. More careful planners take their alternative environments seriously and follow through the logic of the simple strategic planning model but using the redefined interests and multiple environments. In doing so, they prepare contingent strategies to cope with the alternative environments, as in Figure 1.3.

A study that followed this model would prove useful to policy makers who can quickly shift from one strategy to another and who lack ability to influence their environment. Clearly, contingency planning is useful in many circumstances. However, long-range planning almost always seeks to facilitate present decisions, and present decisions frequently can follow only one strategy, not several. For instance, once one builds a navy around large carriers, one may be unable for decades to shift to strategies requiring a predominance of small, fast ships.

This complex, contingency model also possesses a second, more subtle, but sometimes equally fatal defect. It disregards the influence of one's own short- and medium-term decisions over the evolution of environment. Sometimes this problem does not exist because one's decisions have in fact little influence over the environment. For instance, Luxembourg's military planning for the next 15 years could rightly proceed according to a model that assumed that Luxembourg had little influence over its environment. But, for an American strategic planner to make a similar assumption would be absurd. For instance, whether the United States lives

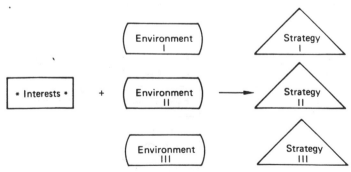

Figure 1.3   Complex strategic planning model—contingency version

in a cold war world or a detente world depends substantially, although not exclusively, on U.S. decisions. In the extreme opposite situation, where the planner disposes resources sufficient to determine his environment, as would have been the case for some of the Roman emperors, this model might also have its uses. The planner could project his interests and alternative environments, and then project separate strategies for each environment in order to determine which environment to choose. But the situation of the United States today is intermediate and more complex. The United States has such great influence over the environment that its models cannot afford to ignore it, yet other actors are sufficiently powerful, and the consequences of U.S. actions are sufficiently unpredictable, that one can never be sure that the consequences of America's great impact on the environment will take the desired form. Similarly, in many Third World countries a few industries so dominate the economy, and a few firms so dominate those industries, that the firms' actions will heavily influence the environment—though not always in the directions desired by those firms. Therefore, if the forecaster is to provide useful advice to decision makers, he must invent a new model that will take into account the influence of the decisions over the evolution of the environment. The decision maker, in turn, must be capable of envisioning a single strategy despite the complexity of alternative future environments.

Before discussing how to construct such a strategy, one must first make the planning models a bit more complicated. The diagram of alternative environments in Figures 1.2 and 1.3 is an oversimplification in that no overlap is shown among the alternatives. In the real world there is usually considerable overlap among alternative realistic environments, and this fact can be diagrammed by showing the alternative environments as possessing a common core, as in Figure 1.4.

In addition, it will be useful to include in the diagram an indication

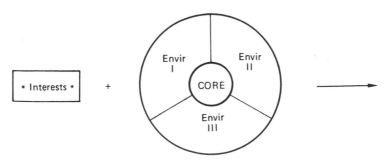

Figure 1.4   The core environment

that, although the alternative environments cover most important contingencies, there are always some contingencies that don't quite fit any of the constructed environments. These few "exogenous contingencies" can be relegated to a halo around the environments, as in Figure 1.5

We can now design an overall strategy, composed of several parts, to cope with this complex situation. First, we can simplify the overall strategic problem by designing a *core strategy* to deal solely with the *core environment* that is common to all of the projected environments. Interests, together with this core part of the environments, are constant and can therefore be employed to generate a specific set of recommendations to policy makers. This core strategy is labeled as such in Figure 1.6. Because the core environment and the core strategy are such useful baselines for policy makers, the forecaster must always devote a great deal of effort to identifying explicitly those core aspects of the environment that are likely to remain constant. Such an emphasis is unusual, because the rapidly changing aspects of the environment always appear more exciting. But, particularly for long-range planning, few things are more useful than a sense of those steady features of the environment that can serve as anchors for policy.

The core strategy is supplemented by a *basic strategy* whose dual purpose is to influence the environment toward the optimal one (hereafter called the *basic environment*) and to facilitate success within that optimal environment. Whereas the core strategy deals with the constants of the environments, the basic strategy copes with the variable features.

But the basic strategy is not sufficient by itself for coping with the variable parts of the environments. What if the basic strategy fails to move the situation into the optimal environment? And, supposing one reaches the optimal environment, what if surprises should occur that are not explicit

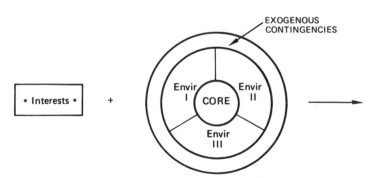

Figure 1.5   Exogenous contingencies

features of that environment? For these contingencies the basic strategy must be supplemented by a *hedging strategy*.

The core, basic, and hedging strategies are diagrammed in Figure 1.6. The core strategy lies at the center, corresponding to the core environment. The basic strategy is an arrow moving one into the basic environment and subsequently maneuvering within that basic environment. The hedging strategy is a set of measures coping with the possibility that one ends up in one of the other environments or has to cope with some exogenous contingencies.

Figure 1.6 distorts the relationship among the strategies somewhat, because, if the core and basic strategies are thoughtfully designed, the hedging strategy will usually turn out to consist of a few measures of diminutive importance by comparison with the core and basic strategies. As Figure 1.6 shows, the hedging strategy copes with the exogenous contingencies and with contingencies arising from the other environments, *insofar as the basic strategy cannot cope with them*. But, invariably, it turns out that a carefully designed basic strategy just happens to be able to deal with many of these other contingencies.

Each of these strategies—core, basic, and hedging—is discussed below in greater detail.

Core Strategy. The core strategy consists of all those elements of policy that remain constant regardless of which environment evolves. It must be based on that section of the environments (if any), here called the *core environment*, which changes very little from one alternative environment to another; that is, on the constants of our models rather than on the variables.

A core strategy is necessarily abstract and extremely flexible. It must be simply and directly stated for the same reasons that mathematical

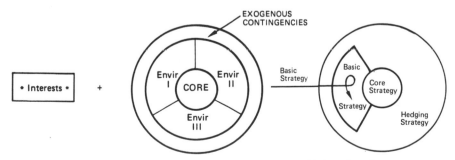

Figure 1.6 Complex strategic planning model—sophisticated version

axioms must be simply and straightforwardly stated. For this reason it is generally convenient to present a nation's core global strategy as an elaboration of a few axiomatic principles that together constitute a *national doctrine*. America's core foreign policy strategies have traditionally consisted of elaborations of one or more such doctrines, but the formulations of both the strategy and its associated doctrine have typically been less than fully deliberate and self-conscious. Among the great and enduring doctrines of American history have been the "no entangling alliances" doctrine expressed in George Washington's Farewell Address, the Monroe Doctrine, the Open Door Policy, and the Truman Doctrine.[2] Most businesses are operated, implicitly or explicitly, according to a few basic principles. Those that are not risk becoming unmanageable conglomerates, or having differing parts of the firm make inconsistent decisions.

Enumeration of a straightforward core strategy entails a great virtue and a substantial problem. The virtue is that the enunciators, their subordinates, the relevant public, and adversaries will all possess a clear guideline to which they can adjust their behavior. Given such a core policy, leaders are less likely to be inconsistent in their decisions, subordinates are more likely to interpret decisions correctly, the public is less likely to become confused and worried, and adversaries are less likely to make misjudgments. Major organizations seldom do well over long periods of time without such a core strategy, or doctrine, or philosophy.

On the other hand, such doctrines tend to become unquestioned gospel and to outlive their usefulness, as did the doctrines of "no entangling alliances" and (in its more extreme form) "containment." This problem, however, is usually more acceptable than its principal alternative—having no core strategy and having leaders, subordinates, public, and adversaries confused and angry. This latter description fits fairly well the situation in U.S. foreign policy in the 1970s. However well-contrived individual policies may be, frequent contradictions among policies in different areas and lack of a generally accepted concept of the nation's overall strategy enhance bureaucratic warfare, fragment political support, erode overall credibility, and elicit accusations of inconsistency or even bad faith from allies and adversaries alike. The U.S. geopolitical confusion of the late 1970s is a potent reminder to both forecasters and policy makers of the danger of focusing on small-scale, immediate, rapidly changing issues, and neglecting the larger, long-term, relatively unchanging aspects of environment and strategy.

Basic Strategy.   Suppose one postulates three alternative political-military environments in the Pacific: a cold war environment like the 1950s, a multipolar anarchy world devoid of alliances and strong political ties, and a current trends model that retains American alliances with several countries, including Japan, and ameliorates U.S. relations with the People's Republic of China and the Soviet Union. None of these environments is a utopia of peace, freedom, and prosperity. All of them are plausible outcomes of current trends, and, given the size of the United States relative to the other actors, it is completely reasonable to believe that the United States can influence regional relationships in the direction of any one of the models. This does not mean that the United States will necessarily be completely successful in exercising such influence, since other powers may oppose that influence, and it does not mean that the United States will not be surprised by the second-order consequences of its influence. For instance, the United States could almost immediately bring into existence the multipolar anarchy model by abrogating the U.S.-Japanese Mutual Security Treaty and the alliance with South Korea. The nation's ability to do so in such a quick and dramatic fashion demonstrates its influence over the structure of the international system. On the other hand, the medium-term consequence of instituting this particular system in such a way might well be a Japanese decision to rearm very quickly with both conventional and nuclear weapons, a decision that would likely lead to nuclear proliferation elsewhere in the world and might well frighten the Soviet Union and China back into a relatively close alignment. Thus, the United States might quickly find itself back in a renewed cold war despite contrary intentions. The point of this is to demonstrate the great influence the United States can exert on the system, but also the fact that great influence does not mean that one inevitably gets one's way.

For the forecaster, the fact that one's own decisions can influence the outcome of trends can be perplexing. The perplexity takes two forms. First, predictions may be self-defeating. For instance, if a forecaster predicts, on the basis of social trends, an eventual communist government in Guatemala, the U.S. government may intervene to prevent the prediction from coming true. Second, the interaction between decision and outcome destroys the carefully constructed partition between the job of forecasting and the job of decision making. That is, if the situation in Guatemala depends upon U.S. decisions as well as Guatemalan social trends, then the forecaster cannot analyze Guatemala's future without also providing a good deal of commentary on U.S. policy. This commentary could well be forbidden domain; the perceived intrusion could then be used by policy makers as a reason for intruding into the forecasting process.

Therefore, as soon as one acknowledges that one's own government or firm is sufficiently able to influence the basic course of events, the job of forecasting becomes inextricably entangled with the jobs of planning and deciding. Delineation of alternative environments by a forecaster defines the choices that a planner or decision maker will perceive. Projection of outcomes by a forecaster presumes some decisions about the range of choices available to the decision maker. The forecaster must make conditional forecasts, which hinge on the decision maker's decisions. Once one goes beyond the core environment and the core strategy to the more amorphous alternative environments and basic strategy, the line between forecaster and decision maker begins to disintegrate. This sets the stage for many of the tensions between forecaster and decision maker that will be analyzed in the following chapter.

The basic strategy concept enables one to cope with the fact that one's own decisions affect the structure of the environment. The basic strategy is a strategy for getting into the optimal environment and for succeeding within that environment. Formulation of a basic strategy thus involves:

1.   Choice of a preferred environment.
2.   Design of a strategy for getting into the preferred environment.
3.   Design of a strategy for succeeding in the preferred environment.

By analogy one could think of the alternative environments as alternative games: chess, checkers, and tennis. Then, a basic strategy would consist of (1) choosing a preference for, say, chess, (2) designing a strategy to get the other players to play chess rather than checkers or tennis, and (3) designing a strategy to win the game of chess. It is appropriate to include (1), (2), and (3) under the single concept of a basic strategy, rather than dealing with them separately, because in any given case they turn out to overlap a great deal.

In choosing a preferred environment, it is essential that the alternative chosen be a practical one. It must not be a utopia; it must be an environment that one can expect to attain with a relatively high degree of certainty, given existing trends and likely reactions of other parties to one's own strategy. If the chosen environment is unlikely to be attained, then the basic strategy is likely to prove ineffective, and the nation or firm will find itself relying on the hedging strategy, which is less coherent and more ad hoc. Such reliance on ad hoc reactions would defeat the purpose of advance planning.

Hedging Strategy.   The hedging strategy is designed to deal with contingencies for which neither the core strategy nor the combination of core strategy and basic strategy is adequate. Such contingencies arise because:

1.   The alternative environments chosen for study can never completely cover the range of possible alternatives.

2. The basic strategy may fail to move the world toward the preferred environment.

3. Surprises that are not part of the structure of the preferred evironment can nevertheless occur within that environment.

A hedging strategy should cover risks to interests resulting from these three kinds of lacunae in the other strategies. However, it must be noticed that there are necessarily tradeoffs between basic and hedging strategies. For instance, a basic U.S. strategy in Asia may seek good relations with China by reducing U.S. presence on the mainland of Southeast Asia, while a hedging strategy might seek to cope with the relatively unlikely contingency of an aggressive Chinese thrust into that area. A good hedging strategy will balance the risks of difficulty in coping with a contingency against the risks of defeating one's own basic strategy.

The more adequate the basic strategy, the fewer will be the contingencies against which ad hoc hedges must be devised. Ideally, the basic strategy would be so comprehensive as to nullify the need for hedges. In any case, the hedging strategy, unlike the core and basic strategies, is simply a set of ad hoc measures and contingency plans rather than the elaboration of a coherent strategic concept.

In a 1972 study, *The World, 1982–1991,* by Herman Kahn, William H. Overholt, and William Pfaff, the Hudson Institute prepared a list of 30 scenarios that most observers would have found improbable, but which would be extremely important if perchance they did occur. By 1976 several of these had already occurred, including the Indian nuclear explosion and the crisis of southern NATO. The crisis of southern NATO depended upon the chance interaction of a Cyprus crisis, Greek and Turkish problems, rapidly rising communist influence in Italy, and the near-simultaneous deaths of the dictators of Spain and Portugal. Because of the postulated number of coincidences, such a scenario seemed unlikely in the extreme. However, something very similar occurred later. This illustrates a fundamental lesson that most forecasters and planners learn only by experience. Although any particular improbable event is by definition unlikely, world history is greatly influenced by unpredictable surprises, and any strategy must be tested for its ability to cope with sudden surprises. Usually this is not done, because bureaucracies are, of course, oriented toward business-as-usual. But the test of strategies is not just the business-as-usual environment; it is the ability to cope with the 1973 OPEC oil embargo, the 1970s change in China's orientation, the 1974 Indian nuclear test, the fall of the Shah of Iran, and Richard Nixon's trip to China, all of which appeared relatively unlikely before they occurred. Particularly when dealing with long-range issues, the forecaster has a responsibility to convey the possibility of important surprises.

SOME DIFFERENCES BETWEEN SHORT-RANGE
AND LONG-RANGE PLANNING

The complex strategic planning model (sophisticated version) discussed above and illustrated in Figure 1.6 copes with crucial problems caused by the increasing uncertainty that one encounters when moving from short-range to long-range planning. But it does not solve all of them. This model reconceptualizes interests, environments, and strategies in ways that deal with long-range uncertainty, but does not reconceptualize the process of getting from interests and environments to the strategies. Going back to Figure 1.1, we have redefined the rectangle, the oval, and the triangle. Now the arrow must come under scrutiny.

It is customary in the national security planning process to project a set of threats that are inherent in the environment and to design a force to cope with those threats. This simple process, however, breaks down in the face of long-range uncertainty. Any attempt to predict, five or ten years in advance, precisely what threats U.S. interests will face, is doomed to failure, for the following reasons:

1. U.S. interests are diverse.
2. A large number of countries, with exceedingly diverse relationships, are involved.
3. Within these countries, decisions are often made by individuals or small groups whose reactions are frequently idiosyncratic, erratic, and otherwise unpredictable.
4. The present state of knowledge does not permit confident long-range analysis of the consequences of current trends. The number of variables and the complexity of interactions are simply too great.

Thus, it would be foolish to attempt to design forces to meet a specific list of projected likely threats. There are so many possible contingencies and threats, to which no confident assignment of probabilities can be made, that a design of forces in this fashion would have to be either (1) quite arbitrary in choosing likely threats, or (2) extremely wasteful because it was designed to meet a very long list of threats only a few of which would ever occur.

Instead of designing forces around attempts to meet individual threats one by one, it is preferable to design a force structure and strategy that can clearly operate in the projected environment, which is clearly within U.S. economic and other capabilities, and which clearly has the capability to meet most low-level and moderate threats that might arise in the environment. Then one can devise a mobilization plan to cope with major threats and with less likely combinations of low- and moderate-level contingencies.

This may sound not very different from standard conceptions, but there are crucial differences. In short-run planning, for instance, military planning for Asia, one faces only a very few important contingencies and can carefully calculate the likelihood of each one, the likelihood that two or more would occur simultaneously, and the specific forces required to meet all likely combinations. In long-run planning one faces dozens of contingencies and combinations of contingencies whose likelihoods are not calculable within reasonable limits. So, instead of picking a specific set of threats and designing forces to meet them, one chooses a *level* of threat for which one requires constant readiness—for instance, a 1½ war strategy. Then one designs a force structure with appropriate mobility. A mobilization strategy can then be designed to hedge against other levels of threat.

This military example is generalizable to all longer-range planning processes. A key to successful long-range planning is to address the planning process at an appropriate level of generality. A U.S. 20-year military plan for Thai contingencies would probably be of little value. But a plan for Southeast Asia or for Pacific Asia would have a geographic scale appropriate to the time frame. The point may be clarified by analogy to physics. In quantum mechanics, one can never predict the position and momentum of individual particles, or of small numbers of particles. However, for large numbers of particles under specified conditions, one can generate statistical laws that yield very high confidence predictions. Similarly, although one cannot predict the extent of insurgency in Thailand over the next 20 years, one can set reasonable bounds on the level of military confrontations likely to arise in Southeast Asia. While this seems obvious, choice of the proper geographic scope and level of generality for planning is seldom easy. When done appropriately, it facilitates solution of two critical problems: sensible long-range policy planning and stable administrative budgeting. The logic of stable budgeting follows the logic of long-range planning. For instance, while no United States intelligence or military budget for Thailand will predictably remain stable over many years, the budget for Southeast Asia, or for North-South issues, may well prove amenable to stable projection. The forecaster must cast his forecasts at an appropriate level of generality for the time under consideration, seeking, like the physicist, to choose variables at a level of aggregation that makes prediction feasible.

A second standard process involved in short-range planning is fragmentation of plans. The military creates a military plan, the State Department creates (or should create) a political plan, and the economists create an economic plan. Each of these functional plans in turn is built up from almost independently created regional plans (for Europe, for Asia, and so on).

For short-range planning, this fragmented process works because over the short range it is possible to assume, for purposes of military planning, that economic and political policies are held constant. Likewise, one can in most cases assume that, except for a few obvious exceptions, interactions among regions will not greatly disturb the calculations. Increasing uncertainty over the long range breaks down these assumptions. Over the long range, interactions among functional and regional policies and trends become so important that dealing with just one fragment becomes like trying to inflate just one part of a balloon.

The source of the problem generates its own solution. Precisely because the planning is long range, it is possible to undertake a more lengthy, less fragmented process of, first, designing a comprehensive but highly abstract national strategy, and then deriving a military strategy consistent with the economic and political parts of the national strategy (or an economic strategy consistent with the political and military parts). It is important to emphasize that detail is not important in designing the national strategy. If the purpose of the national strategy is to provide a context for a military strategy, then the economic part of the national strategy need only deal with a few of the most important economic trends, economic problems, and economic substrategies. Similarly, the forecaster dealing with long-range problems will have to be a different breed from the narrowly compartmentalized forecaster assumed in textbooks on forecasting methods; he will have to deal in broad political-economic-military concepts rather than in narrow, quantifiable terms.[3]

Avoidance of functional fragmentation usually turns out to be more important than avoidance of regional fragmentation. A long-range military plan (say, 10 to 15 years ahead) is meaningless in the absence of complementary economic and political concepts. On the other hand, one can sometimes justify separating out one region of the world for a long-range plan.

OVERVIEW

This analysis does not purport to identify or solve all or even most of the important problems in long-range forecasting and planning, but it does try to analyze some of the reasons why the methods of short-range planning do not apply to planning for the longer range. But there probably will be little dissent to an observation that much of the long-range planning currently done has greatly diminished value because of failure to recognize the breakdown of the assumptions on which short-range planning and forecasting are based.

Finally, it is important to be clear about the purpose of long-range planning and forecasting. That purpose is to improve the quality of decisions made today. In the current state of social science knowledge, detailed prediction of the future is impossible and should be recognized as such. Even in economics, that most quantified social science, the quality of long-range predictions can bring pride to no one. Nobody has ever implemented a detailed 10-year plan or a detailed 20-year plan. And yet, paradoxically, the world's most sophisticated economic planners find 10- and 20-year plans extremely valuable. For instance, economic planners in Japan and Taiwan, who have given their countries the world's highest sustained rates of economic growth, rely heavily on long-range plans. Taiwan uses one-year, two-year, five-year, 10-year and 20-year economic plans. The latter provide an important context and perspective that improve shorter-range decision making.

The solution to the paradox is not obscure. First, some trends, such as multipolarity or Third World consciousness, emerge so slowly as to be undetectable in a two-year time span, yet have great influence over the shape of the future's threats and opportunities. Often, these trends are so ponderous that one doesn't need details to perceive their importance. Second, some problems and trends look very different in long-range perspective. Hudson Institute has a famous graph projecting 1960s rates of growth of research and development spending into the long-range future; by the year 2000, R&D spending becomes larger than the GNP, sending a clear message to the planner. Similarly, the Brookings Institution found that, while the discretionary funds available to the U.S. government for new programs seem trivial over a period of one to two years, major alterations in the shape of the budget can be planned over a 10-year period. The differing consequences of alternative restrictions on industrial pollution appear trivial in a country beginning its industrialization (like Korea in 1960) but appear mammoth over a longer period of time.

Perhaps most important, the process of long-range planning and forecasting changes the way people think. Long-range issues force the economist to think about politics, the political scientist to think about culture, the military technologist to take seriously the possibility that the next war may not be like the last one. In more everyday terms, long-range perspective makes the difference between the adolescent who takes the first opportunity to get out of school and into a job and the one who goes to college. Neither adolescent knows much detail about the future, but one of them has acquired some small pieces of information and some perspectives that help him to make better short-range decisions. In a world of scholarship increasingly divided along rigid lines, and in a world of bureaucracies fragmented into rigid, narrow compartments, such gains of small pieces of information and large differences of perspective can become overwhelmingly important.

It cannot be overemphasized that long-range strategic thinking is qualitatively different from short-range tactical thinking—frequently to the extent of requiring different personalities. The ability to think in terms of the forest rather than the trees, and to cut across the boundaries of particular disciplines and problems, requires cultivation. An example will illustrate the difference. A team of very senior corporate executives was created to deal with the possibility of a major political transformation in an African country. The team identified a list of potential problems: nationalization, loss of export or import licenses, restrictions on profit repatriation, and so forth. They divided the team into committees, each of which was to invent a strategy for coping with one of the problems. After two days, the committee on nationalization had nothing more to show for its efforts than a short list of recommendations that the company communicate with the insurgents, seek a friendly relationship with them, and avoid company policies that would irritate them. These recommendations were sensible, but were such innocuous clichés that the executives were embarrassed. All the other committees also produced clichés. The problem was their bottom-up approach: trying to build strategies out of a collection of tactics directed at individual problems. When a consultant persuaded them to take an opposite, top-down approach, they completed their work within a few hours. They first identified alternative overall strategies: get out of the country immediately, milk the operation slowly for cash, align their policies with the insurgents whenever that could be done at low cost, or spend money to keep the company's policies ahead of the revolution. These alternative strategies generated a rich set of choices for coping with potential nationalization and other specific problems. The difference between the tactical approach, which these senior executives had used exclusively throughout their careers, and the more appropriate strategic approach made the difference between success and failure.

NOTES

1. Table 1.1 is adapted from William H. Overholt, *A Nuclear Posture for Asia* (Hudson Institute, HI-2371/2-RR, April 1977), p. 9. Appendix 1 of that volume consists for an extensive discussion of the anal-

ysis of U.S. national interests. For further elaboration of Table 1.2, see William H. Overholt, *Political Risk* (London: Euromoney Publications, 1982), p. 32.

2. See William H. Overholt and Marylin Chou, "Foreign Policy Doctrines," *Policy Studies Journal* 3, no. 2 (Winter 1974), pp. 185–88.

3. See Chapter 6, on integration of different kinds of forecasts.

Chapter 2

The Needs and Perspectives of Analysts and Policy Makers

INTRODUCTION

Chapter 1 has discussed planning as a *logical* process. This logical perspective is valid, but it must be overlaid with a comprehension of planning as a *social* process. In practice, the planning process is usually divided between analysts, who specialize in describing and projecting environments, and policy makers, who specialize in formulating strategies or making decisions. Analysts and policy makers have characteristic needs, exhibit characteristic patterns of behavior, and interact in characteristic ways. This chapter describes their typical needs, behaviors, and interactions.

Policy makers and analysts are slowly discovering just how difficult it is to provide useful analysis that fulfills its potential in support of policy making. Ironically, as policy makers learn how important the role of analysis is, their demands for better quality and greater quantities of information increase, but the information explosion has inundated policy makers with data they often cannot process, interpret, or even trust. Most information available to policy makers is possibly biased, and this possibility is enough to leave the policy maker in an insurmountable quandary about what to trust, unless an impartial analytical operation can provide guidance through the thickets of contradictory data. Moreover, in response to the demands for higher quality analysis, analysts have all too often responded with pretentious pseudoscientific methodology that actually detracts from the validity of analysis and, hence, from the ultimate quality of decision making. Here, too, the policy maker, usually without the time or expertise to judge analytical methods himself, is in dire need of analytical guidance to see which emperors have no clothes.

Consequently, useful analysis has to guide the policy maker in his own analysis. The proper role of analysis is a "heuristic" one: analysis must instruct the policy maker on how to make sense of the vast amounts of information—often of questionable validity—originating from diverse sources. Analysis must not only provide information in the narrow sense of isolated pieces of data; it must also enable the policy maker to evaluate this information, to know its full meaning, and to incorporate it into his existing base of knowledge and opinion. In the glut of information, useful analysis must distinguish itself by its capacity to make the policy maker master over an otherwise unorganized mass of facts and alleged facts. The direct and most essential conclusion of this diagnosis is that good analysis must be open in displaying its assumptions, its uncertainties, and the context of the phenomena under consideration.

We shall also argue that analysis that is meaningful in this way often encounters resistance, on the parts of both policy makers and analysts, which must be overcome. Psychological and political insecurities can hinder the pursuit of good analysis as well as the utilization of good analysis. Differing needs and perspectives between policy makers and analysts produce conflicts that drain the cooperative spirit necessary for heuristic analysis. These conflicts are all the more insidious because they are rarely recognized.

The purpose of the following discussion, then, is first to elaborate the justifications of analysis as heuristics and then to identify sources of differences and conflicts that can inhibit such analysis. Once the predicaments of the analyst and the policy maker have been defined, the following chapters can begin to address these problems.

In the interaction between analysts and policy makers there are numerous grounds for common cause. Both analysts and policy makers prosper when well-reasoned decisions are based on sensible information supplied and evaluated with a proper appreciation of its strengths and weakneses. It would be misleading, therefore, to cast the analyst–policy-maker interaction as predominantly an antagonistic or adversary relationship. Nevertheless, there are several important strains in the analyst–policy-maker relation, rooted in differences in objectives and perspectives that can lead to miscommunication and mistrust.

POLICY MAKERS' NEEDS

The demands that policy makers make upon their analysts can be separated into two categories: needs for making decisions through reasoned judgment, and additional needs that reflect the policy makers' politics, insecurities, habits, biases, and other motivations extraneous to the specific task of making a rational decision. This is not to say, of course, that the typical policy maker is a neurotic, Machiavellian, or unreasonable person who subverts good intelligence and policy making. More often than not, the opposite is true. But there are characteristic situational pressures that must be acknowledged and then channeled or offset.

Policy Makers' Rational Information Needs

Information provided to policy makers has four intrinsic components:

The specific, manifest content of the information itself
The meaning of this information
The degree of certainty it warrants
The policy recommendations embedded in or implied by the information

Since clarifying each component helps the policy maker to know how to use the information and the risks involved in its use, the following needs arise:

1. Knowledge of the *uncertainty* of the information provided to the policy maker as "factual." This includes an assessment of the reliability of the statistical data employed in the analysis. The policy maker must be aware that all analysis is limited, and understand the particular limitations of each specific analysis. Assessing the uncertainty of analysis also involves knowing how much difference it would make if various aspects of the analysis *are* in error. If the assumptions are incorrect, how different are the conclusions from what they ought to be? If the data are imprecise, does that make a big difference or little difference?

2. Knowledge of where the factual information ends and the recommendations begin. Recommendations disguised as facts (for example, by showing that certain choices will achieve optimal results, but without revealing why these results should be considered optimal) can mislead the policy maker and limit his range of choice.

3. Knowledge of the *context* from which the specific information was derived, so that the policy maker can infer the full meaning of the specifics, understand how to think about the subject matter, and get some additional corroboration on the degree of uncertainty in the specific information provided to him.

4. Knowledge of the *assumptions* underlying the analysis for much the same reasons, in addition to aiding the policy maker in uncovering whether implied recommendations are based on value preferences that he may not share with the analyst.

5. Knowledge of which factors are *relevant* for adequate understanding. In contrast to the preceding needs, which call for an expansion of the informational base at the policy maker's disposal, psychologists have pointed out that the limits of cognitive capacity preclude the processing of too much information.[1] Overly complex information can be as paralyzing as lack of information, as illustrated by the way the glut of information on the U.S. and world energy situation has caused mass confusion for both legislative and executive policy makers. Policy makers' sheer time constraints make it impossible for them to use all available information. This translates into the need for the analyst to provide all of the salient content, but *only* the salient content. The policy maker must know which factors require consideration and which can be safely ignored. All too often attention is focused on factors for which hard data are available, even though "softer" factors are more important.

Policy Makers' Political Needs

The policy maker's political needs are as simple to summarize as they are difficult to fulfill:

1. To be a convincing advocate of preferred policies—hence, to have access to professional-seeming information.
2. Whenever possible, to be correct (that is, to choose policies that, if implemented, produce positive results).
3. When wrong, not to be disastrously so—thus, to make conservative decisions that avoid major risks even at the expense of foregoing certain opportunities.
4. When wrong, to minimize the blame focused on the policy maker.
5. To maintain his decision making discretion.

The informational demands growing out of these political needs focus both on the substance and the appearance of information. In order to maintain his record of "right" decisions, the policy maker requires accurate *and* balanced analysis, but, in order to minimize disastrous mistakes and blame, the information must "excuse" the policy maker if he makes decisions that prove in retrospect to have been faulty. In other words, the demands will either be for information skewed to cover all contingencies *or* or information that will relieve the policy maker's responsibility should anything go wrong.

The information the policy maker chooses to use in *promoting* his preferred policies must appear to be professional, competent, expert, and above all *credible*. But to serve this promotion function it must say what the policy maker wants it to say. A policy maker may signal or pressure the analyst to provide evidence of the right sort, or may be selective in accepting only that information which supports the policy maker's predispositions.

Policy Makers' Psychological Needs

Running at cross purposes to these rational information and political needs are three related habits of thought that are perhaps more prevalent in individuals under pressure to make decisions than they are in analysts. First, there is frequently a demand for *certainty,* to reduce the anxiety of making decisions based on imperfect information about an uncertain world. Decision makers often prefer to presume that certainty prevails, even if not warranted by objective conditions.

Second, the anxiety and frustration of confronting the complexity of almost all decision situations prompt a demand for *simplicity,* for explanations based on uncomplicated causes, simple relationships involving few variables, and clearcut choices. Intricate analysis provokes insecurity through its implication that reality is difficult to comprehend and that situations are hard to control. Hence, uncomplicated analysis is often applauded as decisive, rather than dismissed as simplistic. The policy makers' psychological needs can thus interfere with their informational needs, which require "full disclosure" of uncertainty and are enhanced by comprehensive analysis.

Third, to maintain the policy maker's confidence in his own capacity to understand the world, there is a demand for information that *confirms his already existing views.* This is manifested either by signals to the analyst to say what the policy maker wants to hear or by downgrading the analysis (and the analysts) providing conflicting information. Imagine the reaction of U.S. foreign policy makers in 1977 if *one* analytic source had predicted a revolution in Iran. Even if an analyst has something very original to say, he or she is often at risk in saying it.

ANALYSTS' NEEDS

Analysts also have needs; some are requisites for good analysis, some are psychological, and some are political. Analysts want to be secure, influential, and respected. Analysts are also professionals with disciplinary identifications, loyalties, and desires for respect from their professional peers. To gain professional recognition, analysts are often tempted to use large computer models and arcane methods even if other methods are more accurate and useful. There is also strong peer pressure on analysts to come up with something innovative or original, regardless of whether it is justified. Professional advancement certainly requires the analyst to come up with *something*, even if the best he or she can do, given the limitations on the feasibility of analyzing certain situations, is to offer vacuous verbiage in glossy packages.

The positive function of such professional identifications is that they can offset institutional loyalties that otherwise might have induced the analyst to provide analysis designed to enhance the position of his or her agency rather than to meet the professional standards of impartiality.

Because analysts are generally situated within organizations, their organizational loyalties also play a part in establishing their political needs. Analysis may be distorted to maximize the interests of a particular organization or to confirm its previous positions; analyses prepared by the Navy and the Air Force are likely to differ in ways that reflect differing service interests. Moreover, analysis may be suspected by the policy maker as distorted in this fashion.

Yet it seems clear that, in the long run, accurate analysis that enhances the overall credibility of the analyst's organization is in the best interest of all parties. For analysis to be useful to the policy maker (and, hence, politically useful for the analyst), it must, above all, be credible. If we distinguish between the analyst's persuasiveness with regard to a specific piece of analysis and his long-run credibility, clearly the longer-term considerations ought to dominate. For example, the compulsion of the analyst to be continually relevant, to get the policy maker's attention, and to demonstrate usefulness, can prompt the analyst to depart from reporting the mundane conventonal wisdom even if he believes it, yet in the long run the highly innovative analyst is often wrong in this largely "business-as-usual" world. Ironically, there is some evidence from experiments in cognitive psychology showing that even when analysts provide original and insightful analysis (telling the policy maker something he or she did not know before) policy makers are likely to underestimate the value of such information, as their own perceptions of what they had already known tend to incorporate the new information.

To increase his own usefulness, the analyst must ensure that the analysis is as convincing as it deserves, but the analyst must also convey that he does not always have to be right to maintain a claim of competence. Thus, a corollary to this need to maintain credibility is the need to express the fact that uncertainty does exist in the analysis. This extends not only to direct dealings with the policy maker requesting the information, but also to the policy maker's presentation of the analyst's information to other policy makers and to the public.

The analyst's demand that his input have some impact on policy making creates considerable confusion and dissatisfaction. The problem, it turns out, is not so much that analysts generally lack influence, but rather that it is impossible for the analyst and the policy maker alike to ascribe influence to particular sources. It is extremely rare for a given piece of analysis to have a clearly traceable impact on policy outcomes. The policy maker is not a blank slate; any new piece of analysis, if it is noted by the policy maker, must coexist with previously formed ideas and prior information, some with the same implications for action as the new analysis and some without. Consequently, the impact of analysis is generally impossible to trace, and is quite often indirect. Analysis can change the climate of opinion and the allocation of attention, but the extent to which a particular analyst is responsible usually cannot be determined.

RESULTING CONFLICTS

Because policy makers and analysts have somewhat differing needs and perspectives, conflicts do arise. Some of these conflicts are based on misunderstanding and are therefore remediable; others, based on differences in what the policy makers and the analysts really want and need, are not.

The Pressure for Certainty

The most serious strain between the policy maker and the analyst has been the policy maker's demand for certainty beyond what the analyst legitimately can or wishes to provide. The analyst is pressured to provide single-point, specific forecasts or estimates, rather than ranges of likelihood. This detracts from the analyst's ability to convey the degree of uncertainty that he knows to be inherent in the information. This problem runs deeper than the simple instinctual desire for clearcut answers. Policy makers often find that they can argue more persuasively in favor of their policy preferences if the expert information at their disposal appears to be definitive; and if the policy makers should turn out to have been wrong, they can resort to the defense that they had been misled by faulty—but expert—information. This demand for precise, detailed information pushes the analyst into concentrating on the type of information amenable to precise measurement, estimation, or projection, and on questions amenable to precise answers—even if the analyst does not believe these foci to be as useful as other information or questions of a less precise nature. At the same time, it puts the analyst in the position of appearing wrong when in fact he is legitimately uncertain. Conversely, some analysts go beyond the bounds of reasonable hedging and protect themselves from the risk of error by so muddying the analysis as to abrogate a useful role in helping the decision maker to decide.

The Relationship of Analysis to Decision

The importance granted to analysts in the process of decision making is a second major point of contention. Policy makers confident in their own fundamental understanding of the broad situation with which they are dealing may regard expert analysis strictly as specific information or data. Forecasts and other "technical data" are then treated only as *inputs* to the policy maker's deliberation, which is guided by his own understanding of the situation and his own style of thinking about it. The analyst is not involved in specifying or testing the feasibility of policy objectives.

Hubris or selfishness cannot adequately explain why many policy makers prefer this limited role for the analyst. It may be argued that separating intelligence and forecasting from the other policy-making tasks ensures a certain impartiality on the part of the analyst. His contributions may be less subject to the distortions of wish fulfillment, pressures to say what he believes the policy maker wants to hear, or temptations to manipulate the policy maker's decisions by providing inaccurate information. All of these distortions may occur even if the analyst is cut off from the other policy-making tasks, but they are simply less likely when analysis is maintained as a separate, even isolated, task.

The role of analysis can be vastly increased if it is regarded not as merely the starting point of decision making, but rather as an approach to problem solving. This is not meant to be a semantic trick that simply replaces the term "decision making" with the term "analysis." Rather, it means concretely that the people assigned to do analysis in the usual sense of the term (intelligence, data collection, forecasting, factual evaluation) are also to be involved in all of the other policy-making tasks short of the official authorization of the ultimate policy.

In the forecasting disciplines, this perspective is exemplified by *normative forecasting*, defined as the use of projections to systematically explore and select goals and alternatives. This is an effort to transform the operation of producing forecasts as isolated bits of information into a decision-making process in its own right. In some instances, elaborate decision-making routines have been developed to calculate decisions based on the available "technical" input through explicit optimization routines. If this seems too ambitious a role for forecasting, it should be noted that policy simulation models, for which the analyst not only selects or creates the model but also chooses the range of policy scenarios to be examined, provide an equally extensive role for the analyst.

Finally, there is the *heuristic* conception of the role of analysis, which eschews decisiveness but goes beyond treating analysis as simply input. This is the conception of analysis as an educative aid to the policy maker; not just to inform, but also to instruct him in how to think about the subject under examination. In forecasting, the practical applications of this conception have been the broad, theoretical, "soft" essays on the future, in which specific projections are often conspicuously absent.

This conception of the heuristic (teaching) role of analysis strikes many policy makers as terribly presumptuous, and manipulative as well, insofar as it implies that the policy maker must be steered into thinking the right way. Yet, the analyst can argue that, unless he can convey the way the situation was analyzed, all the specific information provided to the policy maker is taken out of its theoretical context, and thus may be more miseading than useful. The analyst may assert that it is indeed *less* presumptuous to provide a framework for the policy maker to do his own analysis than it is to provide data and projections as if they were the final and absolute truth. In this view, intelligence and projection are to be integrated with the other intellectual tasks of policy making. Instead of projecting isolated trends that quickly lose their vividness, accuracy, and usefulness, the heuristic approach would concentrate on understanding and projecting the dynamics established through analysis of the past and indicated by emerging trends as salient to the future.

Accuracy versus Utility

Policy makers and analysts often differ on the importance of accuracy as a criterion of good analysis. The analyst can point out that, considering the uncertainty inherent in all analysis, the prevalence of self-fulfilling and self-defeating prophecies, and the relatively greater importance of understanding a situation's dynamics than that of having accurate but narrow information, accuracy ought not to be considered as the principal requirement of good analysis. For the policy maker, however, any erosion of the analyst's operating principle of maximizing accuracy destroys the policy maker's security in the "quality control" of the information he must use. From the policy maker's perspective, any sacrifice of accuracy undertaken by the analyst to increase the impact of the analysis—for example, exaggerating a problem in order to promote the policy response appropriate in the eyes of the analyst—undermines the policy maker's ability to make the decision most appropriate in his own eyes.

Even when the analyst refrains from attempts to manipulate analysis to promote preferred policy outcomes, the policy maker's demand for accuracy still may conflict with the analyst's desire to devote relatively less effort to confirming the accuracy of the analysis in order to devote more effort to enhancing the utility of the analysis—explaining the significance of the analysis (on the assumption that it is indeed correct), elaborating on recommendations implicit in the analysis, and so on. This conflict also entails political considerations, this time from the perspective of the analyst. The analyst often wants to reduce the importance of accuracy as a criterion of evaluating the analysis, in order to protect his reputation in case of error. The analyst wants to elevate the relative importance of the *utility* of analysis as a criterion so that his role in the decision making process can be enhanced. Implicit in the forecasting theorists' argument that utility rather than accuracy ought to be the primary criterion is the notion that the analyst's contribution ought to be fully integrated into the decision-making process rather than relegated to the status of "mere information."

Caution versus Relevance

While the *ambitious* analyst, desiring influence in a context of uncertainty, will employ the strategy just noted (namely, seeking to provide interesting information and to downgrade the importance of being wrong once in a while), the *defensive* analyst will react differently. An analyst primarily afraid of being wrong may well confine himself to subjects and methods that provide a high degree of certainty at the expense of relevance. This analyst will, in short, eschew judgment. Since most of the decisions facing a policy maker are matters of fine judgment, the output of such an analyst will prove increasingly worthless. The analyst, who may have been burned in the past for erroneous judgment, will insist on quantifiable data, will insist that he cannot provide answers in the absence of hard facts, and will respond to a request for judgment with an insistence that answers cannot be provided without new resources and without additional time, even though the policy maker may have to act quickly.

Integrity versus Credibility

The policy maker's preference for information that confirms his already formed opinions, either for psychological security or to avoid the appearance of having been wrong before, creates a struggle over the analyst's independence to express his or her own opinions. Assuming that the analyst's information is indeed more accurate than the policy maker's preconceptions, the analyst who conforms to the policy maker's signals risks long-term credibility. If he does not conform, however, the analyst risks his standing with that policy maker, who is more likely to dismiss the analyst's input as implausible, threatening, or of little use.

The Politics of Methods

Policy makers and analysts frequently fight a complex and deceptive battle over methods. It is complex because it touches on many of the motivations and strains alluded to earlier; it is deceptive because, although the issue is cast in terms of choice of methods, in fact many considerations other than the "technical appropriateness" of the methodology come into play.

In terms of the scope of analysts' participation in decision making, analysts wishing to expand their role often advocate methods that incorporate choice-evaluation routines (such as, "figure-of-merit" calculations and optimization routines), which may be opposed by policy makers defending their own prerogatives.

In terms of the *complexity* of analytical method, policy makers are often ambivalent; they prefer complex methods if apparent methodological sophistication makes their arguments (and themselves) seem more sophisticated, but they are rightfully leery of complexity that reduces their understanding of the assumptions and procedures of the analysis. If results or recommendations appear to emerge mysteriously from an incomprehensible analysis (such as a huge econometric model), the policy maker must take these results on faith, reject them, or use them in support of his arguments even if he has no confidence in the method. This can lead to mixed signals from the policy maker to the analyst: "Provide me with a very complex analysis that is simple to understand."

For the analyst, the use of sophisticated methods brings several rewards: personal feelings of mastery, professional (peer) approval, persuasiveness to the extent that the scientific aura of complex methods makes the results also seem "scientific," and a greater opportunity to have a decisive influence insofar as the elaborateness of the method encompasses part of the decision-making routine (for example, optimization). Consequently, sophistication holds some threats for the policy maker if he fears encroachment by the analyst.

Unfortunately, bad analysis and ill-founded decisions often occur when this tension over methodologial sophistication is "resolved," by permitting the analyst to use esoteric methods beyond the understanding of the policy maker as long as their results turn out to support the policy maker's original positions. In such cases, the policy maker loses sight of the assumptions underlying the analysis as well as the dynamics represented through the methods.

In terms of the *explicitness* of method, there are several dimensions of conflict. Sometimes the analyst prefers explicit, usually mathematical methods by virtue of their scientific allure, while the policy maker simply wants easily understandable, informed judgment. Sometimes the policy maker wants explicit methods, either to check on the assumptions underlying the analysis or to give the appearance of sophistication, while the analyst has some judgmentally based knowledge he wishes to convey but cannot do so through a framework of explicit methodology. (These potential difficulties are elaborated on in Chapter 3.) Thus, the educative or heuristic function of analysis, because it is usually carried out through "soft," nonexplicit methods, can be jeopardized by the demand for explicitness.

Soundness versus Surprises

There is a chronic tradeoff between the plausibility of analysis and its sensitivity to surprising outcomes (that is, those of low subjective probabilities). Credibility is risked by producing or acting upon implausible scenarios. The Russian analyst who, in 1970, called attention to the risk that anticommunist Richard Nixon would form an entente with China, was probably fired long before the event. But, since some of these outcomes, should they materialize, would constitute serious dangers (and hence serious political liabilities for the policy maker who does not take them into account), policy makers and analysts are often at odds over presenting implausible scenarios for consideration.

First, the policy maker must indicate that he is aware of all significant possibilities but does not want to be associated with implausible analysis or "hysteria." Policy makers who do not want to take action on low-probability contingencies, to avoid the costs of such policies or avoid being seen as overreacting, may suppress the analysis of these contingencies. Then, if such a low-probability event does materialize, the blame is placed on the analyst. Of course, in practice the strategy is not so Machiavellian or stark; the policy maker simply tries to discourage the analyst from sounding what are probably false alarms. The analyst, in turn, may try to protect his own position by emphasizing all possibilities no matter how remote.

Alternatively, the analyst may try to protect his own credibility in the long run by screening out implausible possibilities that the policy maker *does* want to consider. The insecurity of the policy maker in this situation is exacerbated by the fact that the screening can occur without his awareness and is often far beyond his control. For example, in the operation of formal models (such as econometric and simulation models) whose mechanical operation presumably could insulate the results from the model operator's own biases, there is in fact much plausibility testing that goes along with the parameter estimation and much tinkering with the models when they produce results that do not correspond to the analyst's preconceptions. (See chapters 3 and 4.)

CONCLUSION

What, in the final analysis, does the policy maker want? Depending on his level of political and psychological security, the policy maker is likely to want either *analysis as heuristics* or *analysis as data,* the former being preferred by the secure. Analysis as heuristics provides the policy maker with a basis of understanding that is both selective (since only the important dynamics are reported, information overload is avoided) and rich in contextual meaning (since its assumptions and implications are evident). If, however, the policy maker is impatient with explanations and wants hard data, if he fears intellectual encroachment by the analyst, or if his situation requires that he be armed with precise charts and graphs, the policy maker will demand analysis as data.

As evidence that *analysis as decision making* is not generally accepted by policy makers as the preferred role for analysis, one could point to the decline in the use of explicit optimization routines (that is, explicit programs that calculate the costs and benefits of different strategies) in the past decade, both in corporations (for instance, product rating programs) and in government (like the planning-programming-budgeting system imposed on executive agencies as a budget-formulating device) after such ambitious beginnings in the 1960s. It also appears that forecasting studies that cast their results in terms of policy recommendations rather than as information—even if this information has rather clear policy implications—are less likely to have much impact on the policy makers. The logic of the policy maker's political situation is such that he wants to be aided in finding out what to do, but wants neither to be told what to do nor to appear to be blindly following technical advice.

The analyst's preferences also depend on his level of security. Ambition may call for analysis as decision making, or, along a more intellectual dimension, analysis as heuristics. An insecure or dogmatic analyst may wish the analysis to take the form of hard data backed by precise and formal methods. The preceding considerations of the policy maker's information needs would downgrade the utility of analysis as data, and the considerations of the policy maker's political needs imply that analysis as decision making is likely to be resisted by policy makers. The common ground, therefore, should be analysis as heuristics, even though the insecurities of analysts and policy makers alike pose a serious challenge to establishing this sort of relationship between them.

NOTES

1. George Miller, "The Magical Number Seven, Plus or Minus Two: Some Limits to Our Capacity for Processing Information," *Psychological Review* 63 (1956): 81–97.

Part 2
Forecasting Methods

Chapter 3

Forecasting Methods: Review and Appraisal

This chapter reviews the logic, premises, and properties of the most prominent techniques used in political forecasting and in the related areas of socioeconomic forecasting. There are two distinct reasons for the political forecaster to have some familiarity with the techniques reviewed here. First, the political forecaster obviously must employ some method in his work, either with or without being aware of doing so. The unexamined method is dangerous, because the forecaster remains unaware of the limitations and biases of his own work.

The second reason may be less obvious. The political forecaster spends a large portion of time trying to incorporate and make sense of the other social and economic forecasts that describe the future context of politics. (See Chapter 6.) He must therefore have a basic familiarity with the limitations and biases of the methods others are using to generate these forecasts. Of course, the political forecaster cannot become an expert in all related disciplines in order to generate his own "background" forecasts, but he or she must be prepared to assess the soundness and likely distortions of others' forecasts on the basis of a brief description of the methods and assumptions underlying those forecasts. The descriptions of techniques reviewed in this chapter are not meant to be definitive, but rather to make discussion of their premises, rationales, and limitations understandable.

In keeping with the eclectic approach to methods that we have maintained throughout this volume, this chapter is not a sales pitch for one technique. Rather, it is a guide to the tradeoffs involved in the application of the various techniques, designed to aid the reader in selecting an approach for a given forecasting task or in accepting someone else's background forecast as methodologically adequate.

PRELIMINARY CONSIDERATIONS

Four points should be made at the outset. First, there are no elegant distinctions to be made among the terms "technique," "method," and "approach," although "approach" is generally taken to be more encompassing, the set of methods or techniques applied in a given way. Because the terms are used practically interchangeably in the literature on forecasting, ranging from the most technical concerns of how to smooth data points into an extrapolation, to the integration of forecasting and decision making, there is little merit in making a sharp distinction here.

Second, not all of the methods reviewed here are on the same level. Some pertain to the procedure of making the projection (what the forecaster does to satisfy his own questions about what is likely to happen). Some pertain to the format of presentation (what the forecaster does to convey information to the audience). Others, such as scenario writing, are relevant to both. Nevertheless, they must be discussed together, because method blends are the rule and because the choice of projection procedure and the choice of presentational format are deeply intertwined.

Third, the appropriate choice of method depends not only on the problem, but also on who is making the forecast and under what circumstances. This rather startling fact is true because the viability of a given method depends on how much information and understanding the forecaster has regarding the system under examination. If the forecaster understands a system poorly, any complicated but probably ill-founded theories about it would likely give rise to results that are both incorrect and difficult for the forecaster to perceive as incorrect. One of the great dangers of much of the academic literature on forecasting is the extent to which complex techniques convey a spurious impression of accuracy and comprehensiveness when in fact they simply enshrine unjustified and ill-understood assumptions.

Fourth, before deciding *how* to forecast one should determine *what* to forecast. This decision should be made first, because certain methods simply cannot yield answers in the same terms. For example, sometimes it is not a good idea to forecast quantitative trends, and yet certain methods, inasmuch as they require numerical trends as inputs and produce numerical projections as their outputs, "force" the forecaster to focus on quantitatively defined trends.

CRITERIA FOR CHOOSING A METHOD

The following properties are desirable in forecasting methods:

1. Plausibility testing
2. Capacity to display counterintuitive implications
3. Explicitness
4. Comprehensiveness
5. Sensitivity to nuances
6. Capacity to incorporate well-founded theory
7. Simplicity

The problem is that there are inevitable tradeoffs among these properties. Considered separately, each is attractive, all other things being equal; unfortunately, all other things never are equal.

Plausibility Testing

The capacity to discard or alter results that do not conform with the forecaster's judgments of what is plausible permits the forecaster to screen out silly results produced by forecasting procedures that are misspecified, improperly applied, or otherwise wrong. It is therefore the mechanism that links the human forecaster—with his own judgments of what is plausible and implausible—to the formal method being applied. To the degree that forecasting methods are always in the process of development and refinement, and since we must always have doubts about whether a given forecasting routine is on the right track, plausibility testing is insurance against the tyranny of the method. If, for example, instead of treating a complex model as if it were a black box producing results through unknown intermediate steps, we examine that model's intermediate results to see if they meet the standard of plausibility, we might accept or reject final results on this basis. Or, we might go directly to the model's final outputs, decide whether they make sense, and decide on that basis whether the model is behaving the way we know the world behaves.

The obvious implication of plausibility testing is that we end up second-guessing the model. This is a wise choice if there is reason to expect that we are smarter than the assumptions and relationships expressed in the method; otherwise, it is a sad waste of time. In either case, we are, to a certain degree, discarding the method in order to listen to what we believed anyway.

Capacity for Counterintuitive Implications

The capacity for a forecasting procedure to display the emergence of the counterintuitive implications of underlying premises is often what separates the systematic forecast from the conventional wisdom. Sometimes the implications of plausible premises are themselves implausible. Does it seem intuitively correct that daily doubling of a starting salary of one dollar per day would yield a daily salary of more than $500 million within one month? Such surprises emerge when the human mind cannot easily track the magnitudes of rates of change, when complicated interactions or feedback mechanisms make systems work unlike simple systems, or when trends exceed a threshold that triggers new dynamics. The now famous (and justifiably controversial) Laffer model of supply-side economics produces the counterintuitive result that lower marginal tax rates can yield equal or even higher government revenues. The model is based on the premise that lower taxes may in some cases stimulate greater economic activity, which in turn creates a greater tax base.

A more complicated political example of counterintuitive results is the pattern of democratic collapse in Uruguay in the late 1960s and early 1970s. It probably would have seemed implausible to observers of Uruguayan democracy in the 1950s and early 1960s that the following pattern could emerge:

1. The extensive welfare system increases government indebtedness and other economic problems.
2. The economic problems make it politically more difficult to reform the economy in the face of demands for subsidies to ensure employment, governmental aid to offset the deprivations caused by the economic decline, and so on.
3. The economic decline and political paralysis create dissatisfaction, especially among Uruguay's youth.
4. Manifestations of dissatisfaction provoke a harder line of political response by the government and the army.
5. This response creates even greater dissatisfaction, provoking very severe repression by the government and the army. Latin America's premier welfare state democracy becomes an exceptionally hard-line dictatorship.

Yet this pattern, though of course with greater complexity, led to a snowballing effect of polarization between the government and increasingly extreme leftist opposition, which became a guerrilla operation that provoked a military dictatorship by the 1970s. Perhaps the main reason why it was not anticipated far in advance was that political analysts generally presumed that political systems, and especially democracies, tended to be self-balancing.

Thus, an alternative model in the minds of observers in the 1950s and 1960s may have been that a continuation of the uninterrupted democracy prevailing since the 1930s was the best bet for the future. It is quite conceivable that a political analyst could have accepted all five of the premises listed above, but either have failed to put it all together or simply have had greater faith in his intuition that long-lasting political arrangements will last even longer. With hindsight we accept the validity of these premises and therefore recognize the value of a forecasting approach—in this instance—that would have allowed the counterintuitive implication of military dictatorship arising in South America's apparently most stable democracy to dominate the analyst's own intuitions.

It must be kept in mind, however, that other premises could have been stated, and they could have been wrong. For example, tracing out what would have happened, assuming that the government could adequately appreciate the threat of dissatisfaction caused by economic decline, might yield the prediction that the government would have launched successful efforts to rectify the economic situation despite political opposition (there was a futile attempt at this in 1966). Similarly, the premise that the leftists might have been able to anticipate the danger of military reaction would have yielded the prediction that the guerrilla movement would not have emerged. Similarly, the Laffer model premises may be incorrect, particularly the premise that the increased tax yield from higher economic activity would offset the initial magnitude of tax reductions.

The simple rule is that, if the premises are correct, their implications should be allowed to emerge. The probem, of course, is that the premises may not be correct, in which case the counterintuitive implications are counterintuitive for good reason: they are likely to be wrong.

Explicitness

Explicitness of methods separates the person from the algorithm. When the procedures of generating a forecast are so completely specified that another forecaster could step in, apply the method without having to make independent judgments, and come up with the same results, then the explicitness of procedure has accomplished three objectives.

First, explicitness facilitates assessment of the forecasting method. In contrast to methods in which undisplayed judgment plays a part, the fully explicit method can be taken apart, its components examined for the plausibility of their underlying assumptions, and their consistency checked.

Second, the hidden biases of the forecaster cannot be introduced, because all of the assumptions are expressed within the steps of the forecasting procedure. However—and this is a major caveat—it is frequently no mean feat to determine just what these assumptions are. In other words, although the explicit method allows replication, it does not necessarily mean that the method user understands the implications of the method. For example, as we shall discuss later, the forecaster trying to predict future energy use with a completely explicit regression model may or may not realize that a particular regression model might assume only linear relationships between energy consumption and other factors such as industrial production or population, or, more broadly, that the model assumes that major changes in economic structure will not occur. Thus, explicitness saves the application of the method from the hidden biases of the forecaster, but does not prevent the method from conveying its own hidden biases or preconceptions. It is up to the method user to discover and assess these assumptions.

Third, explicitness allows the individual capable of developing a forecasting framework to go on to other tasks, leaving his "genius" embedded in the method that others can apply. This advantage depends, of course, on the large assumption that the method—without the judgmental input of its originator—is worth replicating.

Comprehensiveness

Comprehensiveness of the factors explored or taken into account through the forecasting exercise is the desideratum that responds to the interconnectedness of all human and social behavior. The contextuality of political behavior, and of social acts in general, is what has prevented the development of simple general laws to account for social and political behavior. The context "out there" establishes the meanings of acts, the complicated channels through which cause and effect operate, and the viable options for the actors whose behaviors are the focus of the forecast. It would not be an exaggeration to say that the most fundamental flaw of political forecasting has been the failure to integrate the interactions among political and other socioeconomic trends.

The ideal is for the approach to be as comprehensive as possible without leading the forecaster into unfounded speculation, whether derived mathematically or judgmentally. The obvious problem with advocating comprehensiveness is that, although it is easy enough to counsel that "everything ought to be taken into account," in practice everyone operates under contraints of time, money, and personnel. Either the forecaster must leave certain factors out of the analysis, or he ends up assuming relationships based on the sketchiest understanding of how the system operates. Therefore, the desideratum of comprehensiveness is for the approach to facilitate at least a perusal of potentially relevant factors, so that the forecaster can decide which, and how many, he can afford to integrate into the analysis.

Sensitivity to Nuances

Sensitivity to the details of the particular case under examination is a requisite because practical forecasting is not a task of theory building, for which detail can be ignored as long as there is progress toward the development of general insights and theories. It is, instead, a task of theory *application,* in which sensitivity to the small points may be essential for determining what theories ought to be applied. Moreover, since the level of detail of the forecast must be congruent with the level of detail needed by the policy maker, subtle differences in the meaning of the ongoing events or in the configuration of factors can be crucial.

Capacity to Incorporate Well-Founded Theory

If the forecaster indeed has a well-founded theoretical understanding of the phenomena under examination, then capacity to incorporate it is obviously important but nonetheless requires care in its application as a criterion. The key question, obviously, is whether the theory is in fact sound. Consider, for example, the task of projecting the strength of an incumbent government's support, in a case for which we have rather certain information on the medium-term economic trends for that country (perhaps because a prolonged upward trend in the prices of that nation's major exports is strongly indicated). If the relationships among high export prices, economic performance, and the support accorded to a government that gets the credit for this economic performance are understood—that is, if we have a theory for linking each element to the others—then it would be justifiable to proceed by developing an analysis linking higher export prices to improved economic performance and hence to a higher level of political support for the incumbent government.

We may proceed by setting up equations that enable us to predict first the overall improvement of economic performance from the improvement in export prices, and then another equation to predict the increase in political support on the basis of the economic improvement. Alternatively, we may proceed by writing scenarios of the likely reactions to economic improvement, based on our theoretical understanding of how these factors interrelate, in order to see whether one or several particular scenarios hold together well in terms of coherence and plausibility. Or we may simply apply our theoretical understanding through implicit judgment, though somehow making sure that these relationships are kept in mind. Using any of these frameworks, we can expand or contract the number of theoretical assumptions or propositions we wish to entertain. If our understanding of the process is more elaborate, we may include more factors; if it is more rudimentary, we may include fewer.

If, however, we do not know whether increased export prices will improve the overall economic performance of the country (after all, they might trigger inflation as the country is inundated with cash from higher export earnings), or if we do not know whether improved economic performance will indeed make the government more popular (it might instead raise aspirations beyond the level that the government can meet in spite of positive economic conditions), then these theoretical expressions may be simply misleading. A less theory-dependent approach, such as simply assuming that the existing trends will continue, might then be more appropriate.

The appropriateness of theoretical content in a forecasting effort thus depends not only on the subject under examination, but also on the knowledgeability of the forecaster. This can create problems for the methodologist who is designing forecasting procedures for future use by unknown individuals.

Simplicity

Simplicity is our last ceteris paribus criterion. Although simplicity, parsimony, or "elegance" is often cited as a desirable quality for aesthetic reasons (particularly with respect to mathematical formulations), there are three considerations that call for simplicity on very practical grounds. First, complicated methods are often difficult to employ, no matter how sophisticated everyone wishes to appear to be. Complicated models, in particular, are cumbersome, difficult to "de-bug," and intimidating to their users and even to their makers. Second, simplicity eases the understanding of the method and of the real-life situation. It has been shown that the usefulness of complicated methods is often reduced by the lack of understanding of the forecast users.[1] Finally, the simpler approaches are generally easier to assess in terms of consistency and the plausibility of their underlying assumptions. Simplicity cannot, of course, redeem a method that is inappropriate.

TRADEOFFS AMONG CRITERIA

Some of the tradeoffs among these desiderata are quite obvious. We may begin with the nearly opposite objectives of plausibility testing and the capacity to express counterintuitive implications. The procedure that applies the standard of plausibility—that is, what strikes the forecaster as plausible—may perforce screen out the counterintuitive results.

Another rather obvious tradeoff is the limitation that explicitness places on the ability of the forecaster to discard (but not to identify) results that seem implausible. If, for example, the forecaster is instructed to operate a complex econometric model mechanically, without the opportunity to alter the model so that outputs fall within the range of plausibility, then the forecaster simply has no opportunity to produce results—with the model—that conform to his own standards of plausibility. Of course, the forecaster may have the option of simply disregarding what the procedure has to say—but then the forecast would not have been made through an explicit algorithm, but rather through the implicit judgment of the forecaster. Looking at this tradeoff from another angle, explicitness enhances the emergence of counterintuitive implications, insofar as it precludes plausibility testing.

The criteria of comprehensiveness and simplicity are often, but not inevitably, at odds. There are innumerable instances of unnecessarily simplistic approaches to specific problems that require more elaborate (often eclectic) treatments. On the other hand, the broad outlines of how to go about examining the complexity of a particular situation can be rather simple and straightforward. The key question, then, is whether the simplicity of the approach is consonant with the complexity of the real-world situation it addresses, and with the level of understanding the forecaster has of this complexity.

A less obvious but equally important tradeoff holds between explicitness and comprehensiveness. Explicitness exercises a subtle constraint on a procedure's capacity to represent reality fully in two different ways. First, the amount of context encompassed by an explicit procedure is limited because the forecaster must discard those factors which are of some relevance but lack clearcut, consistent relation to the outcomes. Thus, for example, the possibility that a regime will lose or gain legitimacy when it fails in a conflict with an outside power is often relevant for assessing the survival of a government (for instance, the survival of the Iranian and Iraqi governments should either lose their war), but it is not easily formulated as an explicit premise or proposition. One might begin with the proposition that "loss leads to lower legitimacy," but there are numerous historical counterexamples, such as Belgium's 1960 loss of the Congo to the independence movement (which had no discernible impact on King Baudouin's reign of now more than 30 years) and Haile Selassie's defeat at the hands of the Italians in 1936.

One might then formulate a more complex explicit proposition, such as "defeat against obviously overwhelming odds stimulates identification and support, whereas defeat that is perceived as avoidable provokes the withdrawal of support." If this formulation also proves to lack general validity—as the counterexample of the fall of the French Fourth Republic following the loss of Algeria would indicate—then one could go for even more elaborate formulations. But at some point the specifications of the relationship will become so complex, or the pivotal factors so subtle or idiosyncratic (such as with the unique historical circumstances of the Ayatollah Khomeini's rise against the Shah of Iran and his "foreign devil" allies), that the formulation of an explicit rule—established prior to the consideration of this particular case—is very unlikely. Yet the impact of defeat still needs to be considered.

Second, there is a finite limit on the number of relationships that can be included in an explicit formulation. The limited resources of any forecaster imply a limit on how much of the reality that could in principle be formulated explicitly actually ends up in an explicit formulation. To be sure, there are econometric models with equations numbering in the hundreds. But most of these equations represent a rather limited number of kinds of relationships, disaggregated in their application to specific industries, types of investments, and so on. To expand these models in order to capture the interactions among factors not yet specified as directly related—such as monetary and fiscal policy responses to inflation and growth trends—would take an enormous amount of work, even presuming that these reactions were well understood.

Whereas completely explicit methods cannot break through the confines of these limitations to achieve full complexity, methods that permit implicit or judgmental considerations can in principle incorporate as many subtleties as the human mind can encompass. Of course, this should not be overestimated; basically stupid computers that can outstrip our own capacities for tracing through implications involving numerous calculations have shown us where some of these limits lie.

THE PROPERTIES OF METHODS

If any forecasting effort is examined carefully, one can identify and analyze the method or methods used, including the residual category of implicit procedures usually labeled "judgment." Each of these methods has its own rationales, strengths, and weaknesses.

However, a more accurate way of understanding how forecasters go about their work is to consider these methods as building blocks often used in combination by the forecaster in the approach to any given problem. One trend may be extrapolated and another regressed on the basis of the first, while a third is projected judgmentally on the basis of the first two. Or the forecaster may apply two or more procedures to the forecast of the same trend and then choose a blended summary projection, based on a (usually unspecified) weighting scheme that reflects how much credence he believes each method deserves.

The following conclusion of the compilers of the National Bureau of Economic Research assessment of short-term forecasting techniques and accuracy illustrates the prevalence of such blends:[2]

> The methods used may vary from a very naive technique to the most sophisticated econometric models. Often, the forecaster uses more than one method to obtain his forecasts. He may use one method to forecast another set of variables. Or, he uses the forecasts from one method as his prime forecasts and those obtained from other methods to make adjustments.

It should also be kept in mind that the merits of different forecasting methods will vary between political and other social phenomena. To the degree that political phenomena are more difficult to capture meaningfully through quantitative measures than economic phenomena, quantitative methods are less applicable to political forecasting.

SOME METHODS AND THEIR LOGIC

Extrapolation

Extrapolation is the projection of a historically based quantitative trend at a constant rate. This sounds much simpler than it really is, for three reasons.

First, the constant rate may refer to the numerical rate of increase, the percentage rate of increase, the doubling rate (the amount of time it takes for the number to double), the rate of acceleration of increase, or any other quantitative measure of change that the forecaster presumes will be constant.

Second, historical data points rarely all fall on a straight line, thus necessitating a procedure for establishing which line fits the historical data best. There is now a vast literature on the best criteria and means for fitting the data and the line, most of it highly technical and not generally of much concern to the political forecaster.[3] Nonetheless, it should be recognized that "the trend" does not always leap out at the forecaster.

Third, if the historical trend is not perfectly straight from its beginning to the present, the decision of where to start in determining the rate to be projected is necessarily somewhat arbitrary. This is a much more important problem than the second point, because utterly different implications can be drawn from starting the extrapolation at different points in time.

Figure 3.1 provides a striking example of this problem. The "real"

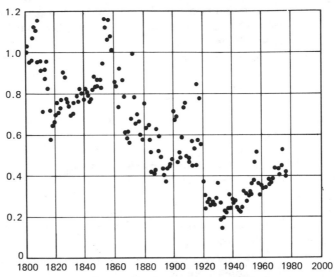

Figure 3.1   The scarcity of copper as measured by its price

price of copper over the past 180 years is shown by the price of copper as a ratio of the Consumer Price Index. Julian Simon, whose book *The Ultimate Resource* presented this scattergram, argues that the general downward trend in the relative price of copper since 1800 indicates that raw materials are becoming less rather than more scarce, more rather than less affordable, and that the current preoccupation with constraining industrial growth because of resource shortages is therefore a misguided overreaction.[4] However, if the extrapolation begins around 1930, the best-fitting linear trend is clearly one of increasing prices and scarcity.

Which is correct? This question cannot be answered through extrapolation alone. If the basic long-term dynamic of the past 180 years (probably having to do with cumulative improvements in mineral resource extraction technology) still operates, then the long-term downward trend is likely to prevail despite the shorter-term cycles seen in the past and, Simon would argue, in the present. If, on the other hand, the structure of the world economy since the Great Depression is sufficiently different from its structure prior to the Depression, then only the last 50 years of the trend are relevant. One can certainly point to post-Depression changes in structure and in economic conduct (such as the practice of Keynesian economics) which might mean that pre-1930 patterns no longer apply, but this remains a question for further analysis and certainly cannot be addressed by simply arguing over the data.

The most obvious property of extrapolation is its severely atheoretical nature. We "let the numbers do the talking" because we do not wish to add much more theoretical input to the forecasting effort. This is not necessarily laziness. It may simply be modesty—the recognition that our theoretical understanding of the phenomenon under examination is inadequate for introducing anything fancier.

The second obvious property of extrapolation is that the procedure is largely explicit. It is not fully explicit because of the discretion involved in deciding where the historical trend is to begin and in choosing how the data are to be smoothed into a single line. Nevertheless, once these decisions are made, extrapolation is fully explicit, allowing the forecast user to see every step of the exercise.

A related property of extrapolation is that it obviously dispenses with efforts to introduce theory into the forecasting effort. It makes no pretense to explain how the world works, except that it tacitly assumes that social interaction is marked by a high degree of continuity, and that all of the factors that influenced the trend in the past will continue to do so.

Regressions

Regression analysis is the next technique encountered as one moves toward greater complexity among the explicit methods of forecasting. Forecasting through regression analysis is, basically speaking, the prediction of one trend or event based on its relationship with one or more other trends. One can predict the levels of a variable using standard regression analysis, and can make predictions about events (the probabilities that events will or will not occur) through several variants of regression analysis, such as discriminant function analysis or probit analysis.[5]

The relationships can hold within one case for the "time series" variables for that case (for example, U.S. energy use levels and U.S. GNP levels) or across cases (for example, energy use and GNP combinations for all the industrialized nations, at one or more points in time). Usually these presumed relationships are linear (the change in the predicted trend is proportional to the magnitude of change in the other trends on which the prediction is based). A very closely related notion from economics is elasticity, the percentage change in one variable, such as demand, to be expected as a result of a one percent change in another variable, such as price.

If the trend under examination is presumed to depend on other, more basic trends in a consistent and straightforward way, the regression equation

Predicted Variable = Constant A + (Constant B1 × Basic Variable 1)
+ (Constant B2 × Basic Variable 2) + . . .

can be used to predict future values for the predicted variable, by first finding values for the constants (usually called parameters), and then plugging values of the basic variables into the equation so that the predicted variable can be calculated.

Note that there is no limit to the number of basic variables that can be introduced into the regression equation, although often only one is used. The more variables included, the less reliable the estimated parameters become.[6] This is an important limitation, because it means that regression analysis cannot be expanded without limit to encompass more and more factors.

Of course, most variables take on different values at different points in time, so the variables must be distinguished by the time periods to which they refer. This gives rise to two variants of forecasting through regression: predicting the future levels of the dependent variable on the basis of simultaneous future levels of the basic variables, and predicting them on the basis of earlier levels of the basic variables. In other words, the second variant presumes that the predicted variable can be considered as a "lagged" result of the other trends.

Generally, the task of finding appropriate values for the constants, which in a sense represent how much change in the predicted variable a given magnitude of change in each basic variable would produce or account for, is accomplished in a way similar to fitting the extrapolation line to the actual historical data—the constant chosen is the one that produces the closest fit between the actual and the predicted data points. It is conceivable, however, that, in the absence of past data, the regression coefficients could simply be generated through a theoretical understanding of how the system works. For example, without data on the relationship between price and demand for gasoline in price ranges beyond historical experience (as occurred after the oil price rise in 1973), many economists simply stipulated elasticities of demand for their oil consumption models. This is not, however, the norm; generally, regression analyses are justified on the grounds of their fidelity with known, objective historical patterns. Consequently, regression as most commonly employed is a form of extrapolation with greater causal or theoretical content, as well as somewhat greater comprehensiveness.

The relationships posited by the regression equation can represent theoretical considerations of how the predicted variable depends on other trends. However, the basic variables can also be discovered inductively—that is, by exploring many potential variables in order to discover those that have been highly correlated with the trend under examination. The danger of an inductive search for basic variables is that one may derive spurious relationships that held for idiosyncratic reasons in the past but have no real theoretical basis, and hence are unlikely to hold in the future. On the other hand, if theory is weak and yet striking correlations do appear, the tactic of "letting the figures do the talking" has the same appeal for regression as it does for extrapolation.

The principal rationale for regression as a forecasting method, compared to more elaborate explicit methods, is that certain trends are primarily determined or conditioned by one or a few other trends. This position does not deny that the real world is more complicated, but rather questions whether it is worth trying to discover and express these complexities, given that the complexities of intricate relationships are often too subtle to be detected in historical data contaminated by many other factors. For example, since energy is largely used to serve individual-level needs of heat, light, and other home uses and to run the nation's industry, it is not unreasonable to predict energy use as a function of gross national product (which increases along with population, higher disposable incomes for energy-using appliances, greater industrial activity, and so on). If economic growth can be projected, then the trend of energy use can be calculated on the basis of this projection. Certainly the relationship between economic growth and energy use is in fact more complicated, but perhaps not in easily understandable ways. The advocate of regression would argue that it is best to stick with a few straightforward, "robust" linear relationships that express the fundamental direction.

Regression has two vulnerabilities as a forecasting method. The first is that the constants that link the predicted trend to the basic trends reflect the past and present structure of the system, so that if this structure changes there is no reason to expect that the constants would still represent the relationships among trends. This occurred after the 1973 oil price increase, when the energy consumption per unit of industrial activity declined because of conservation efforts. On the other hand, if one has no theory of how the relationships among trends are likely to change in the future, the existing relationships may be the best bet.

The second vulnerability of regression is that its validity depends not only on whether the relationships between the predicted trend and each of the basic trends are correct, but also on the projection of each of these basic trends. In the example of predicting energy use from gross national product, an underestimate of GNP will yield an underestimate of energy consumption even if the GNP-energy relationship is correctly specified.

However, if the predicted variable is the lagged result of the basic trend, with a sufficiently great time lag (for example, college enrollments may be considered the lagged result of births of roughly 18 years before), then the future values of the predicted variable depend on already historical values of the basic trends, thus eliminating the problem of projecting the basic trend. Unfortunately, time lags like this are frequently unavailable and the task of establishing the proper and consistent time lag is usually difficult.

Leading Indicators

The leading indicators approach to forecasting is a more modest variant of the regression approach. The direction of change in the trend under examination is presumed to depend on, or at least to be signaled by, earlier changes in the directions of other trends. These leading indicators can be identified inductively by examining the time series of numerous indicators to see if any behave in a consistent and characteristic way prior to changes in the trend of interest (for instance, inventory changes presage business contractions and expansions). Or they can be identified through theories of how events are sequenced. Leading indicators are often used in economic forecasting. In political risk assessment, there is a parallel use of warning signs presumed to occur in advance of important events: troop mobilizations that precede the outbreak of war; loud denials that often precede the denied action, such as resignations and currency devaluations; and the various omens of prerevolutionary dissatisfaction.[7]

The rationale of the leading-indicators approach is that, even in inadequately understood systems, there are regularities in sequencing that permit the forecaster to discover, either inductively or theoretically, what to look for by way of advanced signs. However, it is presumed that these relationships are not so well understood, or perhaps not so completely regular, as to permit more ambitious formulations. Thus, the leading-indicators approach does not explicitly tell the forecasters precisely how to project the trend on the basis of the leading indicator's values. To do so would shift the approach to a standard regression or complex-model framework.

The use of such a method, which strives to predict the direction of change but cannot explicitly estimate its magnitude, makes sense for some applications in economics; for example, in selecting stocks that are likely to go up in value or in anticipating business-cycle turning points. Yet the adequacy of predicting the direction of change, while failing to predict its magnitude, is questionable for many other applications.

Complex Models

Complex models (see chapter 4) approach both desiderata of explicitness and comprehensiveness—but neither as fully as is commonly believed. "Complex" models encompass a range of approaches that have one thing in common: they specify two or more explicit propositions that share at least one factor or variable.[8] Their combining of multiple, interconnected propositions (that is, outputs of one become inputs of another, or solutions must satisfy several equations simultaneously) can explicitly express feedback mechanisms, mutual causation, balancing effects, and other complicated dynamics.

Among the many variations of complex models, the two most prominent have been the econometric model and the systems dynamics model. The controversy concerning the rivalry between these approaches illuminates many of the prominent tradeoffs in forecasting.

Econometric models are distinguished by their reliance on equations whose constants are (as in mainstream regression analysis) estimated on the basis of existing, actual data. "Econometric," after all, literally means economic analysis entailing measurement. Once these parameters are estimated, the equations are "solved simultaneously," which is the economist's way of saying that values for the variables involved are found that satisfy all of the equations.[9] Naturally, this procedure of estimating the parameters limits the specification of econometric model equations to variables and relationships for which historical data exist. The econometrician says that this is the strength of the method—it ensures a solid base in experience for the propositions accepted as part of the model. Critics say that this is the limitation preventing econometric models from incorporating relationships expected to become important in the future, even if existing data cannot speak to what these relationships are like.

System dynamics models, most closely identified with Jay Forrester and his associates at MIT, are distinguished by their procedure of repeatedly updating the whole set of equations by one short period at a time, thus capturing the nearly simultaneous mutual causation that marks complex social systems.[10] But their approach of generating constants or parameters is even more distinctive: even if a constant cannot be derived from fitting the equations to past patterns, the system dynamics modeler can frequently derive parameters that make theoretical sense. They can be based on experimental research (for example, a pollution-impact model may have a parameter for the level of pollution-related deaths attributable to elevated air-pollution levels that is inferred from experiments with laboratory animals), data-based estimation, elaborate theory, or common sense.

These methods free the system dynamics model from the constraint of having to depend only on variables and relationships for which historical patterns permit estimation of the parameters. This permits system dynamics models to encompass more diverse factors and longer-term relationships. It was the system dynamics approach to projection of long-term environmental and resource constraints that caused such a furor in the early 1970s when the Club of Rome study, *The Limits to Growth,* seemed to "scientifically prove" that unchecked world industrialization would lead to catastrophe.[11] The scope, time horizon, and comprehensiveness of this model went far beyond anything that econometricians would dare formulate.

Yet the inevitable tradeoff is that the system dynamics model is less testable and less easily substantiated. The formulation of its relationships (including the parameters) is always open to attack by skeptics who can argue that the model is only the image—or the fantasy—of the modeler's mind. This was certainly the complaint lodged against *The Limits to Growth* study, which was criticized as arbitrarily disregarding or underestimating the capacity of technological advances to overcome resource scarcities and pollution hazards.[12] In contrast, the econometric modeler can claim that his model at least has been subjected to the test of whether there is any set of parameters that can be found to allow the model's results to fit actual past patterns. This feature of econometric models does not guarantee that the model's specifications will be correct for the future, but it does eliminate some relationships that may have seemed reasonable but in fact do not correspond to how the world has behaved.

The defenders of system dynamics modeling respond that, where there is uncertainty as to which formulation is correct, the modeler can try alternative formulations to see whether the results are sensitive to varying assumptions and, if so, in what ways. This procedure of sensitivity analysis is not attacked in principle by the critics of system dynamics, but the critics can point to the difficulty of tracing—and presenting—the sometimes bewildering array of possible outcome differences that just a few combinations of alternative assumptions can represent. (Some system dynamics modelers claim that the models can be tested in a sense by "backcasting"—reversing the direction of time in the models to see whether they end up at actual historical configurations. However, the logic of backcasting is arguable, and it is often inapplicable insofar as the controversial parameters and relationships have to do with the behavior of factors at future extreme levels, such as the impact of very high pollution levels.)

Both of these forms of complex models could—in theory—be operated mechanically. Once the equations, constants, and exogenous (external) factors are specified, the model can be allowed to come to its results without any further intervention by model operators. In other words, the models can be operated without any further plausibility-testing procedures. In fact, system dynamics models have been applauded for precisely this quality. Forrester, Mass, and Ryan have written:[13]

> Although assumptions may be explicitly stated, the human mind is not well adapted to determining the future time-varying consequences of those

assumptions. Different people may accept the same assumptions and structure, and then draw contrary conclusions. . . . Computer simulations can be used to determine without doubt the future dynamic implications of a specific set of assumptions.

Econometric models can also be operated mechanically. Economist Ray Fair developed an econometric model that, unlike the standard models used by econometric forecasting services, used simple extrapolations for the external variables instead of leaving these to the judgment of the model operators.[14]

However, despite the feasibility of using complex models in a mechanical, nonjudgmental way, in the vast majority of cases neither econometric nor system dynamics models are actually run that way. For the system dynamics models, the continual interplay between the modeler, who has many alternative formulations and scenarios to subject to sensitivity analysis, and the model, which is in a continual state of revision and (presumably) improvement, yields model operators' interpretations that tend to converge to the operator's understanding of the world. This is well illustrated in the following interpretation given by Forrester of one of the "computer runs" of his World Dynamics Model:[15]

> The dynamics from this model that follow the peak in population should be viewed skeptically, especially the sudden rise in quality of life that occurs in most of the computer runs. Future examinations of the model will suggest modified structures that would give more likely behavior. But the path that lies beyond the population peak is for now of minor importance. Of immediate interest are the limits to growth, the path from here to any peak that will be imposed, and the policy choices that are open. With respect to these issues, the model appears to be giving reasonable answers, even if the conclusions are contrary to present world expectations.

These paragraphs show that the model implications are dismissed when they diverge from Forrester's expectations that the dynamic in question (involving high industrial investment and rather high population growth— the two bugaboos of the limits-to-growth school of thought) would lead to deterioration rather than improvement in the quality of life; yet the model's implications are supported when they agree with Forrester's openly unconventional expectations of limits to growth. Where the model contradicts his expectations, "modified structures that would give more likely behavior" are promised; otherwise, the model's specifications are left intact.

Forrester may or may not be right in dismissing some but not all of the model's implications. The point of showing his inconsistency in this regard is not to demonstrate whether Forrester's own views on the future are right or wrong, but rather that the discussion of the model's results—which is the final product as far as the bulk of the consumers of this forecasting exercise are concerned—is heavily influenced by Forrester's notions of what is plausible.

For the econometric model, the plausibility testing is more disguised and yet, if anything, even more pervasive. Economist Bert Hickman, surveying a large number of actual econometric forecasting operations, notes that econometric modelers ensure plausible results by:[16]

> changing the preliminary assumptions on exogenous variables and constants until the resulting forecast falls within the range thought to be reasonable. . . . From this point of view, the model serves primarily to assess judgmentally the general implications of the forecaster's assumptions on future exogenous developments, including his ad hoc adjustments for anticipated changes in structure since the sample period, and for the correction of apparent specification errors.

Thus, given the flexibility to choose the values of external variables and constants so that the model's results turns out plausibly, the econometrician can bring results into conformity with his or her preconceptions far earlier than the discussion-of-results stage. In fact, unless the modeler is unusually open about these arcane maneuvers, the forecast consumer would never be aware that this form of plausibility testing is occurring.

It is interesting to note that the "mechanical" model developed by Ray Fair performed very poorly compared to the "judgmentally" operated econometric models. (This is by no means a criticism of Fair's work, since the rationale behind developing and operating this model was not to apply it to practical forecasting, but rather to test how much of the econometric model's performance is caused by model specification and how much by its operator's intervention.) One might suspect that this performance could be explained by the poor (inaccurate) choices of external factors generated mechanically for Fair's model. However, as a general rule, econometric models perform worse (in terms of their accuracy in predicting such basic trends as quarterly or annual GNP changes) when the actual values of exogenous variables are used than when the model operators put in their own erroneous estimates of these exogenous variables. This seeming paradox can only be explained by concluding that choosing exogenous values to bring the models' projections into line with the model operators' ideas of plausibility corrects for errors in the models' equations and parameters.[17] Whether this is an indictment of complex modeling forever, or only for the current state of the art, is considered in Chapter 4.

The issue of the comprehensiveness of complex models is as complicated as the question of whether they are explicit. It may be hard to imagine that a 400-equation model is anything but comprehensive. There are, however, three countervailing considerations.

First, the elaborateness of complex models is somewhat misleading, since the large number of equations in the typical econometric or system dynamics model reflects disaggregation—the separation of broad categories into multiple narrower categories, with the consequent proliferation of relationships. For example, an energy-use model may first be formulated in condensed form, linking overall energy demand to overall economic activity. It may then be disaggregated according to demand for different fuels (gasoline, diesel, heating oil, coal, and so on), with each of these fuels then linked to each of the economic activities (home heating, heavy industry, truck transportation, and so on) that make up the total demand. Similarly, population growth models can break up the population according to age, race, urban or rural residence, and income levels, with these different components and cohorts then related to the factors presumably affecting fertility and morality rates.

The expansion of the number of equations caused by disaggregation does not necessarily mean that the breadth of explanatory factors is increased. The disaggregated energy-use model may explain the demand for each fuel by each source of economic activity in a simplistic way—for example, by positing that demand is proportional to the level of activity— with no consideration of price or technological factors. Or the population model may simply assume that the same fertility and mortality rates applying currently will hold in the future. In neither case does the model aspire to comprehensiveness of explanation, no matter how many equations are included. For the standard econometric models used in economic forecasting, the same explanatory framework that characterized their smaller precursors in the late 1950s still holds today, despite the fact that some models have more than 500 equations. This framework includes the theoretical components for Keynesian economics, such as various components of demand, prices, employment, and so forth, but gives short shrift to the factors emphasized by monetarists and completely excludes social, political, and policy-response factors.

Second, the requirements of explicitness and quantification limit the formulations to those factors that can be quantified and to those relationships that are consistent. Idiosyncratic (that is, case-specific) relationships do not sit comfortably in explicit quantitative formulations. Often, the intuitive awareness that a particular factor is relevant to another factor in intricate ways for a specific case cannot be translated into an explicit formulation.

Third, the greater comprehensiveness of complex models compared to other, more modest methods such as extrapolation and regression is predicated on an always arguable assumption that the system under examination is well understood. The capacity to incorporate well-founded theory is at issue. The act of specifying theoretical relationships in explicit, mathematical form does not establish the correctness of the relationships. Models express assumptions but do not validate them. Even if the modeler is so cautious that he or she includes only relationships "proven" by past experience, there is no guarantee that they will hold in the future.

Thus, the boldness of elaborate modeling comes at the potential cost of going beyond what is reliably known. The greater boldness of the systems dynamics models in their incorporation of factors that cannot be measured econometrically is the crux of the dispute between system dynamics advocates and econometricians. System dynamics models are, by their very nature, capable of greater comprehensiveness, although the extensions of system dynamics models beyond well-known relationships naturally leads them into more dangerous territory. The implication that the choice of method depends on how well the system is understood and how completely the outcomes can be explained by econometrically measurable factors brings into question the utility of the abstract debate between the two positions.

Curve Fitting

Curve fitting is another explicit method, which can rest on two distinctive rationales. First, the forecaster who is modest about his or her theoretical understanding of the system may find a pattern in the data that is expressible as a curve or cycle. Thus, induction, without a theory of the dynamics of the trend, can lead the forecaster to posit patterns that seem more sophisticated than extrapolation, but essentially the method is equivalent to extrapolation. In fact, they are formally equivalent as long as the curve or cycle can be expressed mathematically, since that mathematical expression can be regarded as the constant extrapolated rate of growth of the trend.

However, more often the rationale behind curve fitting is the premise that a powerful, simple, consistent dynamic underlies the past and future pattern of the trend. Thus, curve fitting typically relies on broad, parsimonious theory rather than on the elaborateness of the econometric model or the induction of the regression approach. The curve-fitting approach posits that the macroscopic pattern of the trend under examination is subject to a predetermined pattern that can be described straightforward through a mathematical equation. This pattern or curve may be a concave or convex simple curve, the S-shaped logistic curve representing first accelerating and then decelerating growth, a continuous cycle, or any other relatively simple pattern. The curve may even be a straight line, but this convergence of curve fitting and extrapolation does not negate the possibility of a difference in mentality and rationale between the two approaches. The curve fitter may propose that a pattern will be linear for theoretical reasons (such as a theory of equilibrium-maintaining mechanisms), rather than because he or she has insufficient understanding to do better than the statistics in pointing to the future's likely direction.

Once the type of curve is selected, the curve fitter has to determine the specific shape or parameters for that particular trend. This is most commonly done by estimating the parameters with traditional econometric means: the parameters are selected which best fit historical data (that is, the shape of the curve thus far). Thus, once the type of curve is established and the estimation technique chosen (the latter is a basically technical matter that is unlikely to have much impact on the results), the procedure is explicit and mechanical. Of course, the choice of the curve type is a matter of judgment, or, looking at it from another viewpoint, a matter of theory.

Of all the methods reviewed so far, curve fitting most strongly dismisses the importance of the detailed context of the case. Curve fitting presupposes that only a few macro factors largely account for the trend. In demographic forecasting, for example, Malthus argued that population increases geometrically while food supplies increase only arithmetically, until the food supply proves inadequate and famine produces a population decline. This sort of simple depiction, disregarding such factors as family-size choices and other culturally or economically determined factors, found its counterpart of the more recent past in Raymond Pearl's logistic curve theory, which hypothesized that the S-shaped curve representing first exponential and then leveling-off population growth can be derived solely from considerations of a fixed resource base.[18]

Today the use of curve fitting can be found in cycle theories of the economy. For example, Kondratieff's empirically based theory of roughly 50-year cycles of boom and depression has been modernized and given more theoretical content by Jay Forrester's theory of the phases of capital-goods and consumer-goods industries and by W. W. Rostow's theory of boom and stagnation of commodities industries in response to the relative prices of commodities and manufactured goods.[19,20]

Other economic trends besides aggregate growth can also be projected through macroscopic curves. On the basis of cross-national data on economic growth levels and income distribution, Simon Kuznets identified the well-known Kuznets curve of initially worsening and then improving income distribution when nations are arrayed from the poorest to the richest. The inference seems to be that, as countries develop economically, their income distributions first deteriorate and later are restored to greater equity, although the cross-national comparisons do not really prove that the dynamic, time-series trend actually holds for individual countries.[21] Other curve-fitting approaches can be found in forecasting technological advances, for which a summary curve encompassing the cumulative progress of successively more advanced technologies is often used.

In political science, curve fitting is rare except in two circumstances. Occasionally, one aspect of political behavior seems to adhere to a consistent pattern, or at least a common tendency can be identified from the characteristics of many cases. For example, over time the electorate's loyalty to a particular political party and to the existing political system rises. Sociologist Philip Converse has plotted this trend on the basis of the Almond and Verba *Civic Culture* attitude surveys from the United States, Great Britain, Germany, Italy, and Mexico.[22] Taking into account the effects of personal partisan experience, intergenerational transmission of party preferences, and "forgetting," Converse constructs an idealized curve representing the increasing stability of party preferences over time, driven by the effects of these factors on successive age cohorts of the population. Using the five-country data as the basis for estimation, Converse formulates an S-shaped curve of increasing stability for which "maturity is essentially approached after about two and one-half generations . . ."[23] The example is striking not only for the ingenious meshing of data and theory, but also because it shows how susceptible the choice of curve is to the assumptions underlying the theory, and how much caution is necessary in interpreting the cross-national implication. Converse is too sophisticated to maintain that this pattern is inevitable or even necessarily to be expected in any given case; rather, it is the central tendency of the somewhat varying patterns of individual cases.

The other use of curve fitting in political analysis is in the quantitative expression of political cycles, with all of the inherent limitations of assuming political trends to be cyclical. The alternations of war and peace have long been subjected to empirical examination in the search for predictable cycles. Pitirim Sorokin noted that, by the time of his writing, periods of 50, 111, 300, 500, 600, and 675 years had all been claimed as cycles.[24] Electoral behavior is also frequently alleged to be cyclical. In certain countries, two political parties or factions seem to alternate in their presidential electoral victories (this had been the case in the Philippines prior to 1972 and in Mexico prior to 1982), or whichever party holds the presidential power seems to lose support in the congressional by-elections (as in the United States). In these cases, the electoral support for either party would appear to be cyclical if expressed as a percentage of the total vote.

The mystique of cyclical theories has to be tempered by the distinction between predictively useful cycles and mere fluctuations. For a fluctuation to be of predictive value, it is helpful if it has regularities in magnitude, and it is essential that it have regularity in period (the length of each cycle phase). Without regularity of the cycle period, the prediction says little more than that "someday" the trend will turn around. For many subjects, the arguments *against* the likelihood of fixed-duration cycles rest first on the premise that modernization speeds up the pace of change itself. Mass communications, the interconnectedness of the modern world, and the high stakes of potential nuclear confrontation have telescoped events and phases to shorter durations than ever before. Earlier centuries do not show evidence of devastated nations rising economically, as Japan and Germany have done, within a few decades.

The second basis for rejecting fixed-duration cycle theories of social trends is the phenomenon of learning. Actors in the social process learn to avoid at least some of the mistakes of the past; they learn to identify the danger signs of cyclical downturns and sometimes learn to avert them. Although this is no guarantee that repetitions of counterproductive patterns— such as the alternation of military and weak civilian governments in many Latin American countries—will always be avoided, it does bring into question whether assuming otherwise is a sound basis for prediction. There is no question, of course, that many trends "go up and down"— repeatedly. Retrospectively, one can often find roughly regular patterns. For example, major-power wars can be seen every two decades—if one is willing to be very flexible in selecting and dating these wars. Francis Beer summarizes the status of cycle theories with respect to the occurrence of war.[25]

These periods have been the subject of vigorous subsequent debate. . . . Sorokin's work on European major wars made him extremely skeptical about the existence of any cyclical period of general peace and/or proposed lengths to such a cycle. . . . Subsequently, Richardson reanalyzed Wright's list of major international and domestic violence. . . . He found no evidence of regularity; he saw supposed regular war-peace periods as sheer chance.

More contemporary studies give us the same lesson. Singer and Small's intensive study of world major wars suggests a regular period, somewhat shorter than Wright's, "between 20 and 40 years in the fluctuations of the amount of war *underway* during the 150 years," that they studied. . . . Their data show no regular peace periods when they consider "the intervals between the beginning of successive wars". . . . New wars seem to begin at random intervals.

If particular instances of regular cyclical behavior are indeed discovered in the patterns thus far, any confidence in projecting them into the future must be justified by demonstrating the permanence and the temporal regularity of the specific dynamics underlying them, rather than by the existence of the historical pattern per se.

Forecasting by Analogy

Forecasting by analogy is an allied but less explicit cousin of curve fitting. The broad but simple theory is that the trend under examination fits within a category of cases (of which there may be few or only one other example) that constitute the analogies; their patterns are likely to be followed by the trend under examination. For example, if the future of the home-computer industry is the issue, it may be regarded as yet another infant high-technology industry that will follow the same pattern of initially rapid growth, price reduction, and then market saturation that has been experienced by televisions, microwave ovens, and electronic calculators.

Forecasting by analogy is quite common in political risk assessment. However, the political forecaster frequently stops short of proposing that the current case will necessarily follow the pattern of the analogy, and instead uses the analogy as a framework for understanding the case under examination. This is so because the analogy is often a negative circumstance to be avoided in the future, and the discussion of the analogy serves as a warning and a prescription for how to avoid a repetition of that pattern. The most common analogies of this sort have been the major diplomatic and military fiascos. The presumably avoidable outbreak of World War I, the 1938 Munich Pact (in which Great Britain and France capitulated to Hitler's demands regarding Czechoslovakia), and the Vietnam War have all been invoked to warn of dangers presented by present situations. Similarly, it is commonplace to claim that generals always fight the last war—that military strategy is based on the ostensible similarity of the current situation to the most recent instance of military hostilities.

The rationales of forecasting by analogy are similar to those of curve fitting, but with historical insight partially replacing the role of simple theory. Once it is decided which category (for instance, appeasement), or which single historical analogy (for instance, Vietnam) is appropriate, one need not have an elaborate or comprehensive understanding of how the system operates, but rather the more modest premise that whatever determined the dynamics in the analogous case is likely to operate in the case under examination. For example, we may not completely understand how a population comes to side with the guerrilla forces in a protracted civil war between Marxist insurgents and a government aided by the United States, but we may still attempt to project the developments in Central

America on the basis of the patterns of the Vietnam War. Since the analogy is a real historical case, unlike an abstract theory it can offer as much information as the historical accounts can provide, thus permitting the analyst to explore the parallels between the analogy and the current case at many different levels.

Clearly, the approach of forecasting with analogies depends on, but cannot itself demonstrate, whether the analogy selected is in fact appropriate. As a modest inductive method—"given our lack of solid understanding of how social systems operate, let us choose whatever historical case(s) would seem closest to the current situation"—it shares with extrapolation and curve fitting the potential shortcoming of assuming continuity of patterns. It will therefore be inappropriate when we understand a system well enough to go beyond assuming that the world will continue to operate as it has in the past. As in the case of curve fitting, the phenomena of modernization and learning call into question the assumption that the world will continue to operate as it has in the past, especially when key actors are presumably trying to avoid the failures of the past.

Judgmental Forecasting

Judgmental forecasting encompasses all implicit calculations, whether conducted without recourse to any explicit routines or consisting of the decision to take exception to the results produced by such routines. All social forecasting involves some element of judgment, if only because the forecaster has to judge which approach to use.

It is, of course, difficult to characterize the process of judgmental forecasting, since by its very definition it precludes specifying the routines that the forecaster will adopt in drawing conclusions. Judgment as a forecasting approach is predicated on the assumption that the human mind understands much more about social dynamics than it can express explicitly. The human mind presumably can detect subtleties of meaning that other approaches, which require categorization and formal measurement, cannot capture. Judgment can be comprehensive, if an effort is made to take into account all potentially relevant factors, but of course it need not be. It also provides the flexibility of incorporating the results of other methods without being bound by a rigid or arbitrary weighting scheme.

Judgmental forecasting permits forecasters themselves to assess the "probability" of a forecast's correctness in part by assessing their own level of confidence. Of course, it can be argued that the forecaster is in no position to assess his own knowledge, since the most important information, what he does not know, is inaccessible. But an expert is usually very sensitive to the limits of his own knowledge.

Multiple-Source Forecasting

Multiple-source forecasting consists of compiling and often processing forecasts provided by several other sources. These may be forecasts originally produced for purposes other than the current effort, or they may be solicited specifically for the current effort. Thus, multiple-source forecasting ranges from very modest compilations rationalized on the grounds that "two or more expert heads are better than one," to elaborate efforts to synthesize the results of expert interaction. Multiple-source forecasting shifts the focus of the issue of methodology from the actual generation of a specific forecast to the management of the forecasting effort.

Compilation.   The straightforward compilation of existing forecasts, whether presented in their original forms or averaged in some way, may seem at first glance to be a cheap way of avoiding the task of making a forecast. It often is, to be sure, an inexpensive means of generating a forecast, but it also adds value in at least two ways. First, if it is presumed that each individual forecast reflects the set of considerations taken into account by that forecaster, then the combination of several forecasts expands the range of considerations. The forecasts that are inappropriately low because certain factors have been disregarded will be balanced by the inappropriately high forecasts resulting from the disregard of other factors. If everyone is wrong in the same direction, then the multiple-source forecast is no worse than any single forecast is likely to be, although the compilation, insofar as it seems to be an awesome array of "what all the experts think," may have the negative consequence of inspiring more confidence than the conventional wisdom warrants.

Second, the error of the average is less than or (at worst) equal to the average error of the individual forecasts. (The average error of the individual forecasts is the sum of the discrepancies between each forecast and the true value. The error of the average forecast is its discrepancy from the true forecast. Mathematically, subtracting the error of the mean forecast from the mean error of the set of individual forecasts always yields a nonnegative quantity.)

However, to balance off these seemingly free benefits of the compilation approach, there are two major pitfalls. The first, though seemingly obvious, is far from rare: a compilation that combines forecasts of somewhat different trends, without noticing this fact, is naturally introducing needless confusion, error, and often a false impression of how much disagreement there is in the set of forecasts. This mixing of apples and oranges occurs frequently because forecasters are often fuzzy about exactly what it is they are forecasting; moreover, compilers are sometimes greedy about collecting as many forecasts as they can. For example, many of the compilations of oil supplies include very different definitions of "proven reserves" and "recoverable oil."

This greediness leads to the second problem. There is inevitably some time lag between the already existing forecast's creation and its use in a compilation of existing forecasts. This presents the potentially disastrous problem of allowing obsolete forecasts to be included in the compilation. Since the recency of a forecast is the strongest correlate of its accuracy, this is a very heavy price to pay for the reliance on multiple sources.[26]

Delphi Techniques. When the multiple-source forecast is solicited, the effort often includes provisions allowing the sources to interact with one another, usually in structured ways. The Delphi technique is such an interactive method, which avoids face-to-face intimidation and groupthink by using several rounds of written questionnaires that give the participants feedback on what the others say and why they differ in their opinions. Since on each round the participants are permitted to change their previously expressed opinions on the basis of this feedback, the comprehensiveness of considerations taken into account by each of the participants is likely to be enhanced.[27]

Brainstorming and Commenting. While the Delphi technique has received the most attention of the multiple-source approaches, there is also widespread use of brainstorming (basically unstructured, face-to-face interaction) and the time-honored though mundane-sounding practice of circulating reports authored by one individual and commented on, or cleared, by others. These techniques provide speedy, inexpensive, highly interactive means of integrating expert opinion. They do not, however, address the problem of face-to-face intimidation and groupthink (individuals tend to agree with domineering or higher-ranked individuals, or they dismiss considerations that run counter to the group's consensus in order to facilitate positive social relationships within the group).[28] They also require the services of a competent synthesizer to organize the multiple-source input into a coherent whole. The judgment of this synthesizer can play such an important role in making sense of the various contributions that the final product may be closer to a single-expert effort than a multiple-expert one.

Scenarios and Developmental Constructs

Scenario writing is both an approach to generating forecasts and a format for presenting them. As an approach to generating forecasts, scenario writing consists of gathering propositions on how the system is likely to evolve and then examining the consistency of each set of propositions, discarding inconsistent combinations. The objective, then, is to develop a story about how the future might evolve, with the critical criteria that all the elements of the scenario hold together and that there is a plausible sequence of events for "getting from here to there." If there are several plausible paths and configurations of elements, then several different scenarios are in order. (See Chapter 1.)

Like forecasting through analogy, scenario writing has the advantage of vividness and the potential for richness of detail. More than any other method, the scenario is capable of comprehensiveness. But the open-ended potential for detail creates problems for the interpretation and assessment of the scenario forecast, because the forecast user may have difficulty deciding which elements of the scenario are central—in which case the validity of the entire scenario depends on their correctness—and which elements are unessential detail.

However, if the forecast user has a clear idea of how different elements of the scenario are nested within other, more central elements, then he can decide, as time goes by, how well each scenario is standing up to the comparison with real events. Equally important, the forecast user who is aided in understanding the dynamics of the system through the presentation of vivid and elaborate scenarios can salvage some understanding of the reality even if some parts of the scenario do not occur. Thus, the scenario, unlike the more abstract approaches such as extrapolation, regression, or complex modeling, has a heuristic benefit along with the function of anticipating likely trends.

Developmental constructs are projections of possible future dynamics that the system under examination may experience if given enabling trends materialize. The developmental construct can provide the theoretical underpinning for systematic scenarios. The developmental construct projects, not isolated trends, but rather an integrated set of elements: the dynamics of social or political interaction. In short, it provides the combination of theory and scenario. Harold Lasswell, who pioneered the use of the developmental construct, applied it to the analysis of the possible rise of the "garrison state" (now known in more prosaic terms as the "military-industrial complex"), the "revolution of rising expectations," and a non-Marxist interpretation of the transition to socialism as a possible but not inevitable path for capitalist societies.[29]

The developmental construct, then, is a conditional projection of dynamics. It is predicated on the working assumption that the theory underlying these dynamics is valid and applicable to the case at hand, as indicated by two criteria: first, that they are potent explanations of past and current events; and, second, that existing trends seem to be creating the conditions necessary to make these explanations salient for the case. Thus, for example, Lasswell referred to the development of the security-obsessed, militarist state not as the "garrison state prediction," but instead as the "garrison state hypothesis." The distinction is important in conveying the crucial idea that the future is indeed conditional, inasmuch as it depends both on factors beyond our understanding and on decisions made by policy makers who may be part of the forecast's audience.

The product of the developmental construct approach is, in one respect, more modest than that of the other approaches, in that it focuses on the underlying causal relationships that may emerge in the future without necessarily specifying what specific trends will result. The basic intention of the developmental construct is to instruct the audience in how to analyze the future, rather than to predict specifically what the future is going to be. It is also modest in establishing the construct, not as a universal law applicable in all circumstances (as the explicit methods of regression and complex models imply), but rather as a pattern triggered by other trends. With this focus on theory rather than outcomes, however, the developmental construct is an excellent candidate for the "theoretical input" required of so many other approaches reviewed thus far.

The developmental construct also differs from unstructured scenario writing and the inductive methods in being more explicit about why a particular construct is deemed likely to arise. It is incumbent upon the forecaster first to identify the trends, which are usually a combination of political, economic, and social changes.

For example, two competing developmental constructs for the future of international trade and world politics are North-South polarization (that is, combative relations between developed and underdeveloped nations; the formation of OPEC-like cartels in other raw materials and perhaps even finished goods; increased tariff and foreign-investment barriers; and so on) and increasing world-economy integration. Each represents the tenor and nature of interaction, but neither specifies the outcomes of its dynamic, such as which countries do well and which do not. To assess the likelihood of either of these constructs, it is necessary to identify which trends in economic variables would increase the probability of one pattern over the other; for example, instability in the terms of trade between manufactured and raw materials exports would increase the likelihood of polarization, whereas the collapse of OPEC itself as an effective cartel (to choose an economic-political event as opposed to a continuous trend) would probably discourage the cartel-forming component of polarization.

One excellent example of the use of a developmental construct as a framework of analysis is Markos Mamalakis's analysis of Latin American politics, which is intended as a rival to Marxist analyses that focus on interclass conflicts.[30] Mamalakis posits that sectors (such as industry, agriculture, commerce) clash, uniting individuals of different classes within each sector. However, it is clear that this dynamic of sectoral struggle over economic policy formulation is not always operative. For example, when the same businesspeople operate in more than one sector, or if unions are organized across sectoral lines, there is much less reason to expect political or economic action in favor of one sector at the expense of others.

Thus, recognizing the possibility of sectoral clashes is not enough; one must also determine whether for any particular case the economic actors are becoming unified across sectoral lines or divided along this dimension, and whether the trends point to greater unity or division in the future. In Argentina, the industrial entrepreneurs had been relatively isolated from the landowners producing beef and grain for export, allowing an assessment of the political strengths of these two groups to explain much of the political conflict over protectionist and free-trade policies. Yet, because there has been increased capital flow from the industrial to the agricultural sector, and vice versa, the applicability of the sectoral clash dynamic is now of declining utility for this case. On the other hand, in Peru the dominance of a unified business elite over all economic sectors has gradually been replaced as new elements have established separate sectors in nontraditional export industries. If this trend continues, the sectoral clash construct will become more appropriate in projecting Peru's economic policy, even as it becomes less valid in projecting the pattern in Argentina.

The feasibility of the developmental construct approach depends on having enough knowledge, and enough theory, to understand dynamics and to identify the enabling trends. It therefore makes greater demands for well-founded theory than do the more inductive approaches, but less so than complex modeling. The approach may also be criticized by policy makers who think they want decisive answers, not heuristics. Of course, the advocates of the developmental construct approach could argue that when more than one construct remains plausible, depending on how plausible alternative trends unfold, its modesty is not a weakness, but rather a recognition of unavoidable uncertainty.

OVERVIEW

The numerous approaches to forecasting all have specific virtues and vices, and the practical forecaster may well have use for all of them at different times and on different projects. The political forecaster who needs to know what the structure of the economy (and hence of the pressure-group system) will be a decade hence almost certainly needs to tap into some econometric projections of key economic variables. The economist making long-run economic forecasts that are intended to be of practical use must make explicit or implicit use of scenario-like assumptions about the course of economic policy making.

Given the last generation's emphasis on the scientific qualities of formal, quantitative, computerized models, it is important now to emphasize the indispensability of judgmental projections in the use and manipulation of those formal methods. It is equally important to understand the tremendous sacrifice of comprehensiveness involved in heavy reliance on formal models. The practical bank economist, oil company political risk analyst or manufacturing firm strategic planner must strive for a comprehensive view. The comprehensive view is what strategic planning is all about. Over any extended period of time, comprehensiveness involves such a mixture of quantifiable economic change, hard-to-quantify economic influences, political decisions, and, in many cases, cultural and international factors, that scenario analysis becomes an imperative. This was a central theme of Chapter 1. Chapter 3 has taken this insight and, among other things, related scenario analysis to the use of other methods. Chapter 4 focuses even more detailed attention on the roles and limitations of complex models. Just as we have argued that scenario analysis is logically indispensable in many situations, so we argue that the limitations of complex models are inherent. This goes against the grain of many specialists in model building, whose most basic methodological premise is that, if we could only build a model big enough and complex enough, we would have the ideal analytic system. Even worse, such analysts often prescribe to decision makers that planning efforts should be oriented primarily toward the evolution from big computer models to huge computer models.

This volume argues, on the contrary, that complex models have a place, but that their place is a rather limited one.

NOTES

1. Garry D. Brewer, *Politicians, Bureaucrats, and the Consultant* (New York: Basic Books, 1973); Martin Greenberger, Matthew Crenson, and Brian Crissey, *Models in the Policy Process: Public Decision Making in the Computer Era* (New York: Russell Sage Foundation, 1976).
2. Vincent Su and Josephine Su, "An Evaluation of ASA/NBER Business Outlook Survey Forecasts," *Explorations in Economic Research* 2, no. 4 (Fall 1975): 597–98.

3. Robert G. Brown, *Smoothing, Forecasting, and Prediction of Discrete Time Series* (Englewood Cliffs, N.J.: Prentice-Hall, 1963); George E. Box and G. M. Jenkins, *Time Series Analysis: Forecasting and Control* (San Francisco: Holden-Day, 1970).

4. Julian Simon, *The Ultimate Resource* (Princeton, N.J.: Princeton University Press, 1981), chapters 1 and 2.

5. For the statistical theory, see Norman Draper and Harry Smith, *Applied Regression Analysis* (New York: Wiley, 1966). For applications, see William Coplin and Michael O'Leary, *Quantitative Techniques in Foreign Policy Analysis and Forecasting* (New York: Praeger, 1975), chapter 2.

6. J. Johnston, *Econometric Methods,* 2nd ed. (New York: McGraw-Hill, 1972), p. 160.

7. Stephen J. Andriole, "The Quiet Revolution in the Study of International Politics and Foreign Policy," *Policy Sciences* 14 (1981): 1–22.

8. William Ascher, "The Forecasting Potential of Complex Models," *Policy Sciences* 13 (1981): 247–67.

9. Johnston, *Econometric Methods,* chapter 12.

10. Jay W. Forrester, Nathaniel Mass, and Charles Ryan, "The System Dynamics National Model: Understanding Socio-Economic Behavior and Policy Alternatives," *Technological Forecasting and Social Change* 9 (July 1976): 51–68.

11. Donella H. Meadows, Dennis L. Meadows, Jorgen Randers, and William W. Behrens, *The Limits to Growth* (Washington, D.C.: Potomac Associates, 1972).

12. For a summary of the debate, see Greenberger, Crenson, and Crissey, chapter 5; John Clark and Same Cole, *Global Simulation Models: A Comparative Study* (New York: Wiley, 1975), chapter 1.

13. Forrester, Mass, and Ryan, "System Dynamics," p. 54.

14. Ray Fair, *A Short-Run Forecasting Model of the United States Economy* (Lexington, Mass.: Heath-Lexington, 1971).

15. Jay W. Forrester, *World Dynamics* (Cambridge, Mass.: Wright-Allen Press, 1971), p. 111.

16. Bert G. Hickman, "Introduction and Summary," *Econometric Models of Cyclical Behavior,* Bert G. Hickman, ed. (New York: National Bureau of Economic Research, 1972), p. 17.

17. *Ibid.,* p 17.

18. Raymond Pearl, *The Biology of Population Growth* (New York: Knopf, 1925).

19. Jay W. Forrester, "How the Long-Wave Theory May Explain the Sluggishness in Capital Formation," *Financier* (September 1977): pp. 34–38.

20. Herman Kahn, *World Economic Development* (New York: Morrow Quill, 1979), pp. 208–15.
21. Simon Kuznets, "Quantitative Aspects of the Economic Growth of Nations: Distribution of Income by Size," *Economic Development and Cultural Change* 11, no. 2 (January 1963); Felix Paukert, "Income Distribution at Different Levels of Development: A Survey of Evidence," *International Labour Review* 108, nos. 2 and 3 (August/September 1973).
22. Philip Converse, "Of Time and Partisan Stability," *Comparative Political Studies* (1969): pp. 139–71.
23. *Ibid.*, p. 167.
24. Pitirim Sorokin, *Social and Cultural Dynamics, Vol. III: Fluctuation of Social Relationships, War and Revolution* (New York: American Book, 1937).
25. Francis Beer, *Peace Against War* (San Francisco: W. H. Freeman, 1981), p. 50.
26. Ascher, "Forecasting Potential."
27. See Harold Linstone, *The Delphi Method: Techniques and Applications* (Reading, Mass.: Addison-Wesley, 1975); and Chapter 2 of this volume.
28. Irving Janis, *Victims of Groupthink: A Psychological Study of Foreign Policy Decisions and Fiascos* (Boston: Houghton-Mifflin, 1972).
29. Harold D. Lasswell, "The Garrison State," *The American Journal of Sociology* 46 (1941): 455–68; and *Power and Personality* (New York: Norton, 1948), chapter 10.
31. Markos Mamalakis, "The Theory of Sectoral Clashes," *Latin American Research Review* 4 (1969): 9–46; and "The Theory of Sectoral Clashes Revisited," *Latin American Research Review* 6 (1971): 89–126.

Chapter 4

The Uses of Complex Models

Judging by the volume of research devoted to the development of complex models and the money spent on subscriptions to forecast modeling services, these models have become enormously attractive to many forecast users. This attractiveness, which warrants a separate chapter on complex models, is understandable despite the fact that complex models used in forecasting are generally expensive, cumbersome, time-consuming, and often barely manageable.

TRENDS IN METHODS

In choosing methods, analysts and policy makers alike are naturally swayed by what seem to be the directions of scientific developments in general. Thus, the principal trend in forecasting for at least the past two decades has been the development of "sophisticated" methods, reflecting the rise in the allied sciences of econometrics, sociometrics, cliometrics, politometrics, and so on.

The pursuit of methodological "sophistication" in forecasting has had five related aspects.

Quantification

Numerical and mathematical approaches have been supplanting qualitative and judgmental approaches. It is significant, however, that quantification is not necessary for explicitness or rigor. It became fashionable during the recent era in the social and behavioral sciences to presume an equivalence between quantification and rigorous science. In fact, rigorous explorations (for example, through explicit scenarios) can be undertaken without recourse to quantification.

Explicitness

Explicit statistical techniques have been overlaid on numerous forecasting methods. Whereas extrapolation used to be done with a ruler, it is now done with a regression formula. Correlating energy growth with projections of GNP used to be done implicitly; now it is more often done with the formal apparatus of correlation and regression.

Disaggregation

Trends summarizing several somewhat different kinds of activity or different types of units can be broken down into separate trends for each, with no theoretical limitation on how fine the disaggregation can be. For example, while population growth was once projected as a unitary phenomenon, now it is projected through fertility and mortality rates applied to different age cohorts for different racial components of the population. Energy demand projections for a particular fuel, like petroleum, can be made for each different end use and the results then reaggregated to determine total consumption. The rationale of disaggregation is that each separate, more homogeneous trend will behave in a simpler and therefore more predictable way than the overall trend treated as a single entity. (Sometimes, however, this rationale is false, as indicated by the analogies with quantum mechanics in Chapter 1.) When such disaggregation is employed, the elaborateness of method comes not only in having to project a larger number of more specific trends, but also in summing them up again. Elaborate models for tracking and combining these components often appear to be, and are sold as, the most impressive methodological devices of forecasting. In fact, they are little more than highly detailed but not theoretically complex accounting mechanisms.

Complex Models

All of these developments have set the stage for the shift to explicit behavioral models that go beyond these accounting mechanisms by embodying actual theoretical propositions and assumptions. A complex model has been defined (see Chapter 3) as a set of two or more explicit propositions connected by their sharing of at least one factor or variable. The resulting interconnectedness of propositions can, in theory, capture the complexity of real situations, represent intricate relationships such as mutual causation and feedback, and yield surprise implications that may not have been apparent to the analyst examining each relationship in isolation from the others. Yet complex models can also be intimidating to both their creators and their users, and they are no more valid than the (often unexplored) assumptions that their formidable equations actually express.

Bigger Models

Within this modeling movement there has been a dramatic trend toward bigger and bigger models. While this reflects disaggregation to some extent, it also reflects the tendency to include more complex relationships in these models. With the exception of a few small monetarist models designed more for theoretical explorations than for practical forecasting, econometric models have been growing from the 10-to-30 structural equation average around 1960 to the more-than-100 equation size of today.

THE PERFORMANCE AND POTENTIAL OF COMPLEX MODELING

There is no question that complex models do have unique properties as forecasting tools, just as they do for analysis in general. Multiple, interconnected propositions (outputs of one become inputs of another, or solutions must satisfy several propositions or equations simultaneously) can explicitly and systematically express mutual causation, feedback phenomena, and other intricate relationships. The question is whether these properties can be harnessed to improve prediction and explanation.

To some extent, this potential can be revealed by the existing performance record of forecasting models. Yet it may be argued that complex modeling is such a recent development in practical forecasting that its track record is not an adequate basis of evaluation, because the accuracy of many recent forecasts produced by complex models cannot yet be determined, and current models will presumably be further refined and elaborated through efforts to improve them. But even if the current record of complex models is an insufficient basis of appraisal, the record of forecasting in general reveals much about the nature of forecasting and the nature of the world that the forecasts address. In addition, we may also consider the logical and structural properties of complex models and evaluate those properties with respect to the task of forecasting. Thus, if indeed it is premature to judge the forecasting potential of modeling solely on the basis of the record to date, other bases are available. They are: the nature of complex modeling, the nature of forecasting, and the nature of the practical application of modeling to forecasting. After reviewing the performance record of complex models in forecasting, each of these topics will be considered in turn. Finally, some conclusions regarding the optimal use of complex models in forecasting will be drawn from these considerations.

Judging the Forecasting Performance of Complex Models

Complex models have been prominent in projecting only a few policy-relevant trends. For many years now, econometric models have been used in short-term economic forecasting, and more recently complex models have been employed for energy demand projections. In population forecasting, however, the impressive-seeming models utilized by the Census Bureau are not complex models at all according to our definition, since they lack connected propositions.[1] They are, in reality, elaborate accounting devices, tracking birth and death rates implied by component and cohort-specific fertility and mortality rates, but without any of the interactive effects required by our definition of the complex model. Similarly, travel demand forecasting models, also often formidable in appearance, are nonetheless usually single-equation regression models treating the demand for a particular travel mode strictly as a dependent variable.[2] No matter how many independent variables are included in such an equation, they are not explained or affected by the single dependent variable, but rather projected independently of the models (that is, taken exogenously from extrapolations of other models). Consequently, the performance record of complex modeling rests largely on the economic and energy forecasts, although complex modeling *could* be applied to forecasting in any of the other areas.

In appraising the complex models used in forecasting, there are two questions we may ask of the performance record. The first is how well complex models forecast, either in absolute terms or in comparison with other forecasting methods. The second, equally important question is whether complex forecasting models, subject to considerable refinement and elaboration over the past two decades, have been improving in terms of their accuracy.

To answer these questions, it is useful to take advantage of the fact that complex models do compete with numerous other techniques as forecasting tools. The forecasting performance of other methods provides not only a comparative basis for evaluating the record of complex modeling, but also a benchmark for establishing the intrinsic difficulty of predicting trends of a given period. For example, projecting energy demand trends after 1973 (that is, predicting the demand in particular target years beyond 1973) has been a more difficult task, both for models and for other forecasting techniques such as extrapolation or judgment, than projecting these trends for target years before 1973.[3] Thus, it is very useful to regard the average error of judgmental forecasts as an indicator of the inherent (rather than method-specific) unpredictability or uncertainty of a specific era. By tracking the level of judgmental error over time (that is, of forecasts made in years t_1, t_2, t_3, etc., for target years $t_1 + {}_N$, $t_2 + {}_N$, $t_3 + {}_N$, etc., where N is a fixed length of time, say five or ten years), we can determine whether changes in the accuracy levels of more explicit methods such as modeling can be attributed to changes in predictability. Thus, for example, if the judgmentally based five-year petroleum demand forecasts made during the period 1969–73 (for the target years 1974–78) have a higher average error than the judgmental five-year projections made in, say, 1960–67 (for the target years 1965–72), then our assessment of less accurate complex-model projections made in 1969–73 for 1974–78 ought to take into account the greater uncertainty of the post-1973 period as indicated by the decline in judgmental accuracy.

The Record of Economic Forecasting Models

Econometric models for short-term economic forecasting have been evaluated periodically by the model operators themselves (who generally developed econometric forecasting models initially as theoretical experiments, but increasingly as practical commercial enterprises) and more systematically by an ongoing survey sponsored jointly by the American Statistical Association and the National Bureau of Economic Research.[4] This survey provides the most telling appraisal of how well econometric models forecast.

The ASA-NBER survey indicates that econometric models have not— and still do not—forecast quite as well as the judgmental approach relying on no explicit routines. The most comprehensive ASA-NBER comparison of a large number of economic forecasting sources covered forecasts produced from 1968 through 1973, and found that judgmental forecasting efforts slightly outperformed econometric approaches for quarterly GNP (both nominal and real) and were roughly even in forecasting annual GNP changes.[5]

Although there has been no attempt to repeat so comprehensive a comparison for more recent forecasts, there are some up-to-date comparisons of selected models and noneconometric efforts. The median forecast of the ASA-NBER survey has been used as one benchmark for evaluating the accuracy of prominent modeling operations; the accuracy of forecasts by the Council of Economic Advisors is another noneconometric benchmark. For very short-term forecasts (one or two quarters), Vincent Su found that for the period 1968–77 the ASA-NBER median forecast still outperforms the Wharton model for most variables, but there is little difference for longer horizons.[6] Victor Zarnowitz found that for 1969–76 the annual forecasts of real GNP and the inflation rate by two modeling operations (Wharton and the University of Michigan model) and the two noneconometric sources do not establish the superiority of one method over another. Zarnowitz concludes: "This is in agreement with earlier findings, which strongly suggests that the search for a consistently superior forecaster is about as promising as the search for the philosophers' stone."[7] Finally, Stephen McNees found the same two noneconometric sources to be roughly equal in accuracy to several econometric operations (Chase Econometrics and DRI in addition to Wharton and Michigan) in annual forecasting for the 1961–76 period.[8] Thus, there seems to be no dissent from the conclusion that even the most recent econometric modeling has not offered the advantage of greater accuracy over judgment in short-term economic forecasting, despite the refinement and elaboration of the models.

Does this mean, though, that the models per se forecast with the same general level of accuracy as expert opinion? If so, this would be no mean accomplishment. Yet it is untrue. The prominent econometric modeling services all operate with a considerable amount of judgmental input, introduced either by choosing exogenous variables so that the model's predictions seem plausible to the model operator, or by tinkering with the model specifications or parameters to achieve the same result.[9] Zarnowitz points out that "the genuine ex ante forecasts here considered are all to a large extent 'judgmental.' "[10]

How do we know that pure models (the mechanical operation of the models, insulated from judgment) would not do as well or better than the models as they are run today? There are three pieces of evidence. First, the fact that the modelers leave themselves this leeway indicates their appreciation for adding the polish of judgment. Second, a valiant attempt by economist Ray Fair to operate an econometric forecasting model without judgmental adjustments led to a very poor forecasting record; parallel attempts to operate the Wharton model strictly according to its published specifications led to inferior performance compared with the judgmentally modified forecasts actually released by Wharton.[11] Third, the actual forecasting errors of the models based on runs with parameter values that had to be guessed are lower than the errors produced by operating them with the *actual* values of exogenous variables once these values are known.[12] This superiority of so-called ex ante predictions over ex post predictions is quite startling; knowing the true values of the parameters actually *reduces* the accuracy of model forecasts. This demonstrates that the convergence of plausible results provided by the forecasters' selection of exogenous values (even if they are, in retrospect, incorrect) is needed to offset errors attributable directly to the models' specifications.

The Record of Energy Forecasting Models

Appraising the performance record of energy models is complicated by the widespread use of conditional forecasts in this area, as well as by the fact that most energy forecasting models are designed to project long-range trends, so that their accuracy cannot yet be evaluated retrospectively. A brief methodological digression may clarify the appraisal problems.

When models (such as those used for short-term economic forecasting) produce unconditional forecasts, their accuracy can be evaluated straightforwardly by measuring the difference between the forecasted and the actual results. However, when models are set up to generate conditional forecasts, their performance can be evaluated in two quite different ways. First, the projection indicated as most likely may be considered as if it were the unconditional forecast nestled among other conceivable but less likely possibilities. This most likely projection may then be evaluated like a standard unconditional forecast: retrospectively, by measuring the discrepancy of predicted trend from actual trend; for current forecasting efforts, by examining the spread of most likely projections from several sources.

However, in recent years, particularly since the 1973–74 jump in oil prices, energy forecasters have been far less willing to presume that a particular energy-supply condition, or policy-choice scenario, is more likely than the others. The set of conditional forecasts (or "policy simulations") is offered as an aid to policy makers rather than as a prediction of what they will do.[13] No single projection can be meaningfully regarded as the forecasters' prediction.

When no scenario is designated as most likely, the scenarios must be regarded as exogenous factors, whose likelihoods are not at issue in the modeling exercise. The model produces a set of projections, each posited as correct *if* the corresponding condition or scenario were to hold, but without implying that any particular one will hold or that some are more likely than others. In this case, the retrospective evaluation of forecast accuracy must proceed by first establishing which condition actually prevailed, and then measure the discrepancy between the projection tied to that condition and the actual level of the predicted trend. If it is still too early to evaluate a set of conditional forecasts retrospectively, the spread of conditional forecasts of the same trend for the same target year can be used as one indication of uncertainty or minimum error, but *only if the conditional is the same for every forecast of the set*. For example, one model's prediction of petroleum demand in a specific target year under a particular scenario can be compared only with the predictions of other models for that year and that scenario. The differences among the petroleum demand predictions for that same scenario in that year necessarily reflect error, since only one (or none) of them can be correct.

This last approach is the only feasible one for judging the performance of complex energy models. They are too recent for their accuracy to be judged retrospectively, and they project several different conditionals without designating one as most likely. Because it makes no sense to compare the projections of several models if they take different scenarios as their conditional elements, many apparent opportunities for comparison and measurement of dispersion are precluded. When modelers work independently, there is no reason to expect that any of the scenarios examined will be precisely the same for two or more of them. One cannot say, then, whether differences in projections reflect these scenario differences rather than indicating disagreement, uncertainty, or error.

Comparability *is* feasible, however, when modelers work together to examine the implications of separate models run with a common set of scenarios. The most comprehensive and careful effort in this vein was conducted by the Modeling Resource Group of the National Research Council's Committee on Nuclear and Alternative Energy Systems, with the participation of four modeling groups projecting energy consumption and prices to the year 2010 and beyond, and with limited participation of two medium-range models.[14] Each of the long-term models projected the outcomes of six different policy scenarios, using the same starting points and common assumptions regarding economic growth. Therefore, differences in outcomes from one model to another, for the same scenario, represent at least the minimum degree of uncertainty or error of the models.

There are, in fact, some serious divergences between different models' results. In forecasting energy consumption, the base case projections for the year 1990 vary up to 19% for total energy, and by more than 50% for electricity generation. Some models project five times the consumption of oil indicated by other models. Even when the two extreme projections (of the five models involved in this particular comparison) are dropped, one remaining projection of oil consumption is less than half the levels forecasted by the other two models. One model projects more than twice the consumption of nuclear energy projected by the others.[15]

Most seriously—because the rationale of such simulation exercises is to determine which policies produce optimal results—shifts from one policy scenario to another bring different changes according to different models, especially for the three models most extensively compared in the Modeling Resource Group experiment. For example, the Brookhaven DESOM model and the Stanford University ETA model foresee little impact of a moratorium on nuclear development and limits on coal and shale oil exploration (compared to the base case), while the Nordhaus model (developed by William Nordhaus of Yale University) projects a 20% decline in energy consumption and domestic production under the moratorium condition.

For energy price projections, there are also major discrepancies. While the ETA and DESOM models project only small differences among different scenarios for the 1990 price of oil, the Nordhaus model foresees a 60%–70% greater price under one scenario (limits on coal and shale oil production). Oil prices for the year 2010 forecasted by the ETA and DESOM models are consistently a third to a half greater than those projected by the Nordhaus model. Under all of the scenarios involving constraints on coal and shale oil development, the price of coal is projected to increase twofold or more between 1990 and 2010 according to the ETA and DESOM models, yet the Nordhaus model projects the price to decline by nearly half. For electricity prices, ETA projects sharp increases from 1990 to 2010 under the scenarios of nuclear moratorium and limits on coal and shale oil production; Nordhaus projects declining prices.[16]

Although there are numerous consistencies across models, there are also many inconsistencies. The unavoidable conclusion is that some of the models must be wrong in quite significant ways on policy-relevant issues. It is also discouraging that even the agreement across models need not be an indication of validity; they could all be wrong. For example, all energy models predicting the 1975 levels of U.S. electricity, petroleum, and total energy consumption projected these levels higher than they actually turned out to be.[17] This confident consensus was no guarantee that the models were correct then; any consensus among models' predictions in the future may be equally misleading.

The Nature of Complex Modeling

The key attributes of complex modeling are explicitness and complexity. While complex modeling has no monopoly on either, the combination is unique. Explicitness and complexity are the virtues of complex models— if and only if the models are valid. When models are misspecified, their explicitness forecloses the possibility of adjusting their results on the basis of judgment and plausibility; the model operator must do what the model says. Complexity becomes a burden rather than a virtue for a misspecified model because complexity makes it difficult to determine just where the errors are.

Explicitness.   Complex models are formulated by specifying assumptions and hypothesized relationships as explicit, usually mathematical propositions. While this procedure is often very helpful in uncovering inconsistency and vagueness in the initial ideas or verbal formulations, it cannot establish the correctness of the model's propositions. Models express assumptions but do not validate them. If the modeler tries to ensure the validity of the model's propositions by focusing on disaggregated behavior of presumably greater regularity, the problem of reaggregating these behaviors to model overall patterns becomes another potential source of error. If the modeler only includes relationships proven by past experience, there is no guarantee that they will hold in the future. There is no procedure or format of model specification that guarantees the validity of this specification.

With explicitness and the computational capacity of computers, complex models can combine almost immediate response with the fundamental analysis that an elaborate model—if correct—provides. Other explicit mechanical modes of analysis and forecasting, ranging from trend extrapolation to multiple regression, may be just as quick and automatic but cannot make as bold a claim to represent fundamental understanding of the dynamics of the system under study.[18] If the modeler wishes to convey a detailed image of reality through the model, explicitness will require the model to be large and elaborate. Whereas the analyst relying on judgment keeps the richness of detail and nuance stored in his head, the modeler must commit it all to formal expression. Greater elaborateness has been the most striking trend in model building in the past 15 years.

Yet, as noted in Chapter 3, explicitness also exercises a subtle constraint on the model's capacity to fully represent reality. Explicitness tends to limit the amount of context encompassed by the model, beause the need to formulate explicit, consistent relationships requires the modeler to discard those factors that are of some relevance but without clearcut, consistent relationship to the outcomes. In modeling approaches there is nothing of the notion of a "directed search" to identify contextual factors that may be relevant, but only in particular cases or in idiosyncratic ways. In short, modeling, like extrapolation and other routinized, explicit procedures, tends to simplify and restrict contextual considerations.

The fully explicit model, once formulated, *can* be applied mechanically, independent of any further judgment on the part of the modeler. Although the model represents the model builder's assumptions about how the system operates, mechanical operation can thereafter insulate the results from both the modeler's myopia and his insights about the specific situations being forecast. If the model truly embodies a fundamental understanding of reality with greater sophistication than the casual or less systematically formulated opinion of the model operator, its mechanical operation is a virtue. There are numerous documented instances of analysts incorrectly disregarding the signals of their methods because of personal biases and faulty preconceptions. Yet if the model produces silly results, the lack of intervention by its operators would be a deficiency. Model operators—especially when they are also model builders—are often experts in the substantive area of the model; hence, their judgment might be an important means of screening model results. But this alternative of plausibility testing is correspondingly problematical, as we shall explore later on.

Complexity. The "complexity" of complex forecasting models lies in the existence of several (and often many) interdependent relationships. If some variables (or factors) appear in more than one equation (or proposition), the relationships are "interactive," producing overall patterns of outcomes that would not be obvious from the isolated consideration of each relationship.[19]

This sort of complexity should be distinguished from the elaborateness of the accounting devices included in many models (both complex and not) to recombine disaggregated trends or to keep track of their changes over time. Very often these devices appear to be the most impressive methodological parts of a model; in fact, they represent neither the theoretical complexity of the model nor the behavioral complexity of the phenomena being modeled. For example, an energy model with 50 different equations for the consumption levels of 50 different fuels, and a few more equations to summarize consumption for broader fuel categories, may nonetheless be limited to quite simplistic propositions for each specific trend—for example, that the consumption of a given fuel increases by a fixed proportion each year. In contrast, a model linking the consumption level of one broadly defined fuel category to the levels of a few other broad fuel types (for instance, petroleum consumption limited by a large increase in coal consumption, which in turn is stimulated by lagging nuclear energy generation) may be considerably more complex.

A set of interactive relationships has *emergent properties,* often not apparent to the analyst who examines these relationships one at a time without an explicit model to track the interactions. Though the emergent patterns are indeed nothing more than implications of the basic relationships and the explicitly expressed connections among them, these patterns nonetheless can be surprising, counterintuitive, and inconsistent with expectations.[20]

The Nature of Forecasting

When complex models are applied to the task of forecasting, they enter a field with a track record that antedates complex modeling. Thus, although modeling itself is a recent addition to the tools of forecasting, some insights can be drawn both from a theoretical examination of what forecasting entails, and from the practical benefits and caveats of different forecasting approaches.

A retrospective appraisal of the forecasting record provides the first major source of insight into whether the trends underlying the emergence of modeling as a favored forecasting method are likely to produce better analysis. The record we compiled to evaluate the accuracy and biases of various forecasting methods and sources consists of all available forecasts, up to 1975, of specific U.S. trends in population, energy demand (consumption of petroleum, electricity, and total energy), transportation (airline passenger volume, general aviation fleet size, motor vehicle registrations), economic growth (real and nominal GNP CHANGE), and technology (computer capability and nuclear energy capacity).[21] This record revealed three general findings.

First, *methodological sophistication contributes very little to the accuracy of forecasts,* as evidenced by the following:

1. The introduction of more sophisticated methods in population forecasting, with the elaborate accounting divisions of components and cohorts, has not resulted in more accurate demographic forecasts.

2. Economic modeling and the explicitly quantitative approach of leading indicators have not improved the accuracy of short-term economic forecasting.

3. For energy demand forecasts, correlation and simple trend extrapolation have had the same general levels of accuracy, though the former is a much more elaborate procedure.

4. Separating electricity or petroleum demand into various end-use components does not add any appreciable accuracy over projecting the demand for each as a unitary trend.

5. In transportation forecasting, the more elaborate regression models recently adopted by the FAA to predict both commercial air traffic and the general aviation fleet size have not improved the accuracy record.

Second, *a forecast's time horizon is the strongest and most consistent correlate of its accuracy.* Though there are some exceptions, the general rule is that shorter forecasts are more accurate, often in a nearly linear relationship:

1. Five-year petroleum consumption forecasts have had a median error of about 6%, and 10-year forecasts have had an error of about 13%.

2.   Motor vehicle registration forecasts have median errors in percentages roughly equal to the forecast lengths in years.

3.   Technological breakthrough predictions by expert panels show greater dispersion (indicating uncertainty and greater minimum error levels) for more remote breakthroughs than for breakthroughs perceived to be more imminent.

Third, *all evidence points to the essential importance of the validity of core assumptions antecedent to the choice and application of methods.* Behind any forecast, regardless of the sophistication of methods, are irreducible assumptions representing the forecaster's basic outlook on the context within which the specific trend develops. These core assumptions are not derivable from methods; on the contrary, the method is a vehicle for tracing through the consequences or implications of core assumptions originally chosen independently of (and intellectually prior to) the method. The method selected usually reflects and signifies this preconception of the pattern of future change. For example, envelope curves are chosen as a forecasting method only if the forecaster has a preconception that cumulative scientific breakthroughs will cause the technology improvement rate to take the envelope-curve form. Forecasting by analogy is utilized only when the forecaster believes a particular historical pattern to be analogous. Formal models, too, ought to be viewed as the explicit expression of a set of assumptions, and the operation of the model is the tracking of interactions arising from these presumed relationships.

These core assumptions are the principal determinants of forecast accuracy. When the core assumptions are valid, the choice of method is either secondary or obvious. When these assumptions fail to capture the reality of the context, other factors such as method generally make little difference. This helps to explain why correlational forecasts of electricity and petroleum demand do no better than extrapolation: when one trend is projected by correlating it with a presumably more fundamental, contextual trend (say, industrial production or GNP), its accuracy depends not primarily on whether this correlation is appropriate, but rather on how well the more fundamental trend is forecast. The primacy of contextual assumptions is also consistent with the great dispersion of projections of air transportation forecasting models based on regressions on economic growth: the greatest uncertainty is in predicting the economic growth context.[22]

The importance of both recency and core assumptions makes the problem of relying on antiquated core assumptions particularly serious. This "assumption drag" has been the source of the most drastic errors in forecasting. The worst population forecasts prepared in the 1930s and early 1940s were based on a no longer valid assumption of declining birth rates. Similarly, the electricity demand forecasts of the 1960s continued to project fairly low electricity demand growth, even when the actual growth rates were contradicting this assumption.

These core assumptions are often political. Even for technological forecasting, seemingly far removed from political developments, a major source of uncertainty stems from doubt about the political context. If the variation among predictions of a given technological breakthrough is taken as a measure of uncertainty, it can be demonstrated that developments in technological areas for which advances require large-scale official programs (such as health-care systems, medical education, and space exploration) are more uncertain than developments in technologies depending on engineering refinements and the disaggregated market diffusion of such innovations (such as communications, educational technology, and automation).[23] The difficulty in predicting innovations requiring discrete, high-level, "official" (though not necessarily governmental) policy decisions indicates the pivotal role of political assumptions—both because the political context is important to the development of these technologies and because it is difficult to predict. Political forecasting, perhaps because of the discrete and discretionary nature of political decisions, is the weakest link in the whole range of forecasting trends even remotely affected by policy.

The political context is often ignored (on the dubious grounds that, in the long run, relatively short-lived political conditions or policy decisions will have no net effect), or it is considered in a rudimentary fashion. For example, almost all energy projections made before 1973 totally ignored government responses to energy problems, including the possible responses of petroleum-producing nations to the dwindling real earnings of their oil exports. Even now, long-term energy, economic, and transportation forecasts, if they are based on any explicit assumptions about government policy at all, generally pose a single and stable governmental policy choice, exogenous to the forecasting procedure, as a fixed condition.[24] To ignore the possibility of governmental problem-solving decisions is to limit seriously the validity of any forecast.

The parameters found to fit in the past will hold in the future only if the relationships embodied by the model are invariant. Simply finding a set of relationships and parameters that fit past data in no way guarantees future fit. Some theorists argue persuasively that if such relationships describe aggregate behavior (for example, macroeconomic behavior in the case of economic models), invariance is unlikely even in principle. Aggregate specifications are subject to "parameter drift," if only because individuals' decision rules change from one situation to another, from one set of expectations to another.[25] Robert Lucas points out that even the parameters utilized in the large-scale econometric models as if they had been constant have in fact been drifting, and that this is actually acknowledged by the forecasters through their adjustments of model forecasts on the basis of prior model errors.[26]

We come back to the puzzle of why the large-scale econometric models for short-term economic forecasting are under continual development and yet do not improve in accuracy. This line of reasoning suggests an explanation: the "improvement" of substituting new specifications for old ones merely replaces the representation of the previous context with a representation of the newer context, but without coming closer to a more generally valid representation. There is no a priori reason why there should be a set of aggregate-level propositions that remains generally valid over time.

Implications for Modeling

If, indeed, valid up-to-date contextual assumptions, rather than methodological sophistication, have been the primary determinants of forecast accuracy, there is little basis for confidence that the unique capacity of models to explicitly track complex interactions will materialize in consistently greater accuracy.[27] The advantages of complexity and explicitness may well be offset by the built-in assumption drag of elaborate models, as well as by their tendency to restrict contextual considerations to regular, law-like relationships.

Just as importantly, complex modeling, though it certainly does not preclude the incorporation of policy interactions, has failed to do so. The current generation of complex models developed for economic and energy modeling does incorporate sociopolitical factors, including policy choices, but only as givens, usually expressed through conditional scenarios or parameters. Complex modeling has been particularly slow to incorporate policy response. This omission is illustrated by the approach of William Hogan (organizer of the Energy Modeling Forum at the Stanford University Institute for Energy Studies) and Alan Manne (a principal developer of the Stanford ETA model) in an article on economy-energy interactions.[28] They argue:

> The value share of the energy sector determines the incremental effect upon the GNP. If the 4% value share remained constant, this would mean that a 10% reduction in energy inputs would produce only a 0.4% drop in total output. Thus, for small changes in energy availability, there need not be a proportional impact upon the economy as a whole.

They then go on to say that for large changes in energy availability the critical factor in determining economic growth rates becomes the substitutability of energy inputs by nonenergy inputs (such as insulation or energy-efficient machinery) to compensate for energy supply shortfalls.[29] This formulation may be reasonable if the government is passive or acts only to facilitate the substitution of inputs. But it does not encompass the possibility that the government may react to inflation (triggered by higher energy prices) by enacting recessionary economic policies with much greater impact on economic growth. The commonality of recessionary policies adopted by OECD countries after the oil price increase of 1973–'74 would indicate that this sort of reaction is regular enough to be modeled with some degree of confidence.

The failure to model policy response is, of course, not a mere oversight. It reflects the almost universal commitment of practical modelers to represent aggregate dynamics with aggregate, macro models in which discrete decisions (if not provided as givens) are assumed to be subsumable by general mechanisms of equilibration or optimization.

In principle, disaggregated models based on decision-making agents as the units of analysis (for instance, based on the perhaps firmer principles of microeconomics) can model both discrete responses and the aggregate patterns. If indeed the aggregate behavior of the system follows a pattern of equilibration or optimization as a result of myriad individual decisions—a point not challenged by macroeconomics—a microlevel model can represent such patterns.

THE PRACTICAL APPLICATION OF MODELING TO FORECASTING

The formal properties of forecasting and of complex modeling do not completely determine how complex models are applied in practice to forecasting tasks. There is a range of discretion in the practice of forecast modeling. Choices within this range can make a huge difference in the utlity of complex models.

First, despite the large number of possible model forms—varying in size, format, level of aggregation, propositional form, and so on—in practice complex forecasting models have become highly uniform. Once practical forecasting in a particular area becomes established, there is a strong tendency for the models to converge. Those showing the earliest success drive out the less successful. From the interesting variety of econometric models in the late 1960s, the surviving practical short-term economic forecasting models are remarkably similar: all large, macroeconomic models in the Klein-Goldberger tradition.[30] This could be justified as "survival of the fittest," except that complex modeling as an intellectual enterprise is not advanced enough for all other lines of development to be rejected as inferior simply on the basis of early falterings. In particular, microlevel models have received surprisingly little support and development, considering their initial promise.[31]

Second, thus far, the application of complex modeling to forecasting has also been marked by the related practices of commitment to the same basic structure for long periods of time, continual superficial revision of such models, and plausibility testing of their outputs. Most methodologically sophisticated forecasting efforts are big, expensive, one-shot affairs. Since rigorous, elaborate analysis is time-consuming and expensive, there has been a natural tendency for forecasters to pour their efforts into grand, once-and-for-all projects, carried out only infrequently and yet used long after they are produced because the immense effort makes them seem definitive. This, of course, poses a very serious problem of obsolescence.

In one important way, it would seem that modeling approaches depart from this pattern of one-shot projects because they are automated, ongoing mechanisms that can be updated and can spew out new forecasts at any time. Yet the sunk costs in the development of an elaborate model force it to be a one-shot effort in a more basic sense. Though forecasters may tinker with their model and reestimate its parameters, the model's basic structure remains intact for long periods of time. It is much easier for the modeler to tinker than to scrap the entire model, even though the core assumptions may reside in the model's basic structure. For example, the central mechanism of some energy models is an optimization routine that establishes supplies, demands, and prices so as to maximize benefits under the presumption of competitive markets.[32] Charles Hitch points out that such models (among others) "assume that the economy and its markets will be permitted to function, that prices are not controlled, and that producers and consumers will not be constrained by regulation from responding to appropriate market signals."[33] Yet, after the modeler has spent years developing optimization routines, apparent violations of such assumptions are more likely to be accommodated by patchwork modifications, or disregarded altogether as short-term aberrations, than they are to trigger the abandonment of the model.

Even though these basic structures endure, complex models in practice undergo continual revision. Although the primary emphasis of forecast modeling is usually on the quality of the forecasts rather than on the development of the models, forecasting models (like complex models in general) still represent efforts at theory building—and these efforts are never finished. Therefore, model revision, which seems to the cynic to be an ad hoc effort to keep a fundamentally misspecified model more or less in line with reality, is generally regarded by the model builder as the normal routine of science. In this view, continual revision complements rather than contradicts the durability of basic model structure, because altering the same basic model to keep it consistent with the most recent changes in the phenomena it models saves the modelers from scrapping the basic model itself. There is a fundamental tension, ethical as well as practical, in the simultaneous claims of theory building and practical application. Such tension was particularly dramatic in the case of the Club of Rome members, who held press conferences and mailed copies of *The Limits to Growth* to policy makers, demanding urgent policy response to their model's conclusions of imminent doom, but then responded to criticism of their findings by saying that the model was merely a preliminary effort at theory construction.

Third, plausibility testing is an almost universal procedure in the practical application of forecasting models. This results in part from the commitment to continual model development and in part from the modelers' modesty as to the accuracy of their models. Usually, at least at this stage in the development of modeling, when a model generates implausible outcomes the onus is laid on the model rather than on the modeler's perception of what is plausible. As mentioned in Chapter 3, this plausibility testing proceeds not just by directly rejecting implausible model results, but also through the subtler means of providing exogenous information that makes the model's results plausible.

In energy modeling, a good example of the interplay between exogenous value selection and the plausibility of model results is provided by the treatment of energy prices in the RFF/SEAS Modeling System:

> Since the model does not include a mechanism for determining these prices, our procedure is to develop assumptions about price changes, run the model, adjust prices, and iterate if necessary.[34]

What are the combined effects of these practices? The complex model holds an ambiguous status as both practical device and experiment. When model builders come up with new formulations, should forecast users regard such models as the best devices the modelers can offer for forecasting, or as the latest turn—perhaps a dead end—in the theoretical and methodological search? Most importantly, there is an obvious and direct tradeoff between plausibility testing and the capacity of the model to express the counterintuitive implications of its assumptions. These practices drastically weaken the forecast-modeling enterprise's sensitivity to surprising future possibilities. The homogeneity of models simply reinforces this weakness, as similar models undergoing similar judgmental censorship by modelers holding similar outlooks on the future can so easily reassure all parties that the future is seen with certainty.

It is not clear, however, how long these practices will last. Certain models have become institutionalized, with a life and a durability beyond the active role of their originators. Related to this process of institutional-ization is a growing distinction between model builders and model opera-tors. Innovators like Lawrence Klein and Otto Eckstein are not preoccu-pied with the routine operation of the Wharton and DRI econometric models; they have other, more ambitious things to do.

This development presents both drawbacks and advantages. When methods themselves acquire charisma, their operation can take the place of careful reasoning. Model operators who regard themselves as techni-cians are even less likely than model builders to grapple with the basic structure of an already established model. Hence, the obsolescence of core assumptions embodied in the model's structure will become an even greater risk. If any judgmental input remains in the operation of the model, it will not be from leading economists privy to the discussions at the highest levels of government and industry. Thus, even if the model operators are no less competent as practical economists than prominent model builders, the caliber of inside information used in the remaining practice of plausibility testing is likely to deteriorate.

CONCLUSIONS

The practical issue boils down to this: if complex models as normally operated converge with judgment or, if operated more mechanically, perform no better than judgment, what is the incentive to employ an expensive, formidable model? The current practice of model operation, which is virtually "judgment guided by modeling," is saddled with the predictive weakness of aggregate macrolevel models, without the capacity to reveal surprising outcomes implicit in the component propositions. The possibly emerging practice of mechanically run aggregate models could restore this sensitivity to surprise, but falls prey to the most severe problems of assumption drag, inadequate representation of policy response, and parameter drift.

This dilemma is unresolvable as long as all complex forecasting models are basically alike and are operated alike to pursue the same function. More pluralism in practical forecast modeling is urgently needed. First, the two functions of forecast modeling—to produce consistently reason-able forecasts and to anticipate counterintuitive outcomes—can rarely be pursued by the same model at the same time, but can be as separate enterprises. The former provides credibility for the latter, while surprise sensitivity, as the unique contribution of modeling, enhances the attractiveness of the entire modeling undertaking. Therefore, the operation of some models in the current mode of plausibility testing, and other models in the surprise-sensitive, unconstrained mode, can be mutually reinforcing.

Second, the homogenization of practical forecasting models should be avoided; it not only cuts off promising avenues for developing better models, but also leaves the field to the large-scale aggregate models which (for all the reasons discussed above) will most likely always require plausibility testing. It should be recognized that the really quite modest success of the macrolevel modeling operations (the models *plus* the judgmentally based interventions of the model operators *plus* the adjustments for parameter drift) in terms of performance is no basis for concluding that the models per se are optimal in either specific detail or general form.

This diversity in operating modes and model forms requires considerable sophistication on the part of the models' audiences and funders. They have to be able to recognize which models' outputs are to be regarded as most consistently and plausibly likely, and which are designed to be ultra-sensitive to possible surprises even at the risk of a worse overall record of accuracy. If this is not recognized, forecast users will be disappointed in the first type for not being daring enough, and cynical about the second type for not being accurate enough. Funders must be aware of the widely differing development periods necessary to bring diferent modeling approaches to the point where they start to pay off, and must maintain a broad R&D strategy of cultivating different approaches even when only a few seem superior in the short run. Diversity and a modicum of tolerance will aid in bringing out the potential of complex modeling, without the danger of elevating one complex modeling approach as the panacea for the problems of forecasting.

Most of these comments apply to all forms of complex modeling, and most of the examples of the problems of complex modeling have been drawn from the fields to which complex modeling is most applicable, namely various kinds of economic and energy forecasting. But clearly the problems of complex models are far more severe in political forecasting, where discontinuous leadership changes can frequently change the basic structure of relationships, where changing public perceptions exacerbate the problem of parameter drift, and where the impact of unquantifiable contextual changes is undeniably great. Thus, the political forecaster attempting to use complex models must be doubly wary: he must be somewhat concerned about using complex model forecasts of the economy as inputs to the political forecasting, and he must be particularly skeptical about using complex models to forecast strictly political phenomena.

PROPER USES OF LARGE-SCALE MODELS

The burden of this analysis has been to deflate the ambitious claims frequently made for large-scale, quantitative, computerized predictive models. For most predictive purposes such models simply have not proved more accurate than other methods, and they are far more expensive than competing methods that are easier to keep current. There remain, however, uses for which these models do possess some comparative advantages.

Complex Accounting

While models have not achieved their claims of producing subtle or intuitively surprising results through the interaction of complex substantive assumptions, they do facilitate complicated calculations. That is, when used as calculators rather than as "brains," for accounting rather than analysis, computer models are frequently helpful. For instance, in projecting a balance of payments problem into the future, a model will seldom reveal surprising results, but it will greatly speed up the calculation.

Consistency Checks

Verbal analyses can sometimes conceal internal inconsistencies, particularly when they concern a complex subject or when they represent the combined view of experts with different perspectives. When such complicated analyses can be quantified, or when key parts of them can be quantified, it is frequently useful to check the internal consistency of a paper by formal modeling. For instance, one group analyzing the Chinese economic plans of the late 1970s found that its experts were producing conclusions that were based upon inconsistent premises, and were able to advance their analysis by modeling the inconsistencies.

Sensitivity Estimates

One of the particularly useful forms of accounting that a computer model can perform is the "sensitivity check." For instance, when Japan proposes tariff reductions in response to U.S. demands, a simple computer accounting mechanism can rapidly calculate the approximate effect on the U.S. balance of payments, cutting through the complexity of long lists of detailed changes in rules for large numbers of products. In at least one instance, such a model was used to show very quickly that an apparently responsive proposal was virtually inconsequential.

Policy Simulation

The unique capacity of complex models to trace out the implications of numerous interactions gives these models an advantage over judgment in exploring what would occur if an extensive package of policy changes were to be implemented. Whereas forecasting what *will* happen requires the prediction of policy response—a task that complex models have failed to address—the policy simulation takes a stipulated set of responses as a given, in order to explore its consequences. Human judgment, in contrast, excels in short-term forecasting in a context of limited exogenous change but easily bogs down in calculating the net impact of multiple changes. For example, the consequences of major departures from economic policy or a completely new package of energy regulations can be more easily tracked by a complex model.

Time Estimates

In certain economic situations, models can usefully estimate the time necessary for changes in economic policy or in the economic environment to have a given effect on the economy.

Heuristics

The intellectually most sophisticated use of complex models is the heuristic exploration of an issue. For this use, one creates a model and then manipulates it to see what differences are caused by varying the parameters, the assumptions, and the initial data. For instance, prediction of a country's balance of payments a decade hence is in the strict sense virtually impossible. But by modeling the interactions of principal components of the balance of payments, and then making different assumptions about those components, one can learn much about the dynamics of the balance and the likely limits on change. Such a heuristic use of models is technically just a particularly complicated form of sensitivity testing, but it can be quite enlightening. This use dovetails nicely with the argument of Chapter 2 that analysis-as-heuristics is frequently the optimal contribution the analyst can make to the policy maker.

Finally, it is important to note that the claims for complex modeling techniques are stated both in the present tense and in the future. While complex models have not proved particularly helpful in improving accuracy or insight, it is imaginable that they will improve in the future.

Indeed, modeling efforts that are criticized for failure to improve on other methods almost always assert that the models are in a preliminary phase of development, that one cannot expect immediate results, and that decisive improvements will occur in the future. However, as disussed above, the problems of parameter drift and of critical unquantifiable political and organizational issues impose severe inherent limits on improvements in future models. For the present, most complex, computerized models have created a burdensome expense without corresponding benefits and have detracted from the efforts most vital to successful forecasts: careful analysis of basic assumptions, detailed attention to nuances of context, and frequent updating.

NOTES

1. Except for "identities," equations that aggregate without representing behavioral properties.
2. See Richad Vitek and Nawal Taneja, *The Impact of High Inflation Rates on the Demand for Air Passenger Transportation* (Cambridge, Mass.: Massachusetts Institute of Technology Flight Transportation Laboratory, 1975); and Dale E. McDaniel, "Transportation Forecasting: A Review," *Technological Forecasting and Social Change* 3 (1972): 367–89. J. Scott Armstrong, in *Long-Range Forecasting: From Crystal Ball to Computer* (New York: Wiley, 1978), reports that after extensive searching he was able to find only three transportation models that could be termed "complex" in the sense we are employing.
3. William Ascher, *Forecasting: An Appraisal for Policy-Makers and Planners* (Baltimore: Johns Hopkins University Press, 1978), chapter 5.
4. "Short term" in economic forecasting generally means no more than four to six quarters. The survey of these short-term forecasts is published in various issues of both *The American Statistician* and *Explorations in Economic Research*.
5. Vincent Su and Josephine Su, "An Evaluation of ASA/NBER Business Outlook Survey Forecasts," *Explorations in Economic Research* 2, no. 4 (Fall 1975): 588–618, esp. 600.
6. Vincent Su, "An Error Analysis of Econometric and Noneconometric Forecasts," *Proceedings of the American Economic Association* 68, no. 2 (May 1978): 306–12. It is important to note that the error of the median forecast is not the same as the median error of the set of forecasts.

7. Victor Zarnowitz, "On the Accuracy and Properties of Recent Macroeconomic Forecasts," *Proceedings of the American Economic Association* 68, no. 2 (May 1978): 313–19.

8. Stephen McNees, "An Evaluation of Economic Forecasts: Extension and Update," *New England Economic Review* (September/October 1976): 30–44; and Stephen McNees, "An Assessment of the Council of Economic Advisers' Forecast of 1977," *New England Economic Review* (March/April 1977): 3–7.

9. See the very candid description given by Lawrence Klein in *An Essay on the Theory of Economic Prediction* (Helsinki: Jahnsson Lectures, 1968).

10. Zarnowitz, "Accuracy and Properties," p. 315.

11. See Ascher, *Forecasting* chapter 4; and Klein, *Essay.*

12. Bert G. Hickman, "Introduction and Summary," *Econometric Models of Cyclical Behavior,* Bert G. Hickman, ed. (New York: National Bureau of Economic Research, 1972), p. 17.

13. Congressional Research Service, "Energy Demand Studies—An Analysis and Comparison," *Middle- and Long-Term Energy Policies and Alternatives,* Part 7, Appendix to Hearings before the Subcommittee on Energy and Power, Committee on Interstate and Foreign Commerce, U.S. House of Representatives, March 25–26, 1976 (Washington, D.C.: U.S. Government Printing Office, 1976), p. 2.

14. National Research Council, Committee on Nuclear and Alternative Energy Systems, Synthesis Panel, *Modeling Resource Group, Energy Modeling for an Uncertain Future,* Supporting Paper 2 (Washington, D.C.: National Academy of Sciences, 1978). Two other comparative efforts—reported in Charles Hitch, ed., *Modeling Energy-Economy Interactions: Five Approaches,* Research Paper R-5 (Washington, DC.: Resources for the Future, 1977); and William Hogan, "Reporting on the Energy Modeling Forum," Working Paper (Stanford University, 1977)—did not enforce as much uniformity in scenarios, assumptions, and starting points. In any event, there is much overlap in the models examined.

15. National Research Council, *Modeling Resource Group,* p. 47.

16. *Ibid.,* p. 48.

17. Ascher, *Forecasting,* chapter 5.

18. See the delightful discussion of the fundamentalist-chartist controversy in Martin Shubik, "The Nature and Limitations of Forecasting," *Toward the Year 2000: Work in Progress, Daedalus* (Summer 1967): 945.

19. See Ronald Brunner and Garry Brewer, *Organized Complexity* (New York: Free Press, 1971), Essay 2.

20. The issue of emergent properties is presented most cogently in *Ibid*. The argument that capturing counterintuitive implications is a prime virtue is made in Jay W. Forrester, *Principles of Systems* (Cambridge, Mass.: Wright-Allen Press, 1968); Jay W. Forrester, Nathaniel Mass and Charles Ryan, "The System Dynamics National Model: Understanding Socio-Economic Behavior and Policy Alternatives," *Technological Forecasting and Social Change* 9 (July 1976): 51–68.

21. Ascher, *Forecasting*.

22. *Ibid.*, p. 164.

23. *Ibid.*, pp. 190–91.

24. See McDaniel, "Transportation Forecasting"; Congressional Research Service, "Energy Demand Studies"; and Frederic Dewhurst and Associates, *America's Needs and Resources* (New York: Twentieth Century Fund, 1947), pp. 26–29.

25. See Robert E. Lucas Jr., "Econometric Policy Evaluation: A Critique," in *The Phillips Curve and Labor Markets* Karl Brunner and Allan H. Meltzer, eds. (Amsterdam: North-Holland Publishing Company, 1976), pp. 19–46, at pp. 24–25.

26. *Ibid.*, pp. 23–24.

27. Ascher, *Forecasting, passim*.

28. William W. Hogan and Alan S. Manne, "Energy-Economy Interactions: The Fable of the Elephant and the Rabbit?" in *Modeling Energy-Economy Interactions*, Hitch, ed., pp. 247–77, at pp. 248–49.

29. *Ibid.*, pp. 249–50.

30. Martin Greenberger, Matthew Crenson, and Brian Crissey, *Models in the Policy Process: Public Decision Making in the Computer Era* (New York: Russell Sage Foundation, 1976). Chapter 6 has a discussion of the genealogy of econometric models.

31. For example, see Guy Orcutt, et al., *Microanalysis of Socioeconomic Systems: A Simulation Study* (New York: Harper and Row, 1961) for an early effort; and George Sadowsky, *MASH: A Computer System for Policy Exploration*, Urban Institute Working Paper #5096 (Washington, D.C.: Urban Institute, 1975). Such models have largely been relegated to examinations of local systems or partial analyses of specific policy options (such as income maintenance programs). These applications are discussed in Greenberger, Crenson, and Crissey, *Models*, pp. 107–15.

32. National Research Council, *Modeling Resource Group*, p. 5.

33. Charles Hitch, "Preface," in *Modeling Energy-Economy Interactions,* Hitch, eds., p. iv.
34. Ronald Ridker, et al., "Economic, Energy, and Environmental Consequences of Alternative Energy Regimes, An Application of the RFF/SEAS Modeling System," in *Modeling Energy-Economy Interactions,* Hitch, ed., p. 141.

Chapter 5
The Distinctive Logic of Political Forecasting

The most agonizing challenge for practitioners of political forecasting is to decide how much of the methodology available from other spheres of forecasting ought to be adopted for their own work. Political forecasting is often thought of as amateurish; consequently, there is an understandable yearning for sophisticated methodology. Complex models, regression analysis, Markov chains, and so on, have all appeared in efforts at political forecasting. Yet in too many instances the use of borrowed methods has proved to be counterproductive, with simplistic analyses emerging paradoxically from ostensibly sophisticated methods, which generally are very quantitative. This has resulted in a chasm between the two most common forms of political forecasting—the "journalistic" approach that seems to eschew systematic analysis altogether, and the quantitative approach that has been criticized for its lack of sensitivity to the nuances and complexity of political affairs.[1]

The distinctive nature of politics calls for methods that can cope with political complexity through their comprehensiveness rather than through explicitness and quantification. Both policy makers, and forecasters of nonpolitical trends whose own work must rely on political forecasts, require this comprehensiveness. Systematic analysis in political forecasting is therefore not at all synonymous with the apparently sophisticated quantitative methods employed in other spheres of forecasting. Political forecasting cannot afford the simplifications that come along with quantification of the political forecast per se, but rather must wed theoretical understandings of political dynamics (usually not amenable to quantitative formulation) to the other socioeconomic trends that trigger and condition political action. Political forecasting then becomes a matter of synthesis; nonpolitical trends and the political response are interdependent. Good political forecasting is a sequential process in which political trends and related socioeconomic trends are integrated. These related projections have to be carefully selected and applied by the political forecaster (who must be a "good consumer" of these other forecasts just as the other forecasters must be good consumers of political forecasts), but that does not require mimicry of the methods used to generate these other socioeconomic forecasts.

To explore the existing difficulties and potential improvements in political forecasting, it is useful to raise three questions. First, in what ways are political phenomena distinct from other social behavior? Second, how are the needs of other forecasters and forecast users best served by political forecasting? Third, what implications do these considerations hold for the choice of approaches to political forecasting?

THE DISTINCTIVENESS OF POLITICS AS A FOCUS OF FORECASTING

The distinctiveness of political behavior is important for two reasons. First, one must judge the intrinsic difficulty of political forecasting in order to assess whether current practice is adequate and how much room for improvement one might reasonably expect from better approaches. Therefore, any distinctive characteristics of political phenomena that bear on the difficulty of political forecasting also bear on how much emphasis should be given to casting out the old methods and introducing new ones. The same considerations hold for the issues of how much credence should be given to any political forecast, and, ironically, to what extent political forecasters should be absolved from responsibility for mistaken forecasts. Second, the distinctiveness (or lack thereof) is relevant to the advisability of adopting forecasting approaches popular in other spheres of forecasting. Since the choice of forecasting methods often reflects presumptions about the nature of the phenomena under examination, distinctiveness may call for distinctive approaches.

It must be noted, however, that the predictions of nonpolitical trends, to the extent that they depend on policy choices or political climate, are indirectly affected by the same sources of unpredictability, and indeed by the same dynamics, as the political trends.[2] Nevertheless, as long as the problem of forecasting a policy-dependent or political-climate-dependent nonpolitical trend can be partitioned into two tasks—anticipating the policy choice or climate, and then anticipating the behavior of the nonpolitical trend in the context of that choice—it makes sense to explore whether different approaches to the tasks are appropriate.

The Emphasis on Events

The most obvious distinction between political behavior and most other behaviors subject to forecasting is the greater relative importance of single, discrete events in setting the direction of political developments. Elections, coups d'etat, wars, and policy choices are important per se, rather than solely as incremental additions to a larger pattern. No such discontinuity appears in a projection of gross national product. Moreover, the *meaning* of each such event, resulting from the specific way it unfolds, is as important in affecting the demands and expectations of political actors as is the broad class of events in which it falls.[3] The 190th military coup in Bolivia means something very different from a military coup in, say, contemporary France. Consequently, efforts to aggregate political events according to general categories run the risk of destroying essential information, which is much less of a problem in many nonpolitical areas, such as aggregating economic transactions to calculate the gross national product, or summing births and deaths to calculate the population growth rate.

Because of the importance of prominent political events, the thrust of political forecasting has been prediction of events; hence, the projection of summary measures (like quantitative indicators) has never been the most widely used approach. However, the use of quantitative indicators by some forecast theorists, often those with impressive academic affiliations, has had the effect of denigrating the straightforward prediction of events as somehow insufficiently scientific or rigorous.

Also, because of the importance of prominent political events, political prediction is often cast as an all-or-nothing proposition; the forecast is either right or wrong, as distinct from most other areas of forecasting, in which the forecast, often expressed in quantitative terms (quantities or lengths of time), may be closer or further from the actual outcome on a continuous dimension of error. In fact, the all-or-nothing criterion is misleading; whether a forecast of political events is right depends on how much detail is presented and on where the boundaries are drawn in defining categories of events. For example, the boundary between the outbreak of civil war and an increase in guerrilla insurgency is very fuzzy indeed. The all-or-nothing criterion of validity is especially misleading in the case of predictions of combinations of events (event sequences or scenarios), because certain elements may be correct while others are incorrect. Nevertheless, most political forecasters find themselves in the position of predicting, in either absolute or conditional terms, that particular events will or will not happen.

In predicting events, the political forecaster cannot express the uncertainty of the forecasts in the same way as the forecaster of nonpolitical quantitative trends, for which the range can express the degree of uncertainty (for example, "GNP will be $100 billion ± $15 billion"). The political event predictor has the options of stating flatly that "X will happen"; expressing uncertainty via verbal cues such as "X will probably happen"; or expressing this uncertainty by assigning a numerical probability to the event and stating, "There is a 0.8 probability that X will happen."

Having been stung by accusations that their work is imprecise and unsystematic, many political forecasters have adopted the practice of conveying uncertainty through numerical probabilities, in part as a way of quantifying forecasts even if they are generated through nonexplicit, judgmental means. This has given rise to an ongoing debate over whether the use of quantitative probabilities is an appropriate way to avoid misunderstanding verbal expressions of likelihood (the term "probably" could mean a 60% chance or an 80% chance), or a facade that creates a misleading illusion of precision. We shall argue later that there is a deeper problem in the interpretation of numerical probabilities, because they represent both the forecaster's certainty of understanding and the probabilities inherent in the mechanisms of reality the forecaster thinks he or she understands.

The Importance of Pivotal Choices

A related point is that these prominent events often depend on a small number of individual choices. In general, predictability suffers when the course of the future rides on a few key actions or decisions. In light of this fact, political forecasting suffers if it does not take into account the mechanisms by which these decisions are taken.

There is nothing distinctive about the fact that political events depend on the difficult-to-understand vagaries of human choice; this is a condition of all human behavior. What *is* distinctive about many political developments is that, because a small set of discrete choices makes a big difference, there are very few instances in political behavior in which the law of large numbers applies to smooth out the effects of idiosyncratic decisions, as it so often does in economics, demography, and so on. Even in the case of elections, where (as in energy use or macroeconomic behavior) the simple aggregation of thousands of individual actions reduces the importance of any one individual's idiosyncracies, the behavior of the candidates contesting the election imparts great importance to the role of a few discrete individual choices.[4]

The simple point is that, where individual decisions of great import to the direction of policies are difficult to predict, there is no principle comparable to the law of large numbers to reduce the importance of potential prediction errors. Compare this to the enviable situation of technological forecasting, in which the forecaster need pay little attention to predicting *who* will accomplish the technological breakthrough as long as he can predict that *someone* will successfully make the breakthrough.

A more complicated point is that the prominence in politics of particular individual choices undermines the validity of methods that focus on summary patterns rather than directly representing the "micro process" of decision making. As Brunner and Brewer point out, systems of "organized complexity," characterized by a high-level architecture of interrelations, are far less amenable to explanation and prediction by the standard aggregate statistical methods than are systems that are "complicated" only in the sense of involving many relatively separate actions.[5] Thus, patterns of the political system, which generally display a high degree of organized complexity, cannot be accounted for by aggregate statistical techniques (such as correlation and regression), nor even adequately characterized by aggregate measures.

The Predictability of Political Outcomes

In addition to the problems inherent in predicting patterns highly dependent on pivotal choices, political forecasting faces a distinctive problem in predicting one particularly important class of events because of the balancing mechanisms peculiar to politics. This is the class of *distributive* events, defined as events entailing the actual gain or loss of things of value to the political actors, whether tangible or intangible. Such distributive events are the things most commonly viewed as outcomes: who wins, who loses, who gets what. Distributive events may be distinguished from predistributive events, which are the concrete interactions, classifiable as conflict or cooperation, leading up to the creation and distribution of valued things; they are the behaviors in the processes of "shaping and sharing of values." Distributive events would include victories in wars and elections, policy outcomes, and the distribution of benefits allocated through the political system; predistributive events would include the debate over a particular issue, the state of war, or the formation of coalitions with respect to a given policy before an authoritative decision is taken. Both classes of events can be further distinguished from the dynamics of political interaction, from which events of both types emerge.

Distributive events tend to be unusually difficult to predict because there are at least half a dozen equilibrium mechanisms in political behavior that often operate to bring about roughly even balance to the sides in a political confrontation. Unlike the balances brought about by equilibrium mechanisms in economics, which tend to increase the certainty of outcomes, a balance of political forces naturally tends to reduce the certainty about who wins. These mechanisms include:

The preselection of contested issues, which often emerge only if both or the several sides see a chance for winning;

The tendency of very powerful coalitions to break down, as the big coalition leaders try to reduce the division of the spoils of victory, and the leaders of opposing coalitions offer incentives to the elements being shed from the initially very large coalition (Riker's "minimum winning-coalition principle");[6]

The tendency of political leaders to shift their platforms so as to pick up additional support if their initial support is weak, or to shift back closer to their own true preference in position if their support was initially very great (Downs's "economic theory" of position selection);[7]

The tendency of the powerful to test the limits of their power, thereby often inciting their own countervailing opposition;

The ability of the weaker sides in a conflict to shift it to another part of the political arena in order to enhance their resources;

The tendency of those facing the prospect of major losses to increase their willingness to commit greater resources and undertake costly risks, thereby balancing out the resources actually deployed by each side.

The existence of these mechanisms is hardly controversial, but there are three important caveats. First, just prior to any definitive outcome-determining event (such as an election) there is often a short period during which the positions and coalitions of the political actors are finally locked in, simply because the opportunities for further maneuvering disappear or become too costly. At that point, of course, predicting the distributive outcome becomes much easier; however, it is also, of course, less useful (and less appreciated) than an earlier prediction.

Second, these balancing effects do not impart uncertainty to all facets of politics. Their logic does not apply to predistributive events, because the occurrence of political confrontation is not made more uncertain when political forces are more evenly balanced; on the contrary, balance often increases the certainty that an issue will be engaged. Nor does the logic apply to the various dynamics of political behavior; one can understand *how* politics is played out without being certain as to who will win. Thus, many aspects of political behavior, whether events or propositions about relations among actors or events, are not subject to the same inherent predictive limitations that the balancing tendencies bring to distributive outcomes.

Third, even with regard to distributive events, these mechanisms do not hold in all circumstances. For example, the strategy of reducing one's coalition to the minimum needed to win may be regarded as too risky in conditions of poor information. Alternatively, when no one is in a strong enough position of "coalition leader" to dictate who may remain in the coalition, the strategy may simply be infeasible. As for platform shifting, there are instances in which the positions of various groups become *more* rigid over time, and hence less amenable to support-seeking position changes, as emotional and political attachments to existing positions increase. There is, indeed, the well-known "bandwagon" effect, whereby the increasingly apparent victory for one side or position acts as an inducement for yet more support to shift to the winning side.

Thus, what makes politics distinctive in terms of the difficulty of prediction is not the ubiquity of balancing mechanisms—which would be a gross exaggeration—but rather that these mechanisms occur with considerable frequency. The record of political forecasting is, in a sense, weighed down by the intrinsic difficulty of predicting those distributive events which are subject to the balancing mechanisms. One solace is that the conditions that enable or inhibit the operation of the various balancing mechanisms in specific instances can be identified and monitored. Thus, knowing whether coalition leaders have the power to reduce the size of their own coalition, or whether the platform positions held by a particular group can easily be shifted without incurring high political costs, can aid the forecaster in deciding how much effort should be devoted to predicting the outcome.

More generally, political phenomena depend heavily on interacting combinations of shifts in mass attitudes; realigning coalitions; personal decisions of top leaders; and processes of learning at all levels which frequently enable political groups to counter trends and to avoid past cycles.[8] One can sometimes predict some aspects of attitude shifts. One can analyze certain patterns of coalition behavior. And one can sometimes predict the calculations to be made by key political leaders. But prediction at any one of these levels is usually problematic, and combinations of the three arise in such discontinuous, nonlinear, noncyclical, and often noncumulative ways that complex models seldom apply.[9]

THE NEED FOR POLITICAL FORECASTING

Political forecasters have two important audiences: policy makers and other forecasters. Both interact with political forecasters in intricate ways, providing information as well as receiving information.

Policy Makers' Needs for Political Forecasting

Because the uses of political forecasts depend on the nature of the policy making process, this process is the appropriate place to start in assessing the policy maker's needs. Research on the policy-making process in the real world paints a very different picture from the idealized model of the fully informed decision maker who optimizes through the rigorous application of explicit algorithms. The real-life policy maker, in both the private and public sectors, is a sloppier, more tentative, more human individual.[10] The real-life policy maker *must be* more tentative, more judgmental, and very leery of the information he uses. The policy maker deliberates on, rather than calculates, the measures he ultimately adopts. It is very rare to find a decision maker who plugs quantitative forecasts into a mechanical decision-making model; it is far more likely that the forecast will serve as background information to aid informal, judgmental decision making.

Yet, although the policy maker's use of the forecasts may be informal rather than rigorous, he often requires detailed information corresponding to the level of detail of his own decisions. It is not enough to anticipate the grand changes of war and peace, stability and chaos; businesspeople and government forecast users alike have to understand specific details of their environment and specific reactions to the particular measures they are considering. The risk anticipated in political risk assessment ought not to be simply the risk of total catastrophe—as it often has been conceived— but rather the complex set of risks and opportunities presented by both the general environment and the details of policy, style, and political mood.[11]

The policy maker often faces contingencies that are not—and cannot reasonably be expected to be—anticipated precisely by the alternative scenarios or contingencies considered by the forecaster. Although the forecaster may choose quite plausible conditional forecasts, the policy maker frequently ends up facing partially or totally different conditions.

Finally, the policy maker cannot take for granted that the forecast is correct. He has to make continual assessments about whether the forecast is worth heeding. If the forecast is seen as being at least partially in error, the policy maker still must try to understand the future well enough to make decisions. The utility of a forecast depends not only on how accurate it is, but also on how much confidence the forecast user has in the forecast; this in turn depends on the forecast's plausibility and its preliminary apparent accuracy, as opposed to its ultimate accuracy. Whatever the ultimate accuracy or validity of the forecast, its usefulness from the time the forecast is first stated through the period for which it is supposed to hold depends on how well the forecast *seems* to hold up as the course of events unfolds. For example, the basically correct predictions of decline in the British economy, which seemed off-base when the North Sea oil temporarily held off the more visible signs of deterioration, were probably rejected by some forecast users when the direction of the prediction and the direction of the reality seemed to be diverging.

The Interface Between Political and Nonpolitical Forecasting

The distinction between political and nonpolitical forecasts does not imply that the two are unrelated. The interconnectedness of all human behavior guarantees that the political climate will have at least an indirect effect on the whole gamut of nonpolitical pursuits. Governmental policies in the areas of economics, energy, transportation, and so on, are the outcomes of politics. The obverse is equally true and equally obvious: political trends are conditioned by nonpolitical conditions. Political turmoil in the Caribbean, to take just one example, is at least as much a result of the population explosion and the economic buffeting caused by oil price rises as it is of purely political developments. But if political and nonpolitical forecasting are reciprocally dependent, how can their integration be accomplished?

In the most general terms, political forecasters must be good consumers of nonpolitical forecasts, and vice versa. This entails paying attention only to recently minted forecasts (because recency is of prime importance to forecast accuracy), accepting the forecaster's caveats concerning the uncertainty of the forecast, and striving to understand the underlying assumptions in the choice of method and in the conditions entered into the forecasting analysis.

In more specific terms, there are key elements in nonpolitical forecasting of particular relevance to political forecasting, and vice versa. For the political forecast, the key requirement is to identify nonpolitical trends that:

Change the priority of issues facing the body politic;

Change the leaders, institutions, or social groups critical to decisions;

Shift the resource bases at the disposal of different political actors (for instance, increased wealth or prestige convertible into political leverage);

Activate different political strategies and dynamics than those currently prevailing.

For the nonpolitical forecast, the key requirement is to incorporate the effects of:

Changes in political climate;

Responses of policy makers to the nonpolitical trends as they see them.

While the rationales behind the importance of each of these elements are obvious, the means for tracking the interactions are not. In generating the political forecast, it is necessary to identify nonpolitical trends that may shift the balance of power or change the nature of the political game, but these same nonpolitical trends must also reflect the political trends. As with all such chicken-and-egg problems, one answer is to develop interactive, complex models (though not necessarily equilibrium or optimization models). The other is to pursue cross-impact analyses, formally or informally, by establishing conditional forecasts to convey the impact of each possible political development on the nonpolitical trends, and the impact of nonpolitical trends on politics.

APPROACHES TO POLITICAL FORECASTING

All of these considerations—the need for rich information, the flexibility required of a forecast that must inform the policy maker rather than simply serve as a datum for an algorithm, the impossibility of anticipating all contingencies, the need to assess the reasonableness of the forecast—call for one essential quality of the useful political forecast: it must convey the *configuration* of political conditions, trends, and forces. It is this configuration that the policy makers can rely on to assess the forecaster's plausibility, and can apply themselves in order to infer specific aspects of the environment or to cope with conditions that were not anticipated by the forecaster. Parallel considerations hold for the utility of political forecasting for other forecasters. Like the policy maker, the forecaster of nonpolitical trends must be able to assess the political forecast and to apply it in ways that require a detailed map of the political context.

With these considerations in mind, we now turn to an examination of the viability of alternative approaches to political forecasting. However, we must recognize the complexity of the choice of approach or method.

Forecasting: What versus How

First, one must distinguish between *what* is projected by the political forecaster and *how* the forecaster goes about his work. Obviously, in terms of producing forecasts that are useful to the decision maker, "what" ought to be of paramount importance, and yet far more attention has been devoted to the "how" question, reflecting the fetish for methods that has been as much a part of political forecasting as it has been a feature of political science and of forecasting in general. The consequences are serious not only because of misplaced effort, but also because a given forecasting method can only accommodate a given range of items to be forecasted. Therefore, if the preoccupation with methods predominates, the tail will end up wagging the dog; the trends forecasted or the events predicted will be those most comfortably handled by the most sophisticated-seeming methods, even if there are more useful items to forecast. Moreover, as long as attention is focused on methods, and the subject of what to forecast is neglected, we may continue to take for granted that what we forecast is obviously the correct focus, whereas in fact what is generally forecast is more intrinsically unpredictable, and generally less useful, than more appropriate foci.

Second, the choice of method depends in part on the specifics of each case, because the choice of method, unless it is simply habitual, will reflect the forecaster's preconceptions of the behavior of the system *and* the extent to which he understands the system. For example, the selection of methods tantamount to extrapolation may be based either on a presumption that business-as-usual stability will keep trends going in the same directions, or on an assessment by the forecaster that he knows too little about the behavior of the system to be able to improve upon naive extrapolation. (See Chapter 3.)

What to Forecast

It has long been taken for granted that the primary focus of political forecasting is to predict the distributive events. Because they are the ultimate concern of the poltical actors themselves—their bottom line—it is easy to presume that anticipating such events naturally ought to be the ultimate objective for the political forecaster. Furthermore, when forecasters decide to be quantitative, and start to project quantitative summary indicators, they have most often projected distributive-outcome indicators. Thus, the typical projection of quantitative indicators is not done as an intermediate step in answering the question of who gets what, but rather it *is* the answer, either by directly conveying the power or rewards of a political actor, or by conveying the potential to win that can be translated straightforwardly into the prediction of victory.

However, it is by no means obvious that political forecasting ought to focus so exclusively on the prediction of distributive outcomes, as discrete events or as quantified trends, for several quite compelling reasons. The first reason is, as we have argued above, the relatively greater unpredictability of distributive events whenever coalition formation mechanisms operate. Unless the event is so imminent that the final balance of forces is obvious, it is often simply easier to predict the nature of the confrontation, or to understand how political forces interact, or to project the consequence of alternative distributive outcomes, than it is to predict winners and losers.

The second reason is that, although victory and loss of the political actors of various nations may be *their* bottom line, these events may not be the bottom line for the forecast user, because of the policy maker's and nonpolitical forecaster's needs for more detailed information. Those who would defend the focus on predicting the major distributive outcomes might argue that, since the specific policy-relevant conditions do unfold within the broad framework of major political transitions, these transitions are a more important subject for political forecasting than the lower-level trends in the specific conditions of interest to the decision maker. For example, it is obvious that specific conditions such as a government's predisposition to nationalize particular types of foreign-owned industries, or the chances for economic liberalization policies, or the safety of foreigners within a country, are all strongly influenced by trends in such broad phenomena as overall stability, the victors (for the time being) in the confrontation between capitalism and socialism, and the overall capacity of the government.

Yet, while it is undeniable—perhaps even tautological—that the specific conditions are molded by the broadest level of trends, the specific policy-relevant conditions are not deducible from the distributive outcomes. The actions of the victor depend at least as much on *how* he or she won as on the fact of the victory; the predistributive events establish the political climate, the conditions of political confrontation, and the terms of victory. The initial moderation of Prime Minister Mugabe after his election victory in Zimbabwe was made possible by avoidance of a black-black civil war and the resultant maintenance of an economy that would greatly reward moderate policies and impose huge costs on radical policies, and a political environment that permitted Mugabe's forces to work with other groups. These things were at least as important as the difference between a Mugabe victory and a Nkomo victory. To take another African case, banks doing business with Ethiopian Airlines during Ethiopia's recent revolution and multiple civil wars correctly calculated that imminent war and revolution were less important to their banking relationships than the political esteem in which all competing leadership groups held the airline.

Numerical Probabilities versus Explaining the Mechanism.   Because of the inherent unpredictability of distributive events, one must consider assigning numerical probabilities to alternative outcomes. Political forecasters so often assign probabilities to events that, for one reason or another, they are unwilling to cast as absolute predictions, that the validity of this format is usually taken for granted.

But the probability assigned to an outcome can signify two different things.[12] First, it may reflect *certain* knowledge of a mechanism of reality that can generate several distinct outcomes, at given frequencies or with given likelihoods, as in the simple cases of coin-flips and lotteries. The mechanisms are well understood, and would produce determinable outcomes every time were it not for the practical impossibility of knowing all of the environmental details of each particular occurrence. Alternatively, the probability assigned to an outcome may reflect the analyst's *degree of certainty* that he understands the mechanisms of reality, whether the particular mechanism he *thinks* is correct is deterministic or probabilistic.

In political forecasting, there is good reason to believe that usually probabilities express the degree of certainty rather than conveying the likelihoods of outcomes of a well-understood mechanism. Even when there is an attempt to convey the distribution of outcomes of a given mechanism, the probabilities are also likely to include a component of how certain the analyst is that it is indeed the correct mechanism. What, then, is the forecast user to make of the probabilities so often expressed in political forecasting—probabilities that often seem to make the forecasting effort more quantitative and perhaps even more scientific? Whenever the degree-of-certainty component is present—which is nearly all the time—the forecast user cannot even take the expressed probability as the probability *he* would now assign to the event; *if* the forecaster is wrong in understanding the mechanism—which would be conveyed by his assignment of a probability of less than 1.0 to the "most likely" outcome—he is in no position to assign a probability, whether it reflects his degree of (false) certainty or the likelihood of the outcome. Nor can the forecast user know what the probability of each event would be under the assumption that the forecaster is wrong, because the forecaster, in providing just the probability of the event, has not presented the forecast user with a description of that mechanism. The forecast user cannot form an opinion about whether the forecaster is off-base and, if so, what the probabilities ought to be.

Hence, the responsible analyst must in most cases devote a preponderance of effort to presenting views on how the mechanisms work, how others might disagree, and how the mechanisms generate outcomes.

The Conditional Format.   The importance of pivotal political acts, combined with the difficulty of predicting them and the futility of presuming that they will balance out, leads us back to a critical format issue. Nonpolitical and political forecasts alike are frequently cast in the *conditional* format. Predictions of the form "If X_1 then Y_1; if X_2 then Y_2; . . . if X_n then Y_n," where X is often a political condition or outcome, can be characterized negatively as evading the issue of which X will occur. In light of the inherent limitations of predicting X, however, conditional forecasting ought to be considered as the essence of responsibility. The generation of several conditional forecasts avoids the elimination of possible futures just because one other possibility seems marginally more likely. In acknowledging that he cannot definitively predict the correct direction of future developments, either because the audience includes policy makers with some control over these developments or simply because he cannot know enough to choose, the forecaster employing a conditional format permits the exploration of implications of the other possible political outcomes. By the same token, when nonpolitical background trends are uncertain, the political forecaster need not make an irreversible choice of one of these options, thereby precluding consideration of political developments that might evolve from the other possibilities.

Summary Indicators. Although events are the most commonly forecasted items, there are two other options. One is the *quantitative indicator,* generally a summary measure of events or conditions, such as measures of government capability, levels of violence, military preparedness, degree of inequality of income, and so on, employed either to account for discrete outcomes or to reflect their effects. Within this category of quantitative indicators, one can make a further distinction between indicators representing distributive outcomes and those that do not. Since political power is both a resource and a prize of politics, quantitative indicators of power, such as the capability of a government, must be classified as distributive-outcome indicators.

Focusing on quantitative indices is a deceptively hazardous approach in political forecasting, particularly if they are distributive-outcome indicators that share the previously mentioned pitfalls and some of their own. Yet the projection of quantitative indices is one of the three prime approaches—the others being computer simulation and intricate probability manipulations—responsible for the widespread belief that political forecasting, like other forecasting disciplines, will become increasingly sophisticated methodologically. Ironically, the expectations that somewhere out there one can find methods that, because they are more sophisticated, will do a better job at forecasting, has heightened the dissatisfaction with conventional analytic methods.

But let us explore what "sophistication" means and what "quantification" implies, to see whether equating the two is justified. "Sophisticated" can mean "esoteric" or difficult to understand and utilize, in which case it is no virtue; it can mean "novel" or "unfamiliar," in which case it is not necessarily an advantage or disadvantage; or it can mean "complex" and therefore more difficult only insofar as complexity is more difficult to master.

In what respects is the quantitative index more sophisticated than more conventional methods, beyond its novelty and the sheer mechanical difficulties of its measurement and of trying to remember what it represents? In theory, quantitative indices could be placed in complicated mathematical formulations, but they seldom are. Their complexity is far more apparent than real. In fact, quantitative measures of general applicability are the antithesis of complexity and configuration, for five reasons.

First, for a quantitative indicator to have general validity for a wide range of political systems and over time in each, and to encompass an important part of the political reality, it must aggregate somewhat different manifestations of a broad analytical category of phenomena, such as "violence," "capability of government," or "inequality." Much attention has been focused on the problem of how to weight the events or manifestations that make up each category, but no matter how correct the weighting may be, the summary measure or aggregate loses the composition or configuration of its components. To aggregate is to condense information, often destroying information regarding the relationships among facets of behavior falling within the same category. For example, a summary indicator of the regime capability of the Mexican government might include its ability to collect taxes and its ability to maintain the support of the business elite; yet lumping these together in an overall indicator would conceal the important relationship between *not* collecting high levels of taxes and maintaining business sector support. (See Chapter 10.)

Second, the measurement routine (or "operationalization") of the general purpose quantitative index sacrifices the specific meaning of its class of phenomena in each particular system in order to be applicable more widely. Most commonly, these measures were developed for testing generalizations across countries.[13] The way the index is operationalized may be valid for most countries; for example, in many countries the capacity of the government to extract a tax level that is relatively high in relation to the nation's GNP is in fact likely to correlate highly with general governmental capability. Yet, in any given case, there is a significant chance that the general operationalization does not apply very well. In Mexico the low tax rate is part of a very complex set of conditions cementing a detente between the government and the business community that has given the regime tremendous strength, and the capacity to implement *its* objectives—which often do not require the raising of tax rates.

Third, although aggregate quantitative indices in theory could be inserted into complicated mathematical relationships with other variables, the "lumping" process of aggregation generally permits only rudimentary relationships between summary measures to show through. When theoretically precise and intricate relationships between each aspect encompassed by one broad index and each aspect of another are combined in the correlation of the two indices, the result is usually either the cancellation of countervailing finer-level effects, or a blurred "the greater the X, the greater the Y" type of relationship. Linear relationships are not the way of the political world; they are simply all that remains evident when finer distinctions are blurred.

Fourth, quantification itself, and the requirement of explicitness in interrelating quantitative variables, limits the exploration of interactions to those factors that can be quantified, and to those relationships that are consistent. Idiosyncratic configurations do not sit comfortably in explicit quantitative formulations; often the intuitive awareness that a particular factor is, in a specific case, relevant to another factor in intricate ways cannot be translated into an explicit formulation.

Finally, a purely practical problem: the generation of aggregate quantitative indices is often such demanding work that there is frequently little time left over for refined analysis. Once the thousands of events are counted and weighted, and all the statistical series are squared with one another, the temptation to "let the figures do the talking" by allowing vaguely linear trends to extrapolate themselves can be overwhelming.

Scenarios or Developmental Constructs. The final option of what to forecast is far less commonly recognized, even though every consideration reviewed thus far points to this option as the most useful focus for political forecasting. Instead of projecting trends or predicting events, one can project dynamics of political interaction. Such a projection has been called a *scenario* or a *developmental construct*, a conditional prediction that certain dynamics will apply, but only if the theory underlying these dynamics is valid for the case at hand.[14] (See Chapter 3.) The developmental construct is not a universal law applicable in all circumstances; it is a pattern triggered by other, often nonpolitical, trends. Because each scenario or developmental construct applies only when certain conditions set it into motion, monitoring and projecting the trends that can activate or inhibit such dynamics are essential for selecting from among the infinite varieties of dynamics that conceivably could apply under diverse conditions. Moreover, developmental constructs are superior because they are likely to preserve some analytic utility for the policy maker even when—as always happens to some extent—they begin to unravel.

Compare this to either a sequence of outcomes or a time series of quantitative indicators. For such projections, any divergence of the real pattern from the forecasted pattern leaves the forecast user completely at a loss as to how to salvage some utility from the forecast. This is because neither the outcomes nor the indicators convey enough information for the forecast user to make his own adjustments in order to generate his own forecast of further developments. Furthermore, the forecast user cannot diagnose whether the mechanism of reality that the forecaster had in mind was more or less appropriate, or utterly inappropriate. In contrast, the projection of dynamics through the use of scenarios or developmental constructs is a way of providing the decision maker with a framework of understanding. The framework has its own built-in tests of appropriateness: if the enabling conditions are not met, the scenario or developmental construct is shown to be inappropriate. If parts of it hold but others do not, the decision maker can make this assessment and save what is valid while discounting the rest. If the events that have transpired are not precisely what the developmental construct would have implied, the basic relationships comprising the developmental construct can be adapted to make sense of the new situation.

Thus, there is enormous potential for the *systematic scenario*. Managing the task of scenario writing so that the scenario not only conveys the configuration in a vivid way, but also serves to test the internal consistency of the forecast, may strike many as a surprising possibility, since the scenario is often regarded as an imaginative yarn of the most ad hoc sort. Yet, although the scenario can be as sloppy as any form of unstructured judgment, it need not be. If the scenario is defined as "a statement of assumptions about the operating environment of the particular system," it becomes clear that the scenario, systematically explored, becomes a self-testing instrument.[16] Does the scenario hold together? Are the theoretical propositions linking together the components of the scenario well specified? Are they plausible? Are the other scenario possibilities, once they have been specified, less coherent or plausible? Have all the plausible possibilities been examined? Answering these questions through self-conscious rather than off-the-cuff procedures can avoid many of the pitfalls that scenarios have suffered. The common tendency to give only superficial attention to scenarios other than the "most likely" ones can be overcome by requiring that other possibilities be analyzed in detail. Indications of which components of the scenario depend on which other components—in other words, an indication of the nesting of scenario components—can surmount the problem of not knowing whether partial incorrectness or implausibility of the scenario means that the whole scenario ought to be junked.

The consistency of scenarios may be heightened by ensuring that:

1. Any political actors with some discretion over decisions shaping the outcomes respond to ongoing trends in ways consistent with their intentions (the intentionality principle). For example, a domino theory

scenario of spreading Marxist takeovers in Central America would fail this test if it did not account for the reactions of the rightist governments currently in power, as well as political leaders in the United States, Mexico, and other regional powers.

2.   The events must be consistent with coherent developmental constructs, which in turn must be justified by the plausibility of the appropriate activating trends.

3.   The natural bias in favor of assuming that existing dynamics will necessarily continue must be offset by careful scrutiny of the activating or enabling trends underpinning current dynamics.

4.   Rather than simply assessing the coherence of the scenario as if it came about at one moment in time, the plausibility of the sequence of events necessary to create that scenario must also be examined.

In sum, the forecaster faces a degree of uncertainty and a requirement for detail which the academic scholar does not. The scenario is sufficiently flexible to accommodate any needed detail, and projecting alternative scenarios permits one to cope with irreducible uncertainty. While the scenario initially appears to be undisciplined storytelling, consistency checks, particularly when carried out by a group of well-informed specialists from different disciplines, can make the scenario a highly subtle and disciplined tool.

THE ISSUE OF METHOD

All the considerations reviewed thus far emphasize the serious limitations of the attempts to improve political forecasting through quantitative and probabilistic methods. On the other hand, these methods were developed in reaction to the very real problems of the intuitive, unstructured "crystal ball gazing," which, with its arrogant absolute predictions, often unsubstantiated by data or arguments, gave political forecasting a bad name in the first place. No one wants to go back to unstructured intuition. But as long as these seem to be the poles of choice—intuition versus scientism— the pendulum swings between two unsatisfactory alternatives.

Fortunately, this is a false choice. It only seems that the choice is between unstructured intuition and technical esoterica. In fact, the really important distinction ought to be between systematic and unsystematic approaches, with the term "systematic" referring to the comprehensiveness of the method in incorporating, or at least considering, all potentially relevant factors. *A method can be comprehensive or holistic without being methodologically arcane or the least bit mathematical* if it surveys all the possible influences on the phenomenon under examination. By the same token, a methodologically arcane approach (for instance, correlating the logarithm of one variable with the logarithm of another) is frequently no more comprehensive or systematic than the most off-the-cuff stab of judgment. Indeed, most mathematical approaches are inherently narrow and uncomprehensive (see Chapters 3 and 4).

Being systematic, comprehensive, or holistic is crucial because political events unfold within the configuration and because of the configuration. The forecast is utilizable to the extent that it conveys the configuration. Therefore, any approach that can identify potentially relevant factors and assess their influence, that can preserve an understanding of the structure of the political system and the context of any particular event, has fulfilled this critical requirement.

How much help in this quest for holism in political forecasting can be offered by the discipline of political science? The answer is a paradox. Good political forecasting is, ultimately, good political analysis. However, insofar as "scientific" political science has been preoccupied with theory building rather than theory application, four unfortunate weaknesses in the scientific approach to political forecasting have emerged.

First, the emphasis on developing general theories tends to restrict analysis to propositions, indicators, and dynamics designed to apply anywhere. Unfortunately, as generality increases, the risk of simplism increases as well, since the particular or idiosyncratic aspects of a given case are excluded from the analysis. In seeming contradiction to this point, it has been argued that apparently idiosyncratic political behavior can be subsumed under general rules or explanations once the appropriate equivalencies in function or meaning can be discovered, permitting the analyst to restate the pattern of behavior in more abstract and thus more comparable terms.[15] However, even the most optimistic proponents of this search for general rules in political behavior view the progress in this effort as a gradual replacement of the particular by the general, with great gaps remaining for the foreseeable future in our capacity to account for all important political patterns through generalizations. No one has argued that the progress to date is sufficiently advanced to warrant excluding analysis of idiosyncratic patterns in understanding specific cases. Theory development and testing should not be confused with, nor be allowed to take the place of, the application of both general theory *and* particular knowledge in analyzing any specific political situation.

Second, theory building and testing seem to legitimize indicators designed to be operationalized everywhere. By focusing on the common denominator of the often highly complex and varied behaviors they purport to capture, these indicators trade away their sensitivity to nuance and their capacity to convey the meaning of the behavior in order to permit testing for generality. The same tradeoff cannot be justified for forecasting. The political forecaster cannot defend the tradeoff on the grounds that the validity of the indicator holds in many or even most cases, or that the emerging cross-national pattern is illuminating even if the measurement instruments are blunt, because the political forecast user is interested in developments in specific cases, not in statistical generalizations.

Third, theorizing in political science rarely extends to the level of specific policy selection, the political fortunes of specific parties and coalitions of parties, or the other particulars of political-economic conditions. It is presumed that once the broad outlines of the dynamics of politics are understood the specific implications of these dynamics could be adduced. However, this presumption is almost universally false. No matter how much detailed information one plugs into most current political science theories, one cannot predict detailed outcomes. Moreover, policy makers and forecasters of nonpolitical trends are usually not sufficiently well informed about the politics of any nation to be able to infer all the policy-relevant conditions from broad characterizations of overarching political trends. Therefore, to the extent that the field of political science downgrades detail in favor of generality, the political forecaster will be unable to use the discipline's theories to satisfy the needs of the user audience.

Fourth, general-purpose indicators and general propositions must be explicit if they are to be testable and are to contribute to the cumulative development of theory. However, the requirement that all elements of analysis be explicit has its costs: the elimination of relevant but inconsistently linked considerations, and the absence of judgment or intuition to handle subtleties that have not yet yielded to explicit formulation.

In short, mimicry by political forecasters of research in political science is counterproductive if configuration-limiting methods are employed. The key question then becomes, how can the forecasting effort be organized so as to ensure a systematic search for potentially relevant factors, which can then be assessed with as much theoretical insight as the forecasters can bring to bear? The possibilities will be surprising for those who tend to equate progress with the development of self-contained, technical methodologies.

NOTES

1. For reviews of corporate uses of political forecasting, see Stephen Blank, *Assessing the Political Environment: An Emerging Function*

in International Companies Report No. 794 (New York: The Conference Board, 1980); and Stephen Kobrin, *Managing Political Risk Assessment* (Berkeley: University of California Press, 1982).

2. For example, expert disagreement in predicting technological innovation breakthroughs is greatest when the development or diffusion of such innovations depends on "official" policies. See William Ascher, *Forecasting: An Appraisal for Policymakers and Planners* (Baltimore: Johns Hopkins University Press, 1978), pp. 190–91.

3. Harold Lasswell and Abraham Kaplan, *Power and Society* (New Haven: Yale University Press, 1950), Chapter 1.

4. See the attempt to predict voter reaction to varying campaign emphases in the 1960 presidential campaign, in I. Poole, R. Abelson, and S. Popkin, *Candidates, Issues and Strategies* (Cambridge, Mass.: MIT Press, 1964).

5. Ronald Brunner and Garry Brewer, *Organized Complexity* (New York: Free Press, 1971), pp. 163–70.

6. William Riker, *The Theory of Political Coalitions* (New Haven: Yale University Press, 1962).

7. Anthony Downs, *An Economic Theory of Democracy* (New York: Harper and Row, 1957).

8. Lasswell and Kaplan, *Power and Society,* p. 246.

9. *Ibid.,* pp. 247–50.

10. Much of the literature on the limitations of the policy maker's use of forecasts is synthesized in Robin M. Hogarth and Spyros Makridakis, "Forecasting and Planning: An Evaluation," *Management Science* (1981).

11. See William H. Overholt, *Political Risk* (London: Euromoney Press, 1982), Chapters 1 and 2, for a survey of the needs and purposes of political forecasting.

12. For a summary of the debate, see Abraham Kaplan, *The Conduct of Inquiry* (Scranton, Pa.: Chandler, 1964), pp. 228–30.

13. For example, Michael O'Leary and William Coplin, *Quantitative Techniques in Foreign Policy Analysis and Forecasting* (New York: Praeger, 1975); J. D. Singer, ed., *Explaining War: Causes and Correlates of War* (Beverly Hills, Calif.: Sage, 1979).

14. The term was introduced by Harold Lasswell, and the method was employed in several of his works. See Harold D. Lasswell, *Power and Personality* (New York: Norton, 1948), Chapter 10; and Harold D. Lasswell, "The Garrison State," *The American Journal of Sociology* 46 (1941): 455–68.

15. For example, A. Przeworski and H. Teune, *The Logic of Comparative Social Inquiry* (New York: Wiley-Interscience, 1970); and Moshe

M. Czudnowski, *Comparing Political Behavior* (Beverly Hills, Calif.: Sage, 1976).

16.   S. Brown, "Scenarios in Systems Analysis," in *Systems Analysis and Policy Planning,* E. S. Quade and W. I. Boucher, eds. (New York: American Elsevier, 1968), pp. 298–310, at p. 300. See also Peter deLeon, "Scenario Designs: An Overview," *Simulation & Games* 6 (1975): 39–60.

Chapter 6

Integrating Political and Nonpolitical Forecasts

Frequently, forecasters ask, "Is it better to use political or economic analysis for these kinds of problems?" But there is no meaningful choice to be made between tools of economic analysis and tools of political analysis. The same holds for the other spheres of social action: demography, including population growth and urbanization; sociology, and all the interpersonal relations it covers; resource use and production; ecology; religion; and so on. Politics affects the policies that regulate these spheres, and the general impact of the political climate pervades all aspects of life. It would be hard to imagine any feature of life in Northern Ireland, Vietnam, or Argentina that has not been touched by the political confrontations in those countries.

Conversely, politics is influenced by any social actions that either raise issues addressed by government or affect the distribution of resources among individuals and groups. This follows from two truisms about politics. First, wherever authoritative decisions are made, there is politics. Second, any and all resources potentially can be directed to augmenting political power; wealth, respect, skills, and so forth, are resources as much as they are ends in themselves.

The obvious interconnectedness of politics and other aspects of life raises three issues. The first is a superficial but nonetheless troublesome semantic problem. Although we can distinguish between basically political and "other" spheres, the latter are still political insofar as politics makes a difference. Thus, the terms "nonpolitical trend" and "nonpolitical forecast" are misleading. By the same token, the "political event" is not merely political, nor are its causes to be found exclusively among political factors.

The second issue is the assessment of these other social forecasts in order that reasonable projections can be sorted out from the unreasonable ones. This may seem like an extremely difficult task for the political specialist, inasmuch as it seems to require second-guessing the experts in other fields. Nonetheless, it can be done, because several of the criteria for evaluating these other forecasts do not rest on whether the political forecaster knows more about other experts' specialties than they do, but rather on quite straightforward judgments about the forecasts' recency, explicitness, comprehensiveness, and so forth.

The third issue is how to integrate political forecasting and forecasting of other social trends. This can be viewed two ways. For the political forecaster, the issue is how to use information about other trends that constitute the context of political events. For forecasters of nonpolitical trends, the issue is to model the impacts of political decisions and political climate in order to make their projections of other social trends consistent with the political realities in which they develop.

THE FRAMEWORK OF INTERACTION BETWEEN POLITICAL AND OTHER SOCIAL TRENDS

The relationships between political and other social trends can be viewed as a continuous, two-way interaction involving both politics and policy. Political forecasting attempts to anticipate three classes of trends or events:

1. The *distribution of power* among institutions and individuals (both potential power and power actualized in political victories such as winning elections and armed battles).

2. The *climate of politics,* encompassing how specific instances of political conflict or cooperation are played out, as well as the general levels of security or insecurity, certainty or uncertainty, conciliation or combativeness, and so on.

3. The continuities and changes in *authoritative policy* and in various actors' *strategies.*

Of these three classes of trend and events, the first is the essence of politics as it is conventionally defined. Undoubtedly, the brunt of political analysis focuses on this level. However, the impact of political power distributions and of political victories and defeats on other social spheres is channeled through the other two classes. That is, the economist, demographer, sociologist, or ecologist is not so interested in who gets elected, as in the implications of the election for government regulation, investor confidence, societal tensions, and the like—which result from the nature of the political conflict and the policies of those who assume power.

On the other side of this map is the huge collection of other social trends, ranging from the "hard" material trends in fields like economics, for which quantification seems quite natural, to the "soft" subjective trends in culture, attitudes, and nonmaterial rewards. The difficulties of measuring these soft aspects do not minimize their importance in accounting for political change, although it is common to see political forecasting efforts that rely solely on the hard facts because they seem more reliable and are certainly more easily obtained.

When political forecasts are used to generate forecasts of trends in these areas, the utility of the political forecast depends on how well it is adapted to the time frame and level of detail appropriate for making projections in these other areas. But when we are concerned with making the political forecast itself, our principal preoccupation is with what impact these other trends have on politics. The impact can come about through three channels.

The first channel is in the definition of the political agenda; social changes raise certain aspects of life as public issues while diminishing others. Poor economic performance increases pressure for economic management to become an issue requiring more intensive governmental involvement. Increased income disparities between ethnic or religious groups raise the political issues of discrimination and separatism, as in Nigeria during the Biafran War, in Northern Ireland, in Spain with respect to the Basques, and, of course, in racial relations within the United States. Generally speaking, deteriorating social trends increase the importance of that sphere as a political issue. Therefore, monitoring social trends is the most clearcut way of identifying the likely emergence of newly important issues or issues of considerably greater political importance then before. Economist Albert O. Hirschman has pointed out that it sometimes takes a full-fledged disaster, as in the case of famine in Brazil's drought-prone Northeast, to create sufficient public awareness of a chronic problem so that it becomes a central issue of politics, even if it had been a problem for many years earlier.[1]

The second channel is change in the resources of political actors. Because politics so often involves the translation or conversion of these resources (such as wealth, respect, celebrity, skill, and so on) into political power, changes in these other resources will change the balance of political power.[2] Groups that are becoming wealthier have more money to spend on politics; professions that have gained greater prestige hold more sway in influencing public policy decisions; the removal of social stigma from minority religious, ethnic, or caste groups often enhances their political capacities as well.

The implication of the political importance of changing resource bases is that our monitoring of social trends has to identify not only deteriorations in social conditions, but also those trends that represent different degrees of resource gains by different political actors. Even if one group is not literally gaining at the expense of another, its relatively greater progress in acquiring politically relevant resources will alter our calculations of the strengths of the actors.

The third and final channel is more abstract. In the political forecaster's theorizing about how political dynamics will determine the outcomes of politics, he will recognize that certain other social conditions are prerequisites of, or at least enhance, the operation of some political dynamics but not others. It may be recalled from Chapter 3's discussion of developmental constructs that there are enabling conditions that bring about political dynamics that otherwise might not emerge. Some of these enabling conditions are themselves political (for example, the dynamic of class warfare is made more likely by previous clashes along class lines), but others relate to trends in other social spheres. For example, in the case of policy clashes between industrial and agricultural sectors, as outlined in the discussion of developmental constructs, an economic condition—the concentration of capital within economic sectors—is a crucial enabling condition for this political dynamic to hold. Similarly, the dominance of ethnic clashes can have its origins in increasing social distance between ethnic groups or in deteriorating conditions of well-being for one or more of these groups.

These enabling trends can be identified and monitored only after the theoretical understanding of the political dynamics is accomplished. In other words, we cannot start with an a priori focus on particular kinds of trends, such as deteriorating social conditions leading to issue attention or trends changing resource bases. Instead, we must first examine the alternative political dynamics and then decide which trends are to be monitored in order to anticipate which dynamics will be triggered.

ASSESSING THE OTHER SOCIAL FORECASTS

Since political and other social trends are highly interactive, it is necessary to establish how the political forecaster, without first obtaining advanced training in every other specialty, can separate reasonable from unreasonable social forecasts in nonpolitical spheres. The considerations that the political forecaster ought to take into account can best be presented through a checklist of questions and issues, as in Table 6.1.

A Key Example: The *Global 2000 Report*

To explain how Table 6.1 is to be employed, it is useful to focus on a concrete example, *The Global 2000 Report to the President: Entering the*

Table 6.1   Checklist for Using Other Social-Trend Forecasts

1. Recency
2. Core Assumptions:
   a.   Explicitness
   b.   Plausibility
   c.   Recency
3. Plausible Interconnectedness of Major Trends
4. Likelihood of Source Bias
   a.   Preoccupation Bias
   b.   Vested Interest Bias
   c.   Availability of Alternative Cross-Checks
5. Uniformity of What Is Forecast
6. Political Plausibility of Trends
   Adequacy of Modeling Policy Response
7. Match of Method and Theory
8. Comparability of Forecast Purposes
9. Forecaster's Caveats

Twenty-First Century.[3] This 1980 joint effort of the U.S. Department of State and Council on Environmental Quality (CEQ) is a good example because its laudably frank Summary Volume, in 30-odd pages not counting diagrams, enables the nonexpert to make a fairly solid judgment of the strengths and weaknesses of the approach. Thus, although the study has several serious weaknesses, it provides good material for demonstrating how a set of nonpolitical social-trend projections can be assessed, because it was presented with concern for making its assumptions, methodology, and sources clear. Therefore, it is possible to go through the checklist in order to see how well the study's design conforms to the requisites for a borrowable set of projections.

For the *Global 2000 Report,* a coordinating team from the State Department and the CEQ attempted to project the environmental and resource-scarcity consequences of continued reliance on current government policies of industrial promotion, conservation, and resource exploitation. They, in turn, drew on work, some of it previously prepared, by other U.S. government agencies, such as the Department of Agriculture, the Census Bureau, and the Department of Energy. Therefore, to use the projections of the *Global 2000 Report* is to use projections based on the projections of still other sources—a common situation that calls for extreme caution in checking out the original status and purposes of the component forecasts. The *Global 2000 Report* generated considerable interest and publicity when it was released (not the least of which was because of the magnitude of effort that went into producing it). Yet it immediately drew strong criticism that diminished the impact of its "findings" of gloomy prospects for the environment and for resource availability.

Recency. The recency of the forecast turns out to be the strongest correlate of forecast accuracy.[4] Therefore, it would seem that the *Global 2000 Report* would be of greatest validity immediately, with deteriorating validity as time goes by. However, the study's recency is more problematical because the population and GNP projections utilized to generate forecasts of resource use were actually developed in 1977 (see p. 6 of the *Report*).

Moreover, since several very important structural changes in economic growth, population dynamics, and energy supply occurred between 1977 and 1980, this time lag is of potentially great importance for all of the projections interrelated in the study. These changes included the 1979 oil price boost, with its recessionary economic impact on OECD and developing countries; the growth of energy conservation; and the growing success of population control programs in developing countries such as Mexico. Therefore, reliance on three-year-old projections to generate other, dependent trends compounds the likely inaccuracy of the results. (See the discussion of projecting one trend on the basis of other trends in Chapter 3.) The *Report*'s authors recognize the possibility that circumstances could have changed since the earliest projections were made in 1977, but they reject that circumstances have changed critically. They accompany their summaries of projections with comments on how the projections might be altered; by and large they argue that the alterations are not significant (pp. 8–42).

Core Assumptions. The most important core assumptions of the projections of the *Global 2000 Report* are stated explicitly in the executive summary (pp. 7–8):

> First, the projections assume a general continuation around the world of present public policy relating to population stabilization, natural resource conservation, and environmental protection. . . . There are a few important exceptions to this rule. For example, the population projections anticipate shifts in public policy that will provide significantly increased access to family planning services. The projections thus point to the expected future if policies continue without significant changes.
>
> The second major assumption relates to the effects of technological developments and of the market mechanism. The Study assumes that rapid rates of technological development and adoption will continue, and that the

rate of development will be spurred on by efforts to deal with problems identified by this Study. Participating agencies were asked to use the technological assumptions they normally use in preparing long-term global projections. In general, the agencies assume a continuation of rapid rates of technological development and no serious social resistance to the adoption of new technologies. . . . The projections assume no revolutionary advances—such as immediate wide-scale availability of nuclear fusion for energy production—and no disastrous setbacks—such as serious new health risks from widely used contraceptives or an outbreak of plant disease severely affecting an important strain of grain. The projections all assume that price, operating through the market mechanism, will reduce demand whenever supply constraints are encountered.

Third, the Study assumes that there will be no major disruptions of international trade as a result of war, disturbance of the international monetary system, or political disruption. The findings of the Study do, however, point to increasing potential for international conflict and increasing stress on international financial arrangements. Should wars or a significant disturbance-of the international monetary system occur, the projected trends would be altered in unpredictable ways.

It is clear from this enumeration of basic assumptions that the users of these forecasts can judge for themselves, as time goes by, whether such assumptions as the absence of disruptions in trade or the monetary system are valid. The explicitness of these assumptions is a tremendous asset in assessing the projections and in maintaining their usefulness.

On the other hand, some of these assumptions lack plausibility. If this is indeed a projection of what might happen—the authors are ambivalent on this point, at times stating that the projections "do not predict what will occur" but rather are "conditions that are likely to develop if there are no changes in public policies, institutions, or rate of technological change" (p. 1), and yet repeatedly depicting the results as "findings"— the assumption that public policy would not change, despite the rather disastrous consequences predicted for the environment and resource availability, is not reasonable.

Finally, with respect to the recency of the core assumptions enumerated in the study, it would be hard to fault the study for choosing assumptions that were not part of the up-to-date conventional wisdom. This does not, however, guarantee their correctness. The assumptions on energy demand (pp. 27–29) do not take into account the increasing results of conservation and the oil glut of 1981–83.

Interconnection of Major Trends.   The most obvious failing of the *Global 2000 Report* methodology is the implausible manner in which the major trends are interrelated in the assumptions and procedures employed in making the projections. One does not have to be an expert in forecasting methods, or in any of the substantive areas covered by the *Report,* to recognize that the four basic classes of trends—population growth, economic growth, resource availability, and environmental change—are all mutually causal. Yet, by taking population and economic projections as the basis of resource-availability and environmental projections, but without allowing these latter projections to influence the population and economic change trends, the authors ignored some of the most important interactions:

> With the Government's current models, the individual sectors addressed in the Global 2000 Study could be interrelated only by developing projections sequentially; that is, by using the results of some of the projections as inputs to others. Since population and gross national product (GNP) projections were required to estimate demand in the resource sector models, the population and GNP projections were developed first, in 1977. The resource projections followed in late 1977 and early 1978. All of the projections were linked to the environment projections, which were made during 1978 and 1979. [p. 6]

With this one-way sequential framework, the method is incapable of picking up the following important interactions:

1. Resource scarcities dampening economic expansion.
2. Resource scarcities raising the prices of certain resources, thus shifting the resource-use profiles.
3. Resource scarcities dampening population growth (as through governmental, private-agency, or individual-level family planning in recognition of limited natural resources).
4. Environmental problems provoking either voluntary or governmentally mandated environmental protection efforts, affecting economic growth and resource use; or
5. Environmental problems dampening population growth, either by discouraging large families or directly through higher morbidity rates.

Significantly, these interactions would tend to work against the direction of trends that the *Report* concludes are the most important problems facing the world in the years ahead. Thus, the resource scarcities and environmental problems foreseen by the *Report* are not analyzed in terms of the changes in economics, demography, and resource use that emergent problems plausibly might trigger.

Source Bias.   The likelihood of source bias in the *Global 2000 Report* is rather high. The CEQ, by the very nature of its role and the way its staff must regard their jobs, is preoccupied with environmental dangers. It is less obvious that the CEQ has a "vested interest" in heightening concern over environmental issues, but it is certainly a possibility, considering that budget allocations for environmental research, policy making, and regulation depend on the level of concern among legislative and executive-branch officials.

Given this possibility of systematic source bias, it is useful to ask whether alternative projections are either provided by the study itself, or are otherwise available, to make comparisons. In the Appendix to the Summary Volume, the *Global 2000 Report* authors summarize the projections of five other "global studies" (pp. 43–45), concluding that "the Global 2000 Study's principal findings are generally consistent with those of the five other global studies despite considerable differences in models and assumptions" (p. 43). However, since we are concerned with the impacts of systematic source bias, as well·as the possibility that methods may have also led to biases, we must determine whether these alternative studies were sufficiently different in sources and methods to warrant confidence that the studies are really different.

The suspicion of source bias is not alleviated by the comparison. Three of the five studies were sponsored by the Club of Rome, an organization that has been on the forefront of the efforts to increase awareness of what they see as looming ecological dangers. These studies have been severely criticized, particularly for using methods that arbitrarily ignore society's ability to ameliorate scarcities and environmental problems through technological change and economic adjustment. The other two models, the United Nations World Model and the Model of International Relations in Agriculture, are reported as confirming the increases in food demand and prices that the *Global 2000 Report* emphasizes, but the former study is based on the somewhat artificial framework of asking what it would take "to meet U.S. target rates for economic growth" (thus also taking economic growth rates as a given, rather than as influenced by the other factors), and the Model of International Relations in Agriculture is, as the *Global 2000 Report* points out, only a partial model confined to the agricultural sector (p. 44).

As to whether the methods employed in these comparative studies differed significantly from the *Global 2000 Report,* the answer appears to be emphatically "yes" for the three models sponsored by the Club of Rome (World 2, World 3, and the World Integrated Model), in that all three did contain the mutual linkages among economics, demography, resource use, and environment.[5] The *Global 2000 Report* authors point out:

The Global 2000 Study conducted an experiment with two of the more integrated nongovernment models to answer the question: "how would projections from the Government's global model be different if the model were more integrated and included more linkages and feedback?" The linkages in the two nongovernment models were severed so that they bore some resemblance to the unconnected and inconsistent structure of the Government's global model. Chosen for the experiment were the World 3 model and the World Integrated Model.

In both models, severing the linkages led to distinctly more favorable outcomes. . . . The inescapable conclusion is that the omission of linkages imparts an optimistic bias to the Global 2000 Study's (and the U.S. Government's) quantitative projections. This appears to be particularly true of the GNP projections. [p. 44]

This is a particularly interesting passage. First, by noting that in the comparison with other, more elaborate models the Global 2000 results are optimistic, the authors are in effect bringing to bear additional evidence for their position that the outlook is more pessimistic than what they see as the typical lay opinion on these issues. Second, they make no mention of the rather well-known fact that the entire set of "Limits to Growth" models, of which these are three, has been severely criticized for its pessimistic biases in assumption, most notably the lack of adequate consideration for the contributions of technological change. Whether or not these criticisms are justified, the comparative exercise is misleading if it is construed as a test of the *Global 2000 Report* against a broad range of other studies, approaches, and assumptions.

What do other studies say? Other authors and other models come up with very different scenarios. The Hudson Institute, University of Illinois economist Julian Simon, and Nobel Prize laureate Wassily Leontieff, to name just a few examples, have reached quite different conclusions.[6] This should be taken as an object lesson of two points. First, there are useful and not-so-useful comparisons; one should not accept the source's comparisons unquestioningly, since they may be consciously or unconsciously self-serving. Second, the task of finding useful comparisons may have to be an active one when the original forecast source either does not provide comparisons or may be suspected of being one-sided in the alternative projections offered.

Uniformity of Forecast Objects.   The uniformity of combined or compared forecasts relates to the problem mentioned in Chapter 3 of the pitfalls of treating projections of different trends as if they were forecasts of the same phenomenon. If, for example, the forecast source is attempting to build a

Table 6.2a   M. King Hubbert's "Demonstration" That U.S. Ultimate Reserve Estimates Are "Grossly in Error"—Hubbert's Table

Estimated Ultimate U.S. Crude Oil Reserves

Date	Author	Estimate (Barrels)
1948	Weeks	110×10^9
1956	Department of Interior	300×10^9
1956	Pogue and Hill	165×10^9
1956	Hubbert	150×10^9
1956	Pratt	145×10^9
1957	Hill, Hammar, and Winger	250×10^9
1958	Netschert	372×10^9
1958	Weeks	204×10^9
1958	Davis	165×10^9
1959	Weeks	391×10^9
1959	Knebel	173×10^9
1961	Zapp (U.S.G.S.)	590×10^9
1961	Averitt (U.S.G.S.)	400×10^9
1962	Moore	364×10^9

Source: Energy Resources, NAS 1962.

consensus or composite forecast of, say, world demand for "gas and oil," he or she must make sure that the included forecasts pertain to the same definition of "gas and oil" (does that include natural gas liquids; does it refer to demand for gas and oil for all uses, including petrochemicals, or only demand for gas and oil as energy inputs?), to the same source of demand (whole world or just "free world"?), and for the same time period. If not, the combined forecasts will contain some avoidable error, and the set of forecasts will generally give a false impression of disagreement.

The *Global 2000 Report* does not rely on multiple forecast sources in generating its own projections, since it takes its basic forecasts from single federal agency sources. We can turn to another example to illustrate the importance of examining the uniformity of combined forecasts. A classic case was provided by geologist M. King Hubbert, who wanted to demonstrate that projections of U.S. "ultimate oil reserve estimates" were "grossly in error."[7] Hubbert compiled fourteen estimates of "ultimate reserves" made between 1948 and 1962, and argued that the range of estimates

Table 6.2b Retabulation of the Same Estimates According to Definitions of "Ultimate Reserves"

	On Land Only			On Land *and* Offshore		
At Current	1948	Weeks	110×10^9	1956	Pogue and Hill	165×10^9
Recovery				1956	Hubbert	150×10^9
Rates				1956	Pratt	145×10^9
				1958	Weeks	204×10^9
				1958	Davis	165×10^9
				1959	Knebel	173×10^9
At Future				1956	Dept. of Interior	300×10^9
Recovery				1957	Hill et al.	250×10^9
Rates				1958	Netschert	372×10^9
				1959	Weeks	391×10^9
				1961	Averitt	400×10^9
				1962	Moore	364×10^9
In Ground				1961	Zapp	590×10^9

(from 110 billion barrels to 590 billion barrels) proved that the geologists using the standard methods of reserve estimation did not know what they were doing. Therefore, he argued, Hubbert's own heretical method should be used.

A bit of detective work reveals that the 14 estimates compiled by Hubbert actually refer to four distinct definitions of "ultimate reserves." The lowest estimate referred to the volume of oil recoverable through current recovery technology (as of the estimation date of 1948) from oil deposits on land only; the low middle range estimates referred to oil recoverable through current technology (as of 1956–59) from deposits either on land or offshore; the high middle range referred to land and offshore oil recoverable through improving technology; and the highest estimate actually referred to oil in ground—and was not a recovery estimate at all! The spread of estimates of the second category was 145 to 204 billion barrels, while the spread of the third category was 250 to 400 billion barrels. These ranges are respectably narrow, and certainly do not imply that geologists were hopelessly out of step with one another.

Political Plausibility   The political plausibility of social trends is the one aspect on which the political forecaster is indeed the expert. Many conceivable forecasts of other social trends are not politically plausible, usually because they entail conditions that would not be tolerated by political actors who have enough power to avert them. As long as there is a modicum of controllability of the outcomes by these actors, it is generally not difficult to identify politically implausible trends. In the *Global 2000 Report,* for example, the emergence of disastrous ecological effects, food shortages, and other raw material scarcities would undoubtedly provoke some policy response in the form of new approaches to resolving these problems. As mentioned previously, the study makes no provision for this possibility, on the grounds that it is merely an attempt to demonstrate the consequences of existing policies. Therefore, whatever implication the study might have of representing actual patterns is particularly weak. Of course, the authors do not openly claim that the no-policy-change assumption is realistic. It can be argued that the study, in focusing on where current policies might lead assuming no change in these policies, can concentrate attention on the need for policy change. Yet, in exposing itself to so much criticism for maintaining the unrealistic assumption that there would be no policy response, the study may have discredited the position of environmental alarm.

Match of Method and Theory.   The method of a forecasting effort has to be consistent with the soundest possible theoretical understanding of how the system operates, and the level of knowledge the forecasters have concerning the phenomena underlying the trends. This means, of course, that the methods used to generate the social forecasts that enter into efforts at political forecasting need not be, and in general will not be, the same as those used to make the political forecasts.

There is an optimal level of methodological complexity that can capture what is known, while avoiding mere guesswork where enormous but not always recognizable errors can easily enter. As discussed in Chapter 3, more elaborate or sophisticated methods are justified only when the system is well understood, and simpler methods of more modest theoretical pretensions are called for when the system is poorly understood. At the same time, however, the simplest methods may not do justice to the body of knowledge and theory in which the forecasters can have some confidence. The choice of methods has to find the middle ground.

In the *Global 2000 Report,* it is admittedly difficult to identify and evaluate the appropriateness of the methods used without going deeply into the Technical Volume. However, it is clear, from the above discussions of the *Report*'s failure to take into account the two-way interactions among all important sectors, that the rather simple sequential method is not adequate for representing the growing understanding that has been developing in economics, demography, and related fields of how economic growth and population respond to causal factors such as resource scarcities and ecological conservation policies. The *Report* takes the Census Bureau's mechanical projections of population, which are basically extrapolations of current rates or rates estimated on the basis of birth-control programs, without sensitivity to economic or environmental factors. The projections of grain yields are depicted in a chart in the summary report as a straight extrapolation to the year 2000. These indications of weak methods are reinforced by the *Report*'s own admission that "the effort to harmonize and integrate the Study's projections was only partially successful. Many internal contradictions and inconsistencies could not be resolved" (pp. 6–7). While it is to be appreciated that the authors at least admit these weaknesses, one must wonder why inconsistent results jusify our confidence.

Comparability of Purposes. This is important in determining whether someone else's forecast is likely to have been developed with sufficient care for other applications. For some purposes, only very rough estimates are required of particular elements, which for other purposes may be of central importance and warrant much more careful analysis. For example, a study of world oil supply would require only rough estimates of the supplies offered by each country, as long as the total was sensibly estimated. Yet an application of the supply forecast for one particular country (say, to determine that country's export totals) would naturally call for more detailed analysis.

The *Global 2000 Report* itself seems to make appropriate use of the forecasts it gathers to generate its own projections, since these forecasts were made for the same level—global—and the same 20-year time span as the task undertaken by the *Report*. Any use of the *Global 2000 Report* projections to anticipate world-level trends would be appropriate (assuming that they were to meet the other criteria of quality that would warrant their use). However, plucking out any country-specific projection in order to explore the future of that country (for example, taking the population projection for any given nation) would not be justified, since more intensive studies of such particulars can be found in all likelihood.

Forecaster's Caveats. These are the forecaster's own warnings of the limitations in the certainty, interpretation, and use of the projections. Some of the most serious abuses of forecasts by either forecast users or by forecasters who base their own work on the projections of other trends have occurred when these caveats have been disregarded.

The *Global 2000 Report* illuminates this problem in several ways. First, it makes its own disclaimer about all of its results, asserting that they are not really predictions but rather projections designed to show the impact of the continuation of policies that the study's authors hope will change because of the publication of the study itself. They note: "A keener awareness of the nature of the current trends, however, may induce changes that will alter these trends and the projected outcome." (p. 1) Nonetheless, much of the language of the study implies that it does have the nature of a prediction (for example, referring to results as "findings," basing recommendations on these "findings," comparing the *Report*'s results with other studies that openly claim to be predictions), and the study as been construed as an effort at prediction. For example, *Business Week* stated:[8]

> Early this year the Council on Environmental Quality concluded that by the end of the 21st century global population may reach a level that closely corresponds to the "maximum carrying capacity of the entire earth." Even before then, says the council's *Global 2000 Report*, "serious stresses involving population, resources, and environment are clearly visible ahead. Despite greater material output, the world's people will be poorer in many ways than they are today."

Except for the one ambiguous use of the term "may," this reportage of the *Global 2000 Report* clearly construes the projections as predictions that are "concluded" by the *Report*'s authors.

Equally serious are the problems encountered by the *Global 2000 Report* authors in interpreting the projections gathered for the study from other sources. They take U.S. Census Bureau projections of population growth in individual countries and report these projections as "important findings" (p. 8). Yet the Census Bureau goes to great lengths, in every publication of its projections, to point out that they are mechanical projections of given assumptions on fertility, mortality, and related factors, with no endorsement of any of the series as more likely than other possible projections. In the Executive Summary of the *Global 2000 Report,* the authors discuss the middle series of the Census Bureau projection (p. 8), strongly implying that this series is more realistic. In fact, depending on the assumptions about the success of population control plans, economic influences on family-size decisions, and so on, the other series may be more plausible. To their credit, however, the *Global 2000 Report* authors indicate that they have taken into account the implications of alternative population projections, stating, for example:

One of the most important findings of the Global 2000 Study is that enormous growth in the world's population will occur by 2000 under any of the wide range of assumptions considered in the Study. The world's population increases 55 percent from 4.1 billion people in 1975 to 6.35 billion by 2000 under the Study's medium growth projections. While there is some uncertainty in these numbers, even the lowest-growth population projection shows a 46 percent increase—to 5.9 billion people by the end of the century.

More generally, the *Global 2000 Report* uses the questionable practice of meshing together projections from various sources when this meshing itself is not necessarily consistent with the assumptions used in generating the projections. Each of these sets of projections was developed under assumptions held by their respective agencies, not those of the basic Global 2000 framework that considers resource-use and environmental trends as unilaterally determined by population and economic growth trends.

After going through this nine-point checklist with the *Global 2000 Report*, we have a rather clear view of its strengths and weaknesses as a source of background forecasts for our political forecasting. Its strengths lie in its explicitness, the clarity and assessability of its assumptions, the compatibility of its own component projections, and the authors' exploration of certain alternative projections. Its weaknesses lie in the obsolescence of some of its component projections, the inability of its methods to take traceable interactions into account, the political implausibility of its assumptions, the lack of exploration of more divergent alternative projections, and its ambiguous status as not really a forecast, or, put differently, its status as a conditional forecast of what the world would be like under the extremely unlikely scenario that no policy responses would be forthcoming.

From this assessment, the political forecaster has to decide whether better sources are available. If not, the forecaster must also assess whether the strengths of this study outweigh its weaknesses. Is it worth heeding at all? If not, the political forecaster has the option of commissioning better-designed projections of these social trends, waiting for them to be done, or doing them himself.

NOTES

1.   Albert O. Hirschman, *Journeys toward Progress* (New York: Twentieth Century Fund, 1965).

2.   This framework is worked out in greatest detail in Harold Lasswell and Abraham Kaplan, *Power and Society* (New Haven: Yale University Press, 1950).

3.   Gerald O. Barney, Study Director, *The Global 2000 Report to the President: Entering the Twenty-First Century,* vol. 1 (Washington, D.C.: Government Printing Office, 1980).

4.   William Ascher, *Forecasting: An Appraisal for Policymakers and Planners* (Baltimore: Johns Hopkins University Press, 1978).

5.   See the summary of this class of models in John Clark and Sam Cole, *Global Simulation Models: A Comparative Study* (New York: Wiley, 1975).

6.   See Herman Kahn, *World Economic Development: 1979 and Beyond* (New York: Morrow Quill, 1979); Julian Simon, *The Ultimate Resource* (Princeton, N.J.: Princeton University Press, 1981); and Wassily Leontieff, A. P. Carter, and P. Petri, *The Future of the World Economy: A United Nations Study* (New York: Oxford University Press, 1977).

7.   M. King Hubbert, *Energy Resources,* National Research Council Publication No. 1000-D (Washington, D.C.: National Academy of Science, 1962), p. 50.

8.   *Business Week* (October 5, 1981): 11.

Part 3

A Central
Theoretical Perspective

Chapter 7

Organizational Analysis in Political Forecasting

The thrust of this book's recommendations on political forecasting methods is to emphasize the value of an approach that avoids the excessively simplistic assumptions behind all current quantitative methods, while simultaneously avoiding the equal and opposite dangers of an unstructured journalistic approach. The ideal approach is systematic without being overly quantitative, and also capable of accommodating the enormous complexity and nuance of political behavior.

There are many potential approaches that could theoretically achieve these requirements. The authors of this volume recommend analyzing politics in terms of a framework of *interacting political organizations*. This chapter sketches out very briefly the skeleton of such an approach. Chapter 8 employs this approach in a theoretical analysis of revolution. Chapters 9 and 10 provide case studies that demonstrate concretely how to use the approach. All of the analysis in this book of various methods, various institutional relationships among forecasters and policy makers, and various presentational formats, is independent of the particular approach advocated here. We invite the reader to join us in our advocacy of this particular theoretical approach, or, if you prefer, to regard this simply as an illustration of one kind of systematic, nonquantitative approach.[1]

POLITICS AS ORGANIZATIONAL ACTIVITY: THE CENTRAL METAPHOR

Using organizational conflict and cooperation as the central metaphor of political analysis is appropriate because the central phenomena of politics revolve around organizations. Governments, political parties, and revolutionary insurgencies are organizations. Political regimes are forms of organization. Military and civilian bureaucracies are organizations. Social pressure groups are formal or informal organizations. Interactions among and within organizations are the stuff of politics.

All important political processes can be interpreted in organizational terms, and many insights about political processes are more comprehensible if they are so interpreted. Political leadership change can mean either changes in the occupants of certain organizational roles or changes in the roles themselves. The administration of governments and nations is an organizational phenomenon. The formation of coalitions of groups supporting a regime, the exit of groups from such coalitions, or the emergence of new groups that can potentially influence such coalitions, is another phenomenon of organizational development, as is cooperation or conflict among social organizations. The structures of different kinds of political regimes (such as liberal-democratic, authoritarian, communist, theocratic) are defined in terms of kinds of political organizations that exist in the given systems and the characteristic relationships among these organizations.

THE UTILITY OF THE ORGANIZATIONAL PERSPECTIVE

But why this particular metaphor? Why not analyze politics in terms of the myriad other available metaphors—"the balance of power," "group dynamics," "politics as exchange," "politics as learning," and so on? Our reasons are heuristic, philosophical, and pragmatic.

Heuristically, the organizational perspective reminds us not only that there are people out there, with their own objectives, identifications, and expectations, but also that these people interact in structured, institutionalized ways. The statistical description of their loyalties (for instance, "Ten percent of the population sympathize with the revolution") does not tell us much about this structure; nor does the overall balance of resources or power. By focusing our attention on the organization itself and on how the organization interacts with its environment, this perspective also allows us to distinguish among different types of political resources that are often lumped together in studies that attempt to compare the balance of resources directly. We shall show how to distinguish between the resources that support the organization itself as an institution, and the resources that the organization deploys.

The organizational perspective thus forces upon us the need for fine-grained analysis, even when we are tempted to be abstract and grandiose. In reminding us that political reality consists of individuals interacting with other individuals in settings structured by specific norms, procedures, and resource constraints, we are assured of some contact with the concrete essence of politics.

Finally, this perspective has the heuristic advantage of allowing us to branch out with this metaphor to capture the contributions of each social science in understanding the phenomenon in question. The organizational perspective reminds us of the relevance of the psychology of leaders and followers, the sociology of the group, the economics of the situations the organization faces, and so forth.

Philosophically, this metaphor is laudable because it is not culturally limited. Such an organizational perspective can accommodate both a liberal democratic system where the central government is heavily and directly influenced by social pressure goups, and communist systems where the internal bureaucratic dynamics of the government and the party are much more important than external pressure groups. In short, the organizational metaphor of politics is sufficiently flexible to accommodate more diversity in actual political behavior than, for instance, the interest-group or bureaucratic models of politics. The organizational perspective can embrace them both, if it can be given sufficient content (for which, see the rest of this chapter and the following chapter).

Of course, an organizational perspective on politics must accommodate the fact that many of the groups and social aggregates influencing politics are not *formal* organizations. They may be cabals inside a government, labor movements not yet organized into unions, informal working relationships among certain elites, or even the potential that totally unorganized peasants might be shocked into some kind of informal cooperation to pursue specific interests. In short, the organizational perspective must allow for a variety of degrees of organization, from the formalized structure of IBM or the Executive Office of the President of the United States, to the temporary, informal mobilization of a jacquerie.

Pragmatically, the organizational metaphor has the advantage of guaranteeing that the sequencing of our analysis captures the immediately relevant before it examines the less directly relevant. Given infinite resources—manpower, time, and intellect—work within many different approaches or frameworks can ultimately cover all aspects of any problem. With a realistic appreciation of the resource constraints on any real-world political analysis, however, it is imperative to depend on a framework that begins straightforwardly with the collective units—that is, organizations—directly responsible for the actions that political forecasting tries to anticipate. With an organizational perspective, we begin by asking which organizations and individuals are directly involved in relevant conflicts or in the policies of direct interest. While embedding the analysis of organizations in a framework that permits elaboration along any conceivable line, the organizational perspective focuses first on the institutions of direct political relevance, and then, to the degree that further resources permit, pursues these lines of more intensive analysis.

RESOURCES AND STRATEGIES: FILLING IN THE METAPHOR

Political leaders deploy resources through organizations. At the outset, these organizations may or may not be structured appropriately for the tasks the leaders have set. Part of their leadership strategy is to use this existing structure to best advantage; we call this the "goal attainment strategy." But the other aspect of strategy is to alter the organization's structure to better advantage; we call this the "organizational strategy."

Many political leaders never think to alter the structures of their own organizations, or they lack the intraorganizational resources to do so significantly. Nevertheless, the organizational strategy is often critical to the achievement of the leadership's objectives. It may be that the organization's original structure—its procedures, personnel, customs, beliefs, communications, and so on—render it ineffective. It may be that the actors within the organization adhere to established norms that contradict the goals of the organization's leaders (as in many cases of progressive governments committed to land reform which nonetheless cannot force bureaucrats of middle-class origins to carry out the necessary administrative procedures).[2] Or it may be that the support groups on which the organization initially relies can block changes that the organization's leadership recognizes as essential, perhaps even for the survival of the organization itself. When an economic crisis forces the government to change economic policies or else face collapse, can the government gain the compliance of allied economic sectors that stand to suffer from the new policies? In short, organizational restructuring is often crucially important but is not always undertaken or successful.

With this distinction between organizational strategy and goal attainment strategy comes a distinction between the resources a leader holds within the organization and the resources the organization can wield in its dealings with the outside world. The organizational resources, ranging from charisma to force, from oratory to bribes to fellow members, can be used to direct and to make effective the energies of organizational members. They may be used to mobilize effort, elicit sacrifice, refocus attention, change values, develop expertise, or expand membership. These resources may be vastly different in kind from the resources the organization itself deploys. To cite a graphic example, revolutionary movements and armies alike often rely on camaraderie to maintain internal unity, but they rely on brutality to succeed with the world outside the organization. Moreover, organizational and goal attainment resources are not additive; they do not sum up to an organization's overall capability. Some organizations with enormous potentially deployable resources are nonetheless paralyzed because the leadership cannot mobilize its membership to channel those resources, or because of an impasse within the leadership itself. Therefore, a resource assessment of an organization must evaluate two components: the internally directed organizational resources and the externally directed goal attainment resources. Figure 7.1 depicts the distinctions among internal and external resources and strategies. The situation must be complicated further whenever there are leaders with different objectives.

Internal Resources

Without certain resources, a social aggregate cannot form even an informal organization. The members of the aggregate must be motivated; that is, they must share some interests or some salient goals. For instance, if they are peasants, they might share interests in changing the proportion of their crops that goes to the landlords. They can only organize if there is

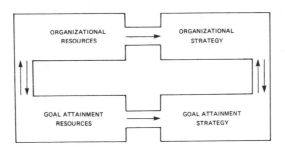

POLITICAL ORGANIZATION – SIMPLIFIED VERSION

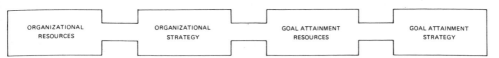

Figure 7.1   Political organization

(or they perceive) some such common interest. Just as importantly, they can only organize if they are mutually aware of or able to define the nature of this common interest. If they perceive themselves primarily as members of the respective landlords' families, then the shared class interest may be invisible to them. In short, the first resources necessary to shared organization are motivational and perceptual: *salient common goals* and *visible common goals*. It may even happen occasionally that common interests are perceived and hence operative even if the perception of common interest is false.

However, motivation is not enough. Organization is impossible if group members cannot *communicate* with one another, if their members lack *skills* to organize, if the potential members lack *available time,* or if some outside force denies them the *autonomy* to organize. For instance, desert nomads may lack sufficient communications to form a viable political group. Illiterate Javanese peasants may lack the skill to coordinate their actions in pursuit of a common national political goal. People who are starving or who have left jobs that require them to work to the point of total exhaustion may lack the time and energy to devote to political organization. This accounts, in part, for the fact that revolutions as a rule do not occur when economic and social conditions are at their worst.[3] A communist government or a village association of landlords may be able to deprive its underlings of the social autonomy required to create an organization. In other words, organization is impossible without the resources listed in Table 7.1. With a bit of each of these resources, organization is possible to some degree. In the total absence of any one of these resources, organization is utterly impossible. The constraints on most social pressure groups consist of lack of one or more of these crucial resources.

For large, modern, formal organizations, lack of organizational resources typically appears in different forms. One is the lack of money. Money can buy communications or organizing time. In the absence of some overarch-

Table 7.1   Organizational Resources

A.	*Motivational*
	1. Visible goals
	2. Salient goals
B.	*Technical*
	1. Communications
	2. Coordination skills
	3. Availability
	4. Autonomy

ing social purpose, money can even provide the motivation for individuals to join organizations. Communications can also fall short for complex organizations, but in different ways. Whereas communication in at least some minimal sense is always present, effective communication in a complex organization is of great importance. In nuclear war, the single most vulnerable aspect of a modern government would be its communications, which are the key to command and control of its military forces and ultimately of the nation itself; during nuclear war, the U.S. government could find itself faced with the same qualitative difficulty as Zimbabwean peasants fighting Ian Smith.

Finally, motivation is an important and often endangered resource of the complex organization. The members of emergent organizations are generally highly aware of the goals of the organization; recency and the struggle to get established ensure the vividness of the objectives. For long-established complex organizations, in contrast, the moral imperative often diminishes or disappears entirely under the weight of bureaucracy and careerism. It is notable that even many revolutionary organizations, such as the APRA party in Peru or the communist parties of many Latin American nations, lose both their fervor and any clearcut sense of mission. Similarly, despite the attractiveness of money for its own sake, it is a commonplace that even modern industrial organizations can quickly get into difficulty when they lose their sense of shared purpose.

The organizational resources available to a given social group or other politically relevant organization derive from the economic, social, cultural, political, and technological context of the group. An authoritarian nation of backward, illiterate landlords and peasants yields a potential landlord organization with certain kinds of resources, potential tenant organizations that lack most kinds of resources, and government and military organizations that must seek to draw resources from the landlords and tenants. A modern, highly differentiated economy yields a different set of groups, a different distribution of resources available to those groups and to government organization, and hence a different variety of possible systems.

Organizational Strategies

Given that a social aggregate possesses organizational resources, some or all of these internal resources will be utilized. One can describe a plan or structure of their utilization that can be labeled an organizational strategy. This strategy or structure may be implicit rather than consciously contrived; it may be institutionalized like IBM or ephemeral like a jacquerie. In short, organizational strategies are patterns of utilization of organizational resources, including especially specification of roles and allocation of resources to these roles. For instance, a potential peasant leader may wish to organize his fellows in order to influence local, or national, politics. To do so, he must choose a structure, which could be a tightly knit revolutionary military organization or, on the other extreme, a loose coalition of farm families who agree to vote in concert. His achievement of a degree of organization may be based on a variety of combinations of propaganda, patronage, bullying, quasimilitary training, and so forth. In a more complex organization, such as Ford Motor Company, the president may wish to move from a highly centralized organization to a relatively decentralized one (such as General Motors), and may seek to do this by appointing a group of highly dynamic individuals as executive vice-presidents, placing them in different locations, and providing each with autonomous control over substantial resources.

Goal Attainment Resources

Depending on the organization's purposes, different resources will be required for it to attain its goals. To avert economic problems for which it is held responsible, a government will need policy expertise and the strength to impose its policy formulations. To win a military battle, an army will need weapons and mobility. To win an election, a party will require a large number of members or supporters to vote with it. To win a commercial battle, a firm will need large amounts of money and perhaps technological skill. To win a propaganda war, an insurgency will need ideas. Clearly, these goal attainment resources can be different from the organizational resources, although they may overlap, and certain basic resources such as money or a monopoly over coercion may be capable of securing both. The kinds of resources that are useful or necessary to attain the organization's goals depend upon the nature of the goals and the strategy with which the organization decides to pursue them.

Goal Attainment Strategies

Goal attainment strategies are the patterns of allocating goal attainment resources by which an organization seeks to attain its goals. There is, of course, an interaction between an organization's resources and its strategies for deploying them. An organization may have to adopt a certain strategy because of resource constraints; at the same time, its strategy will usually generate efforts to acquire additional resources relevant to that strategy. A revolutionary insurgency will emphasize the resources of weapons and secrecy, whereas a democratic political party will emphasize gaining large numbers of members, and a business organization will emphasize money and key technologies.

Each political organization will seek to shape the nature of its competition in such a way as to make its own resources particularly useful. (This is the second aspect of a basic strategy, as discussed in Chapter 1.) A revolutionary insurgency may seek to precipitate social polarization, in order for armed conflict to determine the political outcome. A democratic political party will attempt to coopt opponents, perhaps even from an insurgency, in order to make patronage and votes the determinants of the political outcome. A business organization may seek to shape rules of the electoral game that would allow its funds to buy votes, or to dominate media coverage of the principal political issues.

Assessing Organizational Capability

We can evaluate organizational capability in terms of both specific capabilities to cope with current problems and the general capability to handle future problems that are not yet well specified. Before deciding how to evaluate an organization's capability we must consider what it takes for an organization to be successful at marshalling both internal and external resources. In light of the organization's needs to maintain appropriate and efficient strategies with respect to organizational structure and goal attainment, we propose three requisites or aspects of capability.

First is the *efficiency* with which the organization can deploy its goal attainment resources. Some cultures of the Andes and of Southeast Asia were able to build and maintain vast irrigation networks; others were incapable of keeping up even a fraction of the systems they inherited from these highly capable cultures.

The second aspect is the *adaptability* of the organization as it is forced to confront new challenges. Can a new organizational strategy be implemented, when necessary, to alter no longer efficient resource deployment patterns that may have the prestige of tradition or have acquired vested interests? Can the leadership identify a crisis early enough and overcome the lethargy of established practices?

The third aspect is organizational *unity*. Does the organization fail to deploy resources efficiently because different actors within it are pursuing different interests? Are resources diverted to internal fights rather than to external struggles? Are organizational structures maintained in an inefficient form because those who hold power within the existing structure fear losing it to their adversaries within the organization?

Efficiency, adaptability, and unity depend on the characteristics of three levels of the organization.

Organizational leadership is generally responsible for the choices of organizational and external resource-deployment strategies. Although the leadership cannot often impose strategies that clash with the values of subordinates and the organization's rank and file, good leadership is generally a necessary if not sufficient condition for efficiency and adaptability. From the point of view of the analyst, this is a fortunate fact, because generally the leadership is more visible than the rank-and-file membership of an organization. We can assess leadership in terms of *commitment, unity,* and *competence*. Commitment can be judged in many situationally specific ways, ranging from whether the national leaders of developing countries are willing to educate their children in schools within their own countries to the defection rates of leaders of revolutionary organizations. Unity can be judged either by noting the lack of visible conflicts within the leadership or by assessing whether the values known to be held by the various leaders coincide. Competence must be assessed by inferring skills from training and by evaluating past performance. Naturally, past competence does not always guarantee future competence in the face of new problems.

For medium- or long-term forecasting, we must also pay particular attention to the patterns of leadership recruitment that establish what beliefs and skills qualify an individual for a future leadership position. Examining leadership age cohorts (for example, junior officers within the armed forces, young middle-level party leaders) in terms of their values and caliber will enable the analyst to anticipate the future leadership's commitment, unity, and competence before recruitment into top positions.

The *organizational apparatus,* usually comprising the middle-level functionaries of the organization, serves the dual role of elaborating the particulars of the deployment strategies formulated by the leadership and overseeing their implementation. Hence, the middle-level administrators do more than administer; in implementing general policies in particular ways they are also making policy. Their commitment to the organization and to current organizational objectives can be explored by examining compliance with top leadership directives, rates of defection, and various other indications of loyalty. Unity and competence can be assessed as for the top leadership.

The *rank-and-file* membership, followers, or supporters of the organization are relevant in three respects. First, they constitute a resource of often critical importance for the achievement of organizational objectives, whether through their votes, work, violence, willingness to pass information, or other coordinated actions. Second, as mentioned previously, the broad membership base may represent constraints on what the leadership can dictate, in terms of both organizational strategies and goal attainment strategies, insofar as leadership directives that run counter to rank-

and-file attitudes may jeopardize rank-and-file commitment. Third, just as the organization's middle levels make policy as they oversee the implementation of deployment strategies, the actions of the rank and file per se constitute what the organization actually does. Organizational analysis must take into account the possibilities that soldiers will rape and pillage, assembly-line workers will ignore quality control, or revolutions will go beyond the objectives of their instigators, whether or not organizational leaders order these actions. Thus, unless the leadership and administration of an organization have complete control over the actions of the base, rank-and-file characteristics are important for understanding what the organization will do.

The commitment of the organization's base is generally more fluid than that of the leaders and middle-level administration, for the simple reason that the latter typically receive rewards for their direction of the organization itself. Nonetheless, rank-and-file commitment can be gauged through the same factors of compliance and unwillingness to defect. The unity of the base, which is important insofar as new issues may arise that could set one part of the rank and file against another, has to be assessed through an inventory of their interests and beliefs. The competence of the base, defined according to the actions it may be called upon to perform, must be judged through inferences based on socioeconomic backgrounds, training, and culturally dependent temperaments.

Assessing the capabilities of the rank and file is complicated by the fact that they do not constitute a fixed aggregate regardless of the organizational strategy adopted by the leadership. If, for example, a political party's leadership changes the party structure from a cadre party to a mass party, the very definition of party membership changes as well. Therefore, the medium- or long-term assessment of rank-and-file capabilities must also be linked to a projection of what group or groups will constitute the base of the organization in the future.

THREE ARCHETYPAL SITUATIONS

Much of the complexity of organizational analysis—and of political analysis in general—comes from the fact that organizations often interact with one another. The notion of competition naturally presupposes the existence of more than one organization. Nevertheless, there are some cases in which, apparently, only one organization is visibly involved. In other cases, where organizations do interact with one another, the natures of the interactions are distinctly different. It is therefore useful to outline several of these situations.

"Simple" Task Pursuit

An organization may face the challenge of pursuing particular goals without much immediate relevance of other organizations. When the Dutch built dikes to keep out the sea, or the Incas organized to develop irrigation schemes, or any number of governments attempt to accommodate international economic changes such as the rise in world oil prices or high interest rates, the task is not primarily to compete with other organizations. Figure 7.2 shows the simple diagram of this situation. To be sure, other organizations—"counterelites" who might be in a better position to take over if the dominant organization fails—may well be part of the picture, but the task per se is simple in terms of assessing resources and strategies. There may even be situations in which the issue of political stability depends on whether the government can handle whatever tasks come up, regardless of what they may turn out to be. In such a case organizational survival and external goal achievement merge.

The analysis of organizational capability with respect to simple task achievement is obviously less complex than when several organizations are involved. However, this analytical simplicity does not imply that the tasks faced are by any means necessarily simple. Moreover, if organizational unity is lacking, then the apparent analytical simplicity of this situation does not hold up either. If it turns out that the organization is hindered in accomplishing the task by internal divisions, then we must look to the conflict within. Organizations that face a difficult task but no clearly recognizable enemy often have the greatest difficulty in maintaining internal unity and morale.[4] Since there is no fixed size that defines what does and does not constitute an organization, our perspective allows for the conflicts among different sets of cooperating individuals within the same larger organization as "interorganizational" conflict—which can be analyzed in the same terms that we have outlined above—while at the

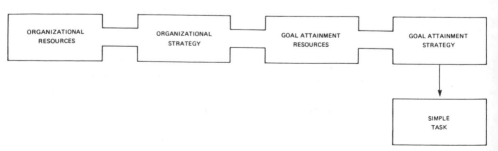

Figure 7.2   Simple task pursuit

same time recognizing that in terms of the larger entity it is intraorganizational.

Limited Conflict

In other situations, organizations compete but they also abide by certain rules of the game that prohibit an all-out effort by any of the organizations to dismantle another. In the cases of elections or competition among lobbying groups to sway policy formulation, organizations impinge upon one another basically through the effects that the deployment of externally directed resources have on the success or failure of one another's efforts. In general—but not always, as the "dirty tricks" of certain U.S. electoral campaigns demonstrate—one political party in a liberal-democratic system affects another by winning or losing elections. Only indirectly, as the victories or losses subsequently influence organizational morale, commitment, strategies, and structures, does one party influence the internal resources and strategies of the other.

The analysis of limited conflict thus requires greater complexity than the simple task situation, as illustrated in Figure 7.3, but the channels of direct interaction are still somewhat limited. One still must assess each organization's leadership capabilities, and each organization's efficiency, adaptability, and internal unity. In addition, one must take account of how each organization is perceived by members of the other(s)—how much of a threat is perceived, how the issues come to be defined, how attractive switching from one organization to another may come to be, and so on. But, most centrally, projecting the strength and success of one organization depends on doing the same for all relevant others. To take an obvious example, no projection of the future prominence of the Italian Communist Party can be reasonably undertaken without a parallel projection of the fortunes of the Christian Democrats.

Figure 7.3   Limited organizational conflict

Insurgency

The insurgency situation differs from the previously outlined cases in two respects. First, when a revolutionary insurgency and a government attack each other, there is a comprehensive effort on both sides not only to defeat the other organization's goal attainment strategy, but also to disrupt its organization and to disperse it permanently by depriving it of one or more of its organizational resources. This process, diagrammed in Figure 7.4, will be developed further in chapter 8. Obviously, the analysis entails even more elaborate examination of interactions between organizations at more levels.

Second, the insurgency situation is complicated by the fact that the competing organizations, by virtue of the fact that one currently rules and the other(s) do not, face very different tasks and organizational problems. The government generally has to reorient its previous preoccupations in order to meet the challenge of the insurgency. If the insurgency is indeed a serious threat, the government must convince its own personnel and support groups of the need to make the necessary sacrifices instead of enjoying the perquisites of power and privilege as usual. Many of the critiques of the conduct of the Vietnam War point out that successive South Vietnamese governments, perhaps because of the reassuring support of the United States, failed to convince key officials and economic sectors of the seriousness of the guerrilla threat until it was far too late. The government must also learn how to suppress the revolt without inciting even more revolutionary opposition. In contrast, the insurgents generally face the problems of scarce basic organizational resources and starting from a weak military position.

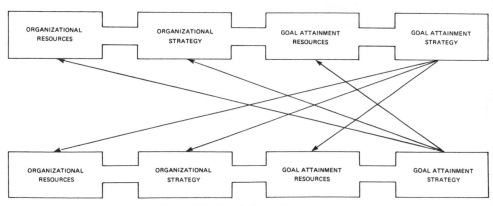

Figure 7.4 Revolutionary insurgency

ORGANIZATIONAL DYNAMICS

There are numerous developmental constructs that can help us to understand the dynamics accounting for both strategic choices and changes in organizational capability itself. For the sake of illustration we list several dynamics pertaining to internal changes and several pertaining to external relations.

Internal Dynamics

Michels' "Iron Law of Oligarchy."[6] One of the most famous formulations of changes within organizations is Roberto Michels' dictum that leadership attitudes ossify over time, as the aging leaders come to value the perquisites of being organization leaders and hence avoid radical objectives that could bring suppression upon the organization and thereby threaten their positions. Michels, who developed this principle for application to the radical political parties of late nineteenth-century Western Europe, nevertheless stated it as a universal principle. However, in keeping with our commitment to regarding such propositions as possible dynamics that are valid in certain times and places but not necessarily universally, we would proceed, in any given case, to search for the conditions and trends likely to trigger the conservatizing of leadership (for example, the existence of sufficiently appealing perquisites of leadership positions, or perception that the pursuit of radical objectives would jeopardize these positions).

Ideological Fractionation. Another intraorganizational dynamic is the emergence of serious ideological disputes within parties, movements, or regimes that can undermine unity and even split the organization. Under the assumption that divisions over ideological matters are more likely to occur where leadership and members consider ideological orthodoxy important, we would expect this dynamic in the presence of the enabling conditions of ideological extremism, lack of personalistic leadership, and insufficiency of immediate material payoffs from unified action.

Bureaucratic Growth. It is very common for organizations to grow in terms of administrative personnel and cumbersomeness, even if this growth is detrimental to effective pursuit of their goals. The transfer of middle-level actors' loyalties from the organization as a whole to the suborganizations within it creates pressures from these actors to expand the subunits. Efforts to circumvent inefficient administrators by creating new administrative subunits ultimately results in greater bureaucratic bloat and inefficiency, if efficiency is measured in terms of productivity per administrative worker. The conditions conducive to bureaucratic growth include the longevity of the organization, the difficulty and breadth of the objectives pursued by the organization, the lack of strong commitment to the objectives defined by the organization's leadership, and the prevalence of careerist as opposed to ideological orientations among organizational personnel.

Bureaucratic Depoliticization. A distinctive dynamic that increases the bureaucratization of an organization can arise from the organizational strategy of removing divisive issues from the political infighting within the organization, sometimes entailing the creation of new institutions.[6] An increasing proportion of issues may thus be removed from active consideration, until or unless dissatisfaction with the fact that so many issues have been insulated causes a rejection of the bureaucratized arrangements. Triggering conditions for the depoliticization may be a history of costly squabbles over irresolvable issues, the perception that internal divisiveness has unacceptable costs, the lack of unified leadership that could resolve the issues straightforwardly, and so on.

Interorganizational Dynamics

Escalation of Interorganizational Conflict. When two or more organizations are in competition, the responses of one toward the other often tend to escalate in their aggressiveness and threat. This is partly due to the momentum of sequential responses, the bargaining logic of appearing to be irrationally reckless, and the need to appear strong in the eyes of the organization's own membership. The likelihood of this dynamic can be increased by dissimilarity and lack of communication between the organizations, by high perceived importance of the issues involved, and by initial animosity between the organizations.

Stereotyping of Adversary Organizations. Very often the members of one organization will adopt exaggerated negative perceptions of the members of adversary organizations, leading to rationalizations for more hostile behavior toward the other organizations. If members of other organizations are seen as unprincipled, prone to violence, and ruthless, aggressiveness toward them appears to be both more urgent and less morally objectionable. The enabling conditions have been identified as a low level of interaction between organizations, cultural or subcultural distinctiveness, and a host of other factors.[7]

Isolation of the Strongest Organization. A typical proposition on the dynamics of coalition formation is that weaker organizations, if they can, will coalesce to confront the one strongest organization.[8] The logic of this coalition choice depends on the strength of the perceived threat that the strongest organization represents, the prevalence of the belief that the bulk of the spoils of victory will go to the strongest among the victors, and the similarities of background and objectives of the potential coalition partners.

In summary, it should be clear that one can not only systematically identify and examine the components of organizational strategy, resources, and capabilities, but also bring to bear large bodies of theory on how organizations work, expressed as developmental scenarios. Because organizations are not simple entities that follow ironclad general laws, the particulars of each organization's structure and the general context in which it operates must also be monitored and interpreted. Armed with these theories, and the ability to identify their enabling conditions, the forecaster is prepared to outline scenarios of organizational development and interaction.

ANALYZING POLITICAL CHANGE

From an organizational perspective, the causes of political change are as follows:

1. The processes of change internal to key political organizations (such as government, military, party, pressure group, or insurgency).

2. Changes in the goal attainment strategies various groups employ, and resulting changes in the distribution of organizational and conflict resources.

3. Economic, technological, social, cultural or international changes that alter the distribution of organizational and goal attainment resources in the society, or that induce changes of organizational strategy or conflict strategy.

The first kind of change is exemplified by the classic pattern of the Chinese dynastic bureaucracy, which began as a highly centralized and capable institution and gradually degenerated into a decentralized, poorly led, undisciplined structure. This pattern is traced in slightly greater detail in chapter 8. Here, the central dynamic of change is the internal evolution of the government organization.

The second kind of change is exemplified by a situation where, in the absence of broader social changes, a democratic political leader in a system that had previously confined itself to rather limited mobilization of elite groups suddenly reaches out to workers or poor farmers and greatly broadens the social base of political competition.

The third kind of change is exemplified by the situation where economic development in a country of landlords and tenants supporting a monarchy suddenly creates a middle class, a modern military, and modern civilian bureaucracies, all of which may oppose the monarchy, and also leads to education of the peasantry and their acquisition of additional organizational resources so that they become an organized political force for the first time. Thus, economic change, which is exogenous to the political system, creates new political organizations and changes the distribution of resources among existing political groups and thereby renders the system vulnerable to upheaval.

USING THE ORGANIZATIONAL PERSPECTIVE

The organizational conflict perspective provides a central metaphor and vocabulary for thinking about political structures and political change. Within that metaphor, it identifies three basic kinds of change. In any polity it highlights key issues:

What are the politically relevant or potentially relevant organizations?

What are the organizational resource constraints of those organizations?

What are the characteristic strengths and vulnerabilities of those organizations?

What goal attainment resources do those organizations dispose?

What goal attainment strategies are those organizations able and inclined to pursue?

What nonpolitical trends influence the distribution of resources and the emergence of new strategies?

So far, however, the organizational conflict perspective is a central metaphor, a vocabulary, and a structure of analysis, rather than a detailed theory applicable to a specific situation. The following chapter applies the organizational perspective to create a theory applicable to a specific issue, namely the issue of political revolution. Chapters 9 and 10 apply the organizational conflict perspective to the problem of stability in South Korea and in Mexico and to certain other problems in Mexico.

NOTES

1.   See William H. Overholt, "A Theory of the Ability of Social Groups to Organize for Political Purposes," paper for the American Sociolog-

ical Association Meeting, Montreal, August 1974. For an extended discussion of the organizational approach to political analysis, see William H. Overholt, *Organization, Revolution and Democracy: Toward a Sociology of Politics* (New Haven: Yale University dissertation, 1972).

2. See James Petras, *Politics and Social Forces in Chilean Development* (Berkeley: University of California Press, 1969).

3. This is documented in James Davies, "Toward a Theory of Revolution," *American Sociological Review* 27 (1962): 5–19, which argues that rising expectations induce revolt when conditions that had been improving suddenly take a turn for the worse. The corollary that revolts generally do not take place when conditions are very bad can rest either on the absence of "relative deprivation" (that is, a visible and salient motivation) or on the lack of other organizational resources.

4. See Lewis Coser, *The Function of Social Conflict* (Glencoe, Ill.: Free Press, 1956), for the classical formulation of this view.

5. Roberto Michels, *Political Parties* (New York: Hearst International Library, 1915).

6. See Francis Rourke, *Politics, Bureaucracy, and Public Policy* (Boston: Little-Brown, 1969).

7. Many propositions are catalogued in Robert LeVine and Donald Campbell, *Ethnocentrism: Theories of Conflict, Ethnic Attitudes, and Group Behavior* (New York: Wiley, 1972).

8. Morton Kaplan, *System and Process in International Politics* (New York: Wiley, 1957).

Chapter 8
Analyzing Revolution

The question most frequently asked of the political forecaster is whether a given regime will experience revolution or stability. When asked this question, the forecaster must first refine the term "instability," since that term can refer to changes in a regime's values, its institutions, its personnel, its policies, or some combination of these. It can even refer to the level of violence present in a society without such changes. This chapter will address the most overwhelming kind of revolutionary change, using a theory that is qualitative but systematic. The theory focuses attention quite intensively on issues of political organization, but employs concepts that can acknowledge the influence of a broad range of political, economic, cultural, social, and military factors.

Although this theory focuses on the great revolution, the analysis of political change as the outcome of conflict among organizations can be applied to virtually any political issue.[1]

AN ORGANIZATIONAL CONFLICT THEORY OF REVOLUTION

A revolution occurs when a domestic insurgent group (or groups) displaces the government of a society by means that are illegitimate according to the values of the existing regime, and when fundamental political institutions are destroyed or transformed and fundamental values of the system are changed dramatically. An abortive revolution occurs when a domestic group attempts to carry out a revolution without complete success. Fundamental political institutions are those without which a regime would be illegitimate in terms of its own values. For instance, competitive elections are fundamental political institutions in the United States because they implement the value of political equality. Fundamental values are those

This chapter is an expanded version of William H. Overholt, "An Organizational Conflict Theory of Revolution," *American Behavioral Scientist,* Vol. 20, No. 4 (March/April 1977), pp. 493–519, © 1977 Sage Publications, Inc.

that serve as basic legitimizing principles for political systems. The reference to illegitimacy of means in the eyes of the old regime eliminates the logical possibility that the changes in groups, values, and institutions would result from the normal and accepted processes of the system, such as from elections in a democracy; such a situation does not conform to most intuitive conceptions of revolution.

This definition includes as revolutions the French, Russian, Nazi, Meiji, Chinese (1911–49), Cuban, and Mexican revolutions, as well as successful revitalization movements and the transformation that occurred in China from the disintegration of the later Han dynasty to the stabilization of the T'ang dynasty. It excludes simple coups, imperial conquest, wars of independence, civil wars that are mere struggles for power, transformations of the international system, political changes that do not overthrow the central government, and nonpolitical changes (though the transformations of institutions and values during a revolution virtually always coincide with major socioeconomic transformations).

THE NATURE OF REVOLUTION

Revolutions are, above all, unlimited struggles between political organizations. An insurgent organization battles with the government organization and with other insurgent organizations for control of the society. Organization has been neglected until recently by theorists in favor of the analyses of sources of discontent, economic trends, ideology, military strategy, and general disharmony.[2] All of these are important, but the creation, maintenance, and destruction of political organizations is the central theme of revolution and the central preoccupation of revolutionaries. Discontent without organization is a mere school of guppies in an establishment sea, and brilliant military strategy not backed by a disciplined organization is just so many squirts of strategic ink.

An organizational conflict perspective on revolution integrates a variety of earlier partial theories. A revolutionary (or governmental) conflict organization in a large and complex society will have a Great Man at the top, surrounded by a Conspiratorial Elite, drawing resources from discontented (or satisfied) Masses, and integrated by Ideas and by a division of labor designed to maximize Harmony. A logic of intense organizational struggle determines the participants, causes, precipitants, strategies, sequences, and many of the consequences of revolution. Each side in the struggle must acquire organizational resources, use them appropriately to build an organization, then acquire strategic resources, and use those to subdue opponents.

THE PARTICIPANTS IN REVOLUTION

Insurgent Organization

A revolutionary party in a large and complex society must eventually face organized, relatively skillful opposition with substantial conflict resources. It must, therefore, be able to cope with heavy decision loads and high need for coordination. It needs an "ability to adapt itself immediately to the most diverse and rapidly changing conditions of struggle."[3] If there is a moderately effective government to combat, these requirements imply emphasis on a small central organization with extremely concentrated organizational resources. Such an organization also maximizes its ability to remain secret and its ability to manipulate other organizations.[4] The successful organization requires extremely high internal cohesion, access to manipulable mass organizations, and good strategic resources and leadership.

The organizational requirements of revolution imply heavy emphasis on acquisition of those resources necessary to organization: *visible and salient goals* (hereafter "motivational resources"), *available time* (or availability), *communications, organizational skills,* and *autonomy,* or funds with which to acquire these. Ideological unity is imperative. Purging or splitting away from dissident factions often becomes preferable to acceptance of weakened discipline. Discussion of varied viewpoints remains acceptable only up to a point, and any sign of organized factions within the larger party or government becomes intolerable. Training of leadership, construction of communication networks, and institutionalization of sources of income to ensure the continuous availability of members become tasks of the highest priority. Discipline is stressed by emphasizing subordination of the individual to the organization, by involving as many aspects of the member's life in the organization as possible, by compromising the members so that they lose their autonomy with respect to nonparty activities, and by emphasizing the viciousness of the enemy. Revolutionary groups that cannot or will not amass sufficient organizational resources and employ appropriate organizational strategies are doomed to failure against all but the most helpless governments.

Some special groups are disqualified from playing sustained roles in revolutions because of their lack of resources. A lumpenproletariat typically lacks organizational skills, leadership, communications, and common purpose. Peasants who live in thinly populated areas with poor communications, and who lack traditions of cooperative organization, are also often disqualified. But other peasants, such as Chinese rice growers, may be packed into dense villages, aware of common problems, with intricate communications nets and a complex network of formal organizations that train leaders and followers in organizational skills.[5] Revolutionary elite nuclei frequently move from one social group to another, seeking appropriate organizational resources, particularly where they face a strong government. Thus, the Chinese Communists initially tried to organize urban workers, then various combinations of rural groups, until they got the proper resources. In modern revolutions, the competitive struggle for organizational resources mobilizes all sectors of society.[6]

Failure to utilize adequate strategies of organization may also render groups impotent in revolution. Anarchists and many contemporary student groups whose ideology is antiorganizational can contribute to social disorder but can never defeat an organized government or insurgent competitor. "Since the acquisition of power requires the development of hierarchy and discipline at some point, an egalitarian movement starts out at an initial disadvantage in relation to its competitors. Sooner or later, if it is to be effective, it must compromise with its initial principles."[7] The Philippine Huks failed for lack of revolutionary organizational strategy as well as for lack of resources; by emphasizing size rather than discipline, and social harmony rather than struggle, they enfeebled themselves.[8] Democratic parties, which usually are loosely organized, are difficult to discipline and usually fall by the wayside in revolutionary struggle.

The importance of organization in revolution does not imply that all revolutions display highly disciplined organizations. Spontaneous disintegration of the government and weakness of potential opponents can provide an opportunity for an insurgent group that is only moderately organized. The Mexican revolution saw the rise of disciplined organizations only in its later phases, and the Cuban revolution was more noteworthy for the organizational weakness of the government and other potential insurgents than for the organizational genius of Fidel Castro's group. Indeed, "Western" revolutions are characterized primarily by the weakness of the government rather than by the initial strength of the insurgents.[9] In addition, organizational strategies improve over time, and organizational resources multiply with economic development, so modern revolutions display greater perfection of organization than most earlier revolutions. Nonetheless, the more highly organized revolutionary party has an advantage that is usually decisive, and there are broad strategies and structures of organization that change only gradually; the conflict parties of medieval cities reminded Weber of the Bolsheviks.[10]

Superficially contradicting the need for a small, highly coordinated revolutionary elite is the obvious need of both government and insurgency for control over broad population groups. Control over such groups is both the goal of and a crucial means for revolution. The contradiction is only apparent, although coordination of additional people requires expenditure of resources. By serving as a reservoir of personnel and funds, mass groups supply organizational resources necessary to the maintenance of the elite.[11] By providing intelligence and (limited) action in response to manipulation by the elite, they supply crucial strategic resources. Coordination of large groups requires precisely the disciplined, powerful elite that is also necessary for strategic reasons. Expenditure of resources is usually minimized because the cooperation of entire groups can often be obtained merely by capturing or coopting their leadership.

Not just any masses will do. Great leverage over a group can be obtained by capturing the leadership of a mass group only if the mass group is itself organized.[12] Otherwise, the "leadership" has no real control over its supposed members. The insurgent and the government must therefore seek organized hierarchical groups and also seek to increase their organization and degree of hierarchy.

Manipulation of a mass group requires access to that group; put another way, it requires motivational resources (visibility and salience of issues) as well as technical resources. The combination of elite and mass groups can be viewed as a single group whose ability to organize can be evaluated. Where leaders of the mass group perceive a common identity or common goals, there are no difficulties so long as the mass group members feel no strong antipathy to the revolutionary elite or remain unaware of the manipulation. Where members of the revolutionary elite are also members of the mass group, and where they possess a minimal level of legitimacy, they can often seize the leadership of the mass group simply by being the most active and highly organized faction within the group. Where the leadership positions cannot be directly captured, the mass group can often be covertly manipulated into active cooperation or friendly passivity through log rolling or (sometimes specious) promises of future support. "Friendly passivity may sometimes decide the outcome of the battle."[13] Any organized group that cannot be manipulated into active support or friendly passivity constitutes a potentially dangerous resource for an opponent; frequently, such groups can be hobbled by depriving them of one or more organizational resources through disrupted communications, assassinated leadership, liquidated financial bases, and induced factionalism.

Government Organization

The government must also be appropriately organized to combat its revolutionary opponents. The quality of governmental organization can be assessed in terms of three components: the executive leadership, the institutional structure, and the social base. The criteria for the executive leadership, which comprises the chief executive and other top leaders, are the degrees to which it is patriotic; honest; politically, militarily, and economically skillful; and unified. The criteria for judging the institutions are those institutions' quality of personnel, performance of their tasks, adaptability in crisis situations, and coherence in the policies they implement. The social base is a strong one to the extent that it consists of organized social groups (military, civil service, middle class, industrial leadership, peasants, and so on) who obey the government and provide it with resources.[14]

If both government and opposition possess sufficient organizational resources and appropriate strategies of organization, then full-blown revolutionary conflict is possible. If all potential revolutionary groups lack organizational resources or are misallocating them, then revolution is extremely unlikely so long as the government is even minimally capable. Conversely, a government that is incapable of maintaining its organization, either because of declining resources or because of catastrophic organizational errors, will fall in the face of any significant revolutionary challenge.

THE CAUSES OF REVOLUTION

The causes of revolution are any events or processes that cast up an insurgent group or coalition that is stronger than the government or that weaken the government until it is weaker than some insurgent group or coalition. The decisive strengthening or weakening can come in the form of improved or worsened organizational resources, organizational strategies, conflict resources, conflict strategies, or some combination of these.

In the theoretical literature on revolution, there is a strong emphasis on the strength of the insurgents or the disintegration of the society. But at least equal emphasis should be placed on potential disintegration of the government. The decline of the central government is the principal feature of the French, Cuban, Mexican, Later Han, 1911 Chinese, Iranian, and many lesser revolutions.[15] The decline of the center may result from a decline in organizational resources. The population may grow discontented and provide fewer taxes, fewer leaders, less obedience, and a weaker communications network than previously. Prerevolutionary regimes frequently experience fiscal crises and partial desertion of their intellectual leadership. A decline in subsidization by a foreign power may produce organizational disintegration in a dependent regime like Batista's Cuba.

Inadequate organizational strategies can also fatally weaken the government. The French and 1911 Chinese revolutions were immediately preceded by disruptive reforms that paralyzed important governmental operations.

Prerevolutionary governments have been seriously weakened by gradual devolution of power to a landed gentry (as in China), by giving key positions to incompetents, and by alienation of the intelligentsia.

Fatal weakness can also result from deterioration in conflict resources or from poor conflict strategies. The most important military-strategic resources are military power, strategic geographic position, and intelligence.[16] Relative military power in the sense of deployable firepower is sensitive to the economic position of the government, which is in turn affected by the extent to which the population supports the government and to foreign supplies. Intelligence, while partially susceptible to outside influence, is primarily a function of the extent to which the government can use the population as a communications net. Given excellent intelligence, a government can destroy a domestic insurgency before it becomes a serious threat. But a government whose population will not supply information because of discontent or fear, or whose officials have lost or failed to seek access to popular knowledge of potential or actual opponents, has lost a crucial battle. Finally, the government that employs inadequate strategies may lose even if its forces are superior in firepower. Chiang Kai-shek's enormous armies constantly humiliated by Mao's tiny forces, and Diem pitifully preparing conventional armies to fight the Vietcong guerrillas, are the archetypes of this form of defeat.

The process of building a strong and successful revolutionary organization is almost a mirror image of the process of weakening a governmental organization. New conflict resources (such as external military aid) may tip the balance between a government and a highly organized committed insurgency. A new conflict strategy (such as heavier reliance on guerrilla warfare) may change the balance of forces. Practitioners of revolution know how important strategy and strategic resources are, but theorists of the disharmony, idealist, and mass uprising variety typically neglect them. Such neglect appears to result in part from the fact that most of the famous and well-studied revolutions began with organizational collapse of the government prior to any powerful military challenge from insurgents. The Chinese revolution was a partial exception to this tendency of great revolutions to begin with governmental collapse, and increasing professionalization of revolutionaries—together with revolutionaries' access to massive external aid—may provide more examples in the future of revolutions against governments that are not organizationally helpless. The outcomes of such revolutions will depend to a greater extent on strategic factors, and analysis of them will require strategic analysis—just as analysis of the 1949 Chinese revolution requires study of Mao's guerrilla strategy.

Nonetheless, there is a sense in which greater stress on the building of an insurgent organization than on strategic factors is justified. Strategic factors have greatly reduced significance so long as there are gross disparities in the organizational capabilities of the opponents; guns are worthless, or even worse than worthless, in the absence of a highly organized army to wield them, but a powerful organization can be formidable even in the absence of the military varieties of strategic resources. It can seek to deny organizational and conflict resources to the government as well as to penetrate and sabotage governmental organization. We therefore focus on the conditions that may lead to creation of a powerful insurgent organization.

Given a discontented group that has accepted a revolutionary ideology and that possesses an adequate strategy of organization, the creation of a powerful revolutionary organization may be a consequence of access to additional organizational resources. Economic growth is an obvious source of such additional resources, for economic growth brings with it new communications, autonomy, and, as a result of urbanization and population growth, increased availability for many groups as a consequence of rising income, and so forth. In addition to the absolute rise in resources, individuals with rising incomes may, without changing their political attitudes, be willing to donate a higher proportion of their personal resources to political groups.[17] These augmented technical resources become available to a variety of groups in the society, usually including the government, and their use by one group does not necessarily deny their use by another group. However, some established governments may be unable to utilize or even recognize increments of resources as effectively as newly organizing groups. For instance, a traditional monarchy cannot tap the resources of the peasants, because it would be overthrown by the aristocracy before it could utilize those resources. For this reason, among others, revolutions frequently, but not invariably, occur in modernizing societies experiencing long-term economic growth.[18]

Revolution caused by acquisition of new resources can also result from processes other than economic or social modernization. An outstanding example is the acquisition by the Chinese Communists of greatly increased autonomy when the Japanese pushed Chiang Kai-shek's troops out of Northern China, thus preventing him from destroying Communist organizations and making village elders more alarmed by Japanese terror than by Communist organizing.[19]

In addition to augmenting the technical resources for organization, social and economic modernization frequently augment the visibility and salience of potential sources of discontent. Modernization produces expectations that cannot always be satisfied,[20] produces disorienting mobility both upward and downward,[21] mobilizes people out of old beliefs and norms before it provides them with new ones, and produces groups of people who cannot tolerate their own identities and seek new identities through violence.[23] Revolutionaries often come from areas or groups whose conditions are improving[24] and at least sometimes tend to be people who assume that they can do better in life than their parents.[25] Discontent may also spread among groups subjected to crime or guerrillas because of the response of other groups to social change.

Construction of a powerful revolutionary organization may be caused by a revolutionary group's acquisition of a new organizational strategy that more efficiently provides new organizational forms for emulation by discontented groups. Ideologies like Leninism provide strategies of mobilization that are especially tailored for revolutionary purposes. Of course, the erroneous emulation of an inapplicable imported strategy can also destroy a revolutionary movement, as was partly the case with the Philippine Hukbalahaps' emulation of Maoist strategy.[26]

STRATEGIES OF REVOLUTION: THE CONDUCT OF REVOLUTIONARY STRUGGLE

Revolutionary struggle between government and insurgent (or insurgents) is conducted in accordance with some explicit or implicit conflict strategies. (Since the goal of revolution is successful conflict, we shall refer in this chapter to "conflict strategies" rather than using the broader but clumsier term, "goal attainment strategies.") Governmental and insurgent strategies can most usefully be analyzed along lines suggested by the basic paradigm of political organization. The opponents attack one another's organizational resources, organizational strategy, conflict resources, or conflict strategy, or some combination of these. (See Figure 7.4) The choice of a particular strategy is dictated by the strategic knowledge of the leaders of each side and by the adequacy and vulnerability of opponents' resources and strategies.

The ultimate goal of the insurgent is to destroy or capture the organizational resources of the government. To the extent that the insurgency fails to attain this goal, the revolution is abortive. The government's goals need not be so all-encompassing. To the extent that the government can protect its own organizational resources and organizational strategy, it wins, even if the insurgent organization remains intact and active.

Within the general category of strategies focused upon the opponents' organizational resources, one can classify strategies according to the particular organizational resource or set of resources under attack. Certain strategies attempt to create a general strain on all of the opponent's resources. For instance, an insurgency may stimulate massive civil disobedience in widely dispersed locations and may attempt to disrupt tax collection; such a strategy maximizes the government's need for resources while minimizing its inflow of resources. Likewise, a government may engage in continuous pursuit of guerrillas in order to impose maximum demands on guerrilla resources and to prevent institutionalization of the insurgent's line of communication.

Other strategies focus on depriving government or insurgency of specific resources that may be particularly scarce or particularly vulnerable. To deprive a government of its motivational resources, an insurgency may employ propaganda and disruptive tactics to create a sense of demoralization. The demoralization could consist of weariness, a sense of inevitable loss, or a sense of illegitimacy. The government may respond by attempting to deprive the insurgency of motivational resources through reforms.

Other strategies within the broad category of those focused on organizational resources attempt to deprive the opponent of key technical resources. In societies where political leadership is scarce, an insurgency may follow the example of the Viet Cong in attempting to disrupt government organization by systematic assassination of provincial leadership. The government could follow the Philippine and Taiwan strategies of massive cooptation of potential insurgent leaders into government. Strategies oriented toward depriving an opponent of communications include technological blockage of radio communications (as with martial law in Poland, 1981–82), prohibitions on meetings of groups that might otherwise organize, and various techniques for overloading a group's communication channels. Strategies focused on depriving the opponent of availability include cutting off food, jailing potential opponents, massive movement of populations away from the insurgents (as was accomplished through urbanization in Vietnam), and even genocide. Finally, strategies focused on deprivation of autonomy include continuous surveillance and threats of reprisal against individuals, families, or villages. Once again, the decision to focus on depriving the opponent of a particular resource is based on calculations of scarcity and vulnerability.

Strategies focused on the organizational structure of the opponent typically attempt to fragment the opponent's organization or to immobilize the opponent's decision making or implementation of decisions. The lines of fragmentation can be religious, political, economic, social, racial, or geographic. Immobilization can be accomplished by overloading the adversary's decision-making processes or by inducing factionalism or structural contradictions. The decision process may be overloaded either by making those processes themselves excessively complex and unwieldy (as is the case with some coalition governments) or by overloading the court system or the legislature with a burden of decisions. A government that succeeds in getting a revolutionary party to focus on winning democratic elections and thereby spreading itself too thin may hobble its adversary through structural contradictions. An insurgency that forces a landlord-based government to appeal for peasant support may hobble a government through structural or policy contradictions.

Strategies focused on conflict resources emphasize obtaining funds, weapons, geographic position, intelligence, and political legitimacy, and denying the same resources to the adversary. Both government and insurgent seek foreign sources of supply, improved tax bases, self-manufacture of weaponry, diplomatic recognition, and various kinds of intelligence apparatus, and they seek to prevent the opponent from obtaining the same. Where the opponents cannot be denied access to needed resources, it is often possible to hamper their use of them or to turn their access to resources against them. The opponents' currency may be inflated by counterfeiting, their supplies of weaponry may be polluted by booby-trapping, their information may be rendered useless by providing false information to confuse them. Strategies for denying conflict resources to the opponent range from the classic military tactic of cutting the adversary's lines of supply to the more sophisticated technique of destroying a political party so that the government will lack the intelligence provided by political lines of communication with peripheral villages.

A final category of conflict strategies consists of those that attempt to render the opponents' conflict strategy and potential strategies harmless without necessarily denying them access to conflict or organizational resources or attempting to disrupt their organizational structure. The simplest kinds of such strategies attempt to render the opponent's strategy impotent or self-defeating through the use of *agents provocateurs* or through infiltrating agents who pervert the opponent's strategy by providing misleading advice or by directly making self-defeating strategic decisions. A second set of such strategies is typified by various applications of game theory and deterrence theory that seek to channel the use of the opponent's conflict resources in ways that sterilize them. Insurgent military forces may lure government forces far from the areas of most significant political activity. The government may permit an insurgent group to develop lucrative economic activities that are not threatened as long as the insurgent behaves within certain bounds. The use of this kind of strategy tends to be tactical when employed by insurgents, because the insurgent must always keep in mind the eventual goal of destroying or capturing the government's organizational resources. However, the domestication of an insurgent through this kind of strategy may sometimes serve as an ultimate government strategy.

POLITICAL-ECONOMIC SYSTEM CHARACTERISTICS

As with most systems, an overall political system is considerably more than the sum of its parts. Having examined a regime's executive leadership, its government institutions, and its social coalition, and having conducted the same analysis of its adversaries, one knows a great deal about the system. However, by looking at the system as a whole, one can arrive at broader characterizations of its strengths and vulnerabilities— that is, of the social processes that strengthen or weaken the opposing organizations. Different kinds of political systems display different characteristic strengths and weaknesses, and a good analysis of a given system should begin from a knowledge of the characteristic strengths and weaknesses of that kind of system and then proceed to more detailed analysis.

Detailed examination of the strengths and weaknesses of all major forms of political systems has of course been a preoccupation of philosophers and political scientists throughout history, and even a brief summary of the resulting accumulation of knowledge would take us far afield. Nonetheless, it will be useful to outline briefly a few examples of the kinds of system analysis mentioned here.

The *classic large empire*, ruled by an emperor through a centralized bureaucracy and a geographically extended nobility, possesses strengths and weaknesses that give it a distinctive life cycle. When a Chinese dynasty, to take one obvious example, is conquering its opponent, it is a highly centralized, highly disciplined, highly meritocratic fighting force. It is highly responsive to the demands of its leader, because disunity would disqualify it as a challenger to the old regime. The leader in turn is a highly disciplined, skillful figure, because outside the functioning of an existing empire no sufficient base of political and military support could be acquired by a leader lacking these qualities. However, once the insurgent dynasty takes power, things begin to change rapidly. The emperors henceforth maintain their position through heredity rather than skill and, given the lack of external discipline, an eventual descent into sloth invariably occurs. Various parts of the bureaucracy eventually acquire exclusive jurisdiction over important aspects of the empire and become relatively autonomous entities. Nobles ruling distant areas of the empire initially hold power only through their official relationship to the emperor, but eventually gain hereditary title to estates and positions and acquire the capability to act independently of the central power. Sloth at the center and the inexorable accretion of power to increasingly autonomous domains at the empire's periphery bring about an eventual loss of unity. Meanwhile, under traditional economic conditions, centuries of peace produce a population that eventually overwhelms the capacity of the economy to support it. These forces eventually render the kingdom vulnerable to internal revolt and external invasion.

The *modern monarch* faces a somewhat different set of problems. The monarch in a modernizing economy must cope with four critical facts. First, he is dependent upon the support of a traditional aristocracy. Second, modernization induces increasing demands from the peasantry for improved social and economic conditions. Third, the security of the country depends upon the development of a modern military, which is likely in turn to see the security of the country as dependent not only upon acquisition of modern arms but also upon economic and social modernization in forms inconsistent with the traditional position of the monarch. Fourth, economic development brings with it an educated intelligentsia and middle class, which are likely to find rule by hereditary monarchy anathema to their meritocratic beliefs.

The king or queen who seeks to retain power by relying on the traditional aristocrats will eventually be overthrown by the gradually mobilizing peasantry, by a modernizing military that fears peasant radicalism, or by a modernizing military and middle class that regard rapid economic development as the key to security from external danger. The monarch who abandons the aristocracy in search of an alliance with the peasantry will antagonize the powerful aristocracy long before the support of the peasants becomes sufficiently organized and active to replace the old support of the aristocracy. Appeal to the military or the middle class is virtually certain to be unsuccessful, because the whole theory of legitimacy and the whole architecture of a monarchical regime will be anathema to modernizing bureaucrats and entrepreneurs. Similarly, any effort to retain the traditional system by impeding the modernization process will eventually antagonize all four major groups because they will be aware of their country's inferiority to more rapidly modernizing foreign powers.

A characteristic modern *military dictatorship* initially has the advantages of decisive action and strong ability to implement decisions when it takes over the government. However, typical difficulties quickly set in. As the society modernizes, powerful social pressure groups emerge and the economy becomes increasingly complex. A small military elite becomes increasingly incapable of handling the resulting complex problems. The difficulty in coping with complex problems is exacerbated because the repression characteristic of a military regime usually deprives it of much needed information about the problems and discontents of the society until those problems and discontents become unmanageably large. Moreover, the political divisions of the society gradually infiltrate the former professional unity of the military, depriving it of its principal advantages, namely unity and decisiveness. Gradually the military regime becomes indecisive, politicized, corrupt, unpopular, and, when it recognizes its position, demoralized.

Democracies characteristically have the advantages of broad public support, ability to change executive leadership as needed, and ability to rejuvenate deteriorating governmental institutions through an alliance of executive leadership and broad popular pressures. In industrialized societies these strengths are balanced against a tendency for liberty to become licentiousness, a tendency for strong beliefs to be watered down in universal skepticism, and a certain institutional flabbiness that appears to develop as a concomitant of long periods of prosperity and of public demands for improved welfare even at the cost of institutional and financial discipline. So far in this century the strengths of the industrial democracies have heavily outweighed their weaknesses.

However, Third World democracies have had their share of problems. In a typical Third World context of weak central government institutions, democracy typically has unintended consequences. Democracy facilitates the organization of strong pressure groups, which press on the weak central government institutions. Those institutions give way, with the result of frequent political disorder. Because powerful labor, business, education, military, and civil service groups all impose financial demands on the weak government, another major consequence is inflation. Typically, in Third World countries, the political parties consist largely of patron-client systems where patronage is the predominant political consideration. Civil service and executive leadership positions are doled out to political supporters who lack competence, thereby perpetuating and exacerbating the problem of weak government institutions. The result is a cycle of disorder and inflation that alienates the military, the middle class, and the peasantry alike, depriving the democratic government of the broad base of public support characteristic of industrial democracies. Moreover, democracies are frequently unable to equalize income distributions, particularly in Third World countries badly in need of land reform. Elected parliaments usually are dominated by landlords and administered by bureaucracies staffed with the sons and daughters of landlords. The parliament will seek to avoid legislating land reform, and the executive will resist implementing reforms if they are legislated. Most democratic legal systems copied from advanced democracies heavily emphasize the protection of property and, even when they do not, the adversary judicial procedures associated with democracy in the West give the landlords enormous advantages in combating resourceless peasants. The result often is a loss of support for the regime even among those groups that could normally be expected most strongly to support democracy, together with violent attacks from a peasantry that perceives democracy as class-based, from a middle class that fears loss of its savings to inflation, and from a military that regards the incompetence and weaknesses of government institutions as a threat to security. Brazil in 1964 and South Korea in 1961 are noteworthy examples of a phenomenon that has occurred throughout much of the Third World.

Communist systems possess the advantages of a disciplined party with a coherent theory of society, an extraordinary intelligence apparatus, and a bureaucratic system that is often quite disciplined or at least firmly under the control of the executive leadership. The characteristic problems of communist regimes are bureaucratic stagnation, ideological obsolescence that impedes modernization and eventually stimulates public cynicism, alienation of the intelligentsia, the problem of keeping an increasingly large and powerful working class under party control, inability to modernize agriculture without abandoning collectivist ideals, and, in the client states of Eastern Europe, a merging of nationalism with social discontent.

OVERVIEW

Viewing regimes and oppositions as complex organizations enables one to analyze the stability of political systems while taking into account the full historical complexity of a society. Currently popular theories can be utilized in many cases as specific components of this larger organizational view. Insights of revolutionary leadership studies can provide some information about the qualities of the executive leadership of a revolutionary organization. The theories of Lenin and Selznick help to analyze the institutional structure of conflicting political organizations. Theories about frustration-aggression and economic inequality can give clues to the possible attitudes of such social groups as workers and farmers. But none of these partial theories provides any solid basis for a forecast in the absence of larger organizational perspectives. The analyses useful to a forecaster consist not of recent volumes but of such earlier works as Aristotle's classic description of the characteristic problems and cycles associated with various kinds of political systems, an analysis that has been helpfully supplemented by Max Weber and Samuel Huntington; Alexis de Tocqueville's description of a disintegrating regime in *The Old Regime and the French Revolution;* Marx's description of rapidly evolving social coalitions in "The Eighteenth Brumaire of Louis Bonaparte"; and biographies of the great conservatives and revolutionaries. A qualitative but systematic theory, focused on issues of political organization, can encompass the partial insights of such authors, and it can facilitate systematic examination of the consequences for political stability of economic and social change.

NOTES

1. See William H. Overholt, *Political Risk* (London: Euromoney, 1982), chapters IV and V.
2. For a survey, see William H. Overholt, "The Sources of Radicalism and Revolution," in *Radicalism: Its Sources, Aspirations, Strategies and Consequences*, Scwcryn Bialer, ed., (Boulder, Colo.: Wantview Press, 1977).
3. V. I. Lenin, *What Is to Be Done?* (New York: International Publishers, 1943), p. 162.
4. *Ibid.*, pp. 116–17.
5. William H. Overholt, "Martial Law, Revolution and Democracy in the Philippines," *Southeast Asia Quarterly* 2, no. 2 (Spring 1972).
6. Samuel P. Huntington, *Political Order in Changing Societies* (New Haven, Conn.: Yale University Press, 1968), chapter 5.
7. Barrington Moore, *Political Power and Social Theory* (New York: Harper, 1965), p. 14.
8. Overholt, "Martial Law."
9. Huntington, *Political Order,* chapter 5.
10. Max Weber, "Politics as a Vocation," in *Max Weber,* H. H. Gerth and C. Wright Mills, eds., (New York: Oxford University Press, 1946), p. 88.
11. Lenin, *What Is to Be Done?*, p. 116.
12. Philip Selznick, *The Organizational Weapon: A Study of Bolshevik Strategy and Tactics* (New York: McGraw-Hill, 1952), p. 81.
13. Lenin, *What Is to Be Done,* p. 121.
14. For an extended discussion, see Overholt, *Political Risk,* chapter IV.
15. For instance, see John R. Gillis, "Political Decay in the European Revolutions," *World Politics* 2, (April, 1972): 344–70.
16. Nathan Leites and C. Wolf Jr., *Rebellion and Authority* (Chicago: Markham, 1970), p. 147.
17. *Ibid.*, p. 147.
18. Crane Brinton, *The Anatomy of Revolution* (New York: Vintage, 1965); James C. Davies, "Toward a Theory of Revolution," *American Sociological Review* 27 (February 1962): 5–19; Gil Carl Alroy, "Revolutionary Conditions in Latin America," *Review of Politics* 29 (July 1967): 417–22.
19. Franz Schurman, *Ideology and Organization in Communist China*

(Berkeley, Calif.: University of California Press, 1966), p. xli.

20.   Davies, "Toward a Theory"; Ted Robert Gurr, "Psychological Factors in Civil Strife," *World Politics* 20 (January 1968): 245–78; Ted Robert Gurr, *Why Men Rebel* (Princeton, N.J.: Princeton University Press, 1970).

21.   Sir William Arthur Lewis, "Commonwealth Address" (1963), summarized in Lawrence L. Stone, "Theories of Revolution," *World Politics* 17 (January 1966): 159–76; A. B. Hollingshead, R. Ellis, and E. Kirby, "Social Mobility and Mental Illness," *American Sociological Review* XIX (October 1954): 577–84.

22.   Mancur Olson Jr., "Rapid Growth as a Destabilizing Force," *Journal of Economic History* 23 (December 1963): 529–52; Karl W. Deutsch, "Social Mobilization and Political Development," in *Political Development and Social Change*, Jason L. Finkle and Richard W. Gable, eds. (New York: Wiley, 1968), pp. 205–26.

23.   Karl Marx, *Capital* (New York: Modern Library, n.d.), pp. 708–09; Eric Hoffer, *The True Believer: Thoughts on the Nature of Mass Movements* (New York: Time, 1963), pp. 13, 42, 62; William Kornhauser, *The Politics of Mass Society* (New York: Free Press, 1959), pp. 108–09; Hanna Arendt, *Totalitarianism* (New York: Harcourt, Brace and World, 1968), pp. 172–75; Erich Fromm, *Escape from Freedom* (New York: Avon, 1967), p. 45.

24.   Alexis de Tocqueville, *The Old Regime and the French Revolution*, trans. Stuart Gilbert (Garden City, N.Y.; Anchor, 1955), pp. 175–77; Lucien Pye, *Guerrilla Communism in Malaya: Its Social and Political Meaning* (Princeton, N.J.: Princeton University Press, 1956), p. 130 *ff;* Alroy, "Revolutionary Conditions," p. 419.

25.   Pye, *Guerrilla Communism*.

26.   Overholt, "Martial Law."

Chapter 9

Korea: A Case Study

To illustrate the use of organizational analysis, this chapter will employ the theory to analyze three periods of modern South Korean history: the collapse of the democratic regime of 1960–61, the stability of the Park Chung Hee regime from 1961–79, and the transition away from Park in the early 1980s.

THE MILITARY REVOLUTION IN SOUTH KOREA

Democracy fell in South Korea after less than a year. To understand why, one must analyze the organization of the regime. As outlined in Chapter 7, this means analyzing the commitment, unity, and competence of three levels of the regime's organization: the executive leadership, the institutional structure, and the social support.

Executive leadership in South Korea during its brief period of democracy (1960–61) provides a case in which a weak top leader reflected the organizational weakness of a whole regime. After the 1960 fall of Syngman Rhee, and after a brief interim government, an election brought to power the Democratic Party and its leader, Chang Myon. The victorious Democratic Party was divided into a new faction led by a weak leader, Chang Myon, and an old faction determined to prevent the success of the new faction. Factionalism ensured the emergence of weak parties and weak individuals in numerous ways. The old faction collaborated with former members of Syngman Rhee's Liberal Party, thereby weakening the Democratic Party. Members of the Democratic Party defeated in nominating procedures simply ran on the party's ticket anyway, thereby ensuring division of the party's votes and defeat of both nominees. The two factions engaged in violent physical attacks on each other. Mutual slander became a principal form of competition between the factions. Moreover, within the new and the old factions, there was equally serious factionalism.

Both factions were led by political weaklings. Chang Myon was a passive, indecisive figure who managed to get on very well during the

Japanese period and therefore lacked strong nationalist credentials. Chang maintained his position in part by reneging on a promise to his principal rival that the latter would receive the nomination for the vice-presidency in 1960, in return for stepping aside in Chang's favor in 1956. After the death of this rival, Cho, the old faction also nominated a weakling, Yun Po Sun, whose main virtue was that he never offended anyone. He also had managed to do well during the Japanese period and had served as an official in the Syngman Rhee government, thereby impairing both his nationalist and his democratic credentials. Chang Myon subsequently became prime minister and Yun Po Sun became president. Chang Myon repeatedly demonstrated political and physical cowardice—for instance, by going into hiding when a conflict was likely. "Yun's ascendence and stature on the political scene was primarily due to his wealth, some interest and ambition in politics, and his inability or unwillingness to undertake any activities such as business or scholarly work."[1]

Turning to the *institutional structure* of the regime, the party structure of the day ensured the rise of such weaklings to the highest political positions. Syngman Rhee's intimidation campaigns weeded out some potentially strong political figures. The rest were weeded out by the determination of the opposition party factions to bring to power weak men whom they could manipulate. Given this background, it was relatively predictable that the regime would behave in inconstant and opportunistic fashion and would quickly fall. Similarly, given the inexperience and frequent disinterest of the principal party politicians in economic and military affairs, and given their focus upon appointing officials in accordance with patronage considerations to the exclusion of merit, it was predictable that the policies would lead to military and economic weakness.

The corrupt, incompetent patronage politics of the democratic regime, its inability to implement its (theoretically quite sound) economic program, and the widespread fear of military incapacity and northern invasion that resulted from its incompetence eroded *public support* for the democratic regime. A purge of the military, the police, and the civil service alienated them without cowing them. Middle class support waned. Students, leftist political groups, and radical labor groups took heart from the evident weakness of the regime and promoted public disorder.

The Korean case also illustrates the democratic regime's lack of another principal virtue, namely *unity*. A regime based on no particular principles other than opportunistic factionalism will invariably be a weak regime. Similarly, a regime built upon strong but conflicting ideologies will likely be weak. Korean factionalism, in North and South alike, provides vivid illustrations of the dangers of factionalism.

As indicated below, the military opposition that overthrew the Korean democratic regime of Chang Myon possessed strengths that corresponded to the democratic regime's weaknesses: unity, principled patriotism, organizational efficiency, and concern for economic and military performance.

REPRESSIVE STABILITY, 1961–79

Just as democratic South Korea provided an outstanding example of leadership and institutional division and incompetence, and resultant loss of public support, so authoritarian South Korea under Park Chung Hee provided an unusual example of regime unity and skill. South Korea had the advantage of being a homogeneous society that had reacted with relative uniformity to the horrible experience of a brutal northern invasion. The society therefore provided the basis for building a unified regime.

The New Executive Leadership

Patriotic, modern, and honest elements within the military outmaneuvered and purged their competitors within the military. Under the leadership of Park Chung Hee, a dedicated patriot who had earned a reputation as the only honest general in the Korean Army, they proceeded to undertake the same kind of institution building within the government that had previously occurred within the military. The result was an imposition of unity upon a previously factionalized polity and the introducion of merit principles into hitherto corrupt bureaucracies run solely on the principle of patronage.

Rather than maintaining direct power, as so many other Third World military regimes had done, the Korean military quickly retreated from direct exercise of political authority, partly driven by its own motives and partly by U.S. pressure, and proceeded to coopt the most dynamic civilian leadership. Wave after wave of the finest available professional talent was drawn into the Korean government by a civilianized leadership determined to impose modernity upon the country. Japanese-trained officials were replaced by American military-trained personnel. Then came a wave of Koreans trained by American civilians, including successively natural scientists and engineers in the early 1960s and economists in the late 1960s, followed by political scientists and sociologists in the 1970s. South Korea, unlike North Korea and even Japan, was remarkably open to foreign-trained leadership and, unlike most other societies in Asia, was open to young leaders in their thirties and forties, rather than being run by old men like Chiang Kai-Shek, Mao Tse-tung, and a series of elderly Japanese leaders. The ability of the South Korean elite to absorb such people was ensured by institutions that will be further discussed below.

Governmental Institutions

Institutions provide the information on which executive policies will be based, implement the policies, and report on the success or failure of the policies. Therefore, if the government institutions are incompetent or corrupt, the executive leadership may be confused by inaccurate information, and its policies may become mere words devoid of consequence.

A review of South Korea's principal institutions indicates that it has achieved institutional qualities parallel to the qualities of its executive leadership.

The South Korean *military* grew out of a history of Yi dynasty insistence upon maintaining civilian control by ensuring the ineffectuality of the military, as well as a later history of Japanese determination not to develop effective Korean military institutions. The United States provided minor training programs for the South Koreans in the late 1940s, but did not emphasize them or fund them well, because the training programs were primarily a public relations screen to justify disengagement from Korea in 1948–49. However, during the Korean War, effective South Korean military units were trained and key institutions were created, namely the Command and General Staff school, the National Defense College, and, above all, the Korea Military Academy, which became a base of near-fanatical patriotism, honesty, and emphasis upon modern military training. Young officers like Park Chung Hee, trained at the Korea Military Academy, then cleaned up small units of South Korean military and later used those units as bases to overthrow the government and to conduct a purge of corrupt and incompetent senior officers.

By the late 1960s, the loyalty and discipline of the South Korean military were unchallenged by any observer. In some ways, their discipline became superior to their American counterparts. Unlike the U.S. Army in Korea, the Korean Army has no drug problem. By the late 1960s, North Korean infiltrators penetrated primarily through the U.S. division because South Korean forces were more efective than U.S. forces in stopping infiltration. By 1971, South Koreans manned the whole border of the demilitarized zone without any serious allegation that military risks resulted from such heavy responsibilities. South Korean troops proved extremely effective in Vietnam, partly because of superior discipline and partly because they did not rely so heavily as Americans on mobility and firepower. A feeling that their performance in Vietman had been superior to American performance finally terminated a morale prolem that had existed ever since the defeat by North Korea in 1950.

The institutional development of the South Korean military reflects an increasing emphasis upon discipline, honesty, and competence, a pattern of consistently superior performance under varied conditions, a willingness to exploit bright and well-trained young men and to promote them quickly even at the expense of influential senior officers, and the creation of numerous think tanks and other institutional innovations to ensure a constant inflow of innovations. Thus, although peacetime military units provide fewer overt indicators of their performance than most other societal institutions, the South Korean military is clearly a highly effective institution.

Similarly, South Korean *educational institutions* exhibit strong indicators of institutional quality. South Korea at independence lacked virtually all the basics of modern education, namely schools, teachers, and literacy. It possessed almost no non-Japanese teachers and virtually no textbooks in any language other than Japanese. Between 1945 and the late 1970s, South Korea's literacy rate rose from 22% to well over 90%. School registrations (primary, secondary, and vocational) rose from 1.4 million in 1945 to 9.8 million in 1980, and teachers from 20,000 to 225,000. During this period, traditional forms of education in the Confucian classics and in humanistic activities that were economically unproductive were transformed into a system that emphasized vocational programs and skills that would directly feed a modern economy. At the same time, the educational system provided a uniformity of access and training that greatly facilitated South Korea's achievement of an egalitarian income distribution. In most Third World countries, by contrast, education continues to emphasize the traditional professions rather than modern technical knowledge and to inure heavily to the benefit of an economic elite.

The system has adjusted rapidly to the changing needs of an extraordinarily booming economy, and began shifting successfully from pure teaching to a teaching and research emphasis. Despite problems, which include a traditional overemphasis on rote learning and a dissonance created by an effort to square democratically oriented textbooks with South Korean political realities, the system performed well in both quantitative and qualitative terms, adjusted to changing social circumstances, successfully attracted an extraordinarily talented cadre of teachers and administrators, changed successfully away from an impracticable American-model administrative system to a more centralized South Korean system, and successfully linked itself to the economic planning institutions and to the president's office through a series of think tanks and other institutional innovations.

A third institutional complex consists of those institutions oriented toward promoting growth of the *urban industrial economy* and of *trade*. These institutions, along with the rural development institutions, have faced a nearly impossible task. "In 1934 the Japanese governor estimated that every Spring he saw about half the Korean farmers scouring the country-side for bark and grass to eat."[2] The Korean economy in the 1950s and the early 1960s grew slowly and was marked by massive unemployment. However, after the institutional reforms promulgated by the Park Chung Hee government, Korea's growth rate soared, based largely on industrialization and trade growth. From 1962–77, Korea's average economic growth rate was 10.3%; from 1970–77, it was 10.8%; in the five years after the 1973 oil embargo, it exceeded 11%. Unemployment largely disappeared. Most social infrastructure kept up with economic growth and with urbanization, although Seoul grew to 8 million people. These economic successes have been surpassed by South Korean trade. Exports rose from $4.8 million in 1962 to $21.0 billion in 1981.

The economic growth successes have not been a hothouse plant. Although South Korea imports most of its energy in the form of oil, growth after the oil embargo was more rapid than growth before the oil embargo. Although South Korea had few exports to the Middle East in 1973–74, it not only surmounted the balance of payments crisis caused by the skyrocketing oil prices, but also managed to balance its trade with the Middle East by 1976 and to earn a balance of payments surplus from the Middle East thereafter. Korea surmounted Western protectionism by responding to limits on export volume with improvements in export quality. Its exports rose more than 20% even in 1975, a year of severe recession. Its export growth rates did not decline as a result of Western protectionism in this period. Although South Korea is highly dependent upon world trade, it achieved its mid-1970s five-year plan (1972–76) goals despite the oil embargo, Western protectionism, and world recession. While the economy got into difficulty, as Park aged and made bad decisions on wage policy and heavy industrial investment, and then suffered major reverses after Park's assassination, institutional strength made substantial recovery possible despite global stagflation, high oil prices, and high interest rates in 1981.

South Korea's economic growth has been planned by government planning units, guided by the credit rationing of the Bank of Korea, led by the development of massive trading companies (13 of which exported over $100 million by 1977), and staffed by executives in their late thirties and early forties who were trained at the best American institutions. Thus, by the criteria of general performance, crisis performance, structural soundness, and personnel quality, South Korea's industrial and export institutions appear very sound indeed.

South Korea's *rural development institutions* have followed a parallel course. Rural development was slighted in favor of urban development until the early 1970s, but in the meantime the government built the basic infrastructure of roads and communications, created an agricultural extension network, introduced new varieties of rice, and subsidized fertilizer. Beginning in 1970, the government introduced the Saemaul program, which provides villagers with assistance in building roads, meeting facilities, bridges, irrigation networks, reservoirs, and water distribution systems, and teaches villagers how to organize for development. The government successfully put the primary onus for planning projects on the villages themselves, and provided assistance only in return for large efforts from the villagers. It rewarded the most successful villages, rather than subsidizing the most unsuccessful. The result was rapid rural development that did not place a huge administrative or economic burden on the central government and that was driven by a chain reaction of expectations of success. As a result, South Korea went from being a major rice importer to being a rice exporter. Farm income has risen roughly in accordance with the extraordinary growth of urban income. The distribution of land and income has nonetheless remained remarkably egalitarian. Villagers who once lived in poverty reminiscent of Pakistan or Bangladesh now universally possess radios, cement, good housing, and piped water, and assume that they will dress well, send their children to competent schools, and even take vacations.

All these developments have put a strain on South Korea's *income distribution programs*. It is generally accepted among economists that economies at South Korea's level of development experience the most intense pressures for income inequality to increase. Moreover, it is generally believed that an emphasis on rapid economic growth tends to exacerbate income inequality. The more rapid growth of urban industry than of rural agriculture enhances unequalizing tendencies. South Korea thus faced extraordinary pressures toward increasing inequality. Despite these pressures, South Korea has not employed the Western techniques of massive income transfers, minimum wages, and unionization. It has, however, conducted a massive land reform, made reduction of unemployment the highest economic priority, emphasized labor-intensive industrialization, enacted progressive tax policies, and adopted massive luxury taxes.[3] It has taken strong action to ensure that educational opportunity is uniform, even to the extent of abolishing five elite high schools that were at one time providing more than half of the entrants into the Seoul National University. The result is that, although South Korea faces extraordinary pressures toward an inegalitarian income distribution, and although econometric models of the South Korean economy show it to be very resistant to income redistribution programs, South Korea has ended up with an income distribution more egalitarian than all but five countries in the noncommunist world. In a 1975 World Bank survey, South Korea was shown to have an income distribution superior to all noncommunist countries except Australia, Canada, Japan, Libya, and Taiwan.[4]

South Korea's *political institutions* represent a more mixed situation. South Korea entered in the 1950s with only a sense of cultural identity as a major political asset. South Korea's sense of nationality was pan-Korean and therefore as much a dividing as a unifying force. The country was ideologically polarized between extreme right and extreme left, and it lacked even the most elemental consensus as to the appropriate means of governance. Outbreaks of rural and urban violence were common. Political parties, government ministers, and the military and police were all divided into contending factions that frequently immobilized them. Bribery and corruption were massive and omnipresent. The tenure of high officials other than the president was typically only a few months.

Since that time, South Korea has achieved an anticommunist national consensus and a consensus on the basic modes of urban economic development, rural economic development, and income distribution, although the presence of a small group of extremely rich entrepreneurs remains the subject of intense political controversy. The National Assembly is elected by honest elections but is a largely powerless institution. Park Chung Hee was elected indirectly by a National Council for Unification, which was in turn an elected Council of nonpolitical figures. The rules confining the National Council for Unification to nonpolitical figures and allowing President Park to appoint one-third of the National Assembly ensured the continuation in office of Park Chung Hee and also ensured continuing political controversy over such a system. Harsh methods in dealing with political opponents also ensured a degree of dissensus.

A government that was relatively small in terms of proportion of the population and proportion of the economy exercised extraordinarily successful control over the nation's economy and other aspects of society. The government as a whole was honest (by the standards of Third World countries or of Massachusetts state government), able to act, highly competent in achieving its goals, and able to attract the best talent available. In addition to ministries of the kind that other governments possess, the South Korean system included a group of think tanks reporting directly to the president on every major governmental function from education to income redistribution. Those think tanks ensured a steady flow of high-powered talent and modern innovations to the center of government. The South Korean system also included a centralized communication and coordination mechanism, the Korean Central Intelligence Agency, which provided sensitive coordination (while at the same time acting as an unusually insensitive tool of political repression). The South Korean government worked effectively with business as well as the military in ensuring that such national goals as security, rapid growth, and egalitarian income distribution were achieved. The South Korean government thus achieved a great deal, including a consensus on many of the major issues, effectiveness of individual institutions, and overall coordination of major institutions.

These achievements were numerous and impressive, but the achievements in creating an institutionalized political system lagged far behind the achievements in creating effective governmental administration. While the consensus on anticommunism and on domestic economic structure were impressive *political achievements*, there was no strong, positive *ideological* consensus. To the extent that South Korea acquired a dominant ideology, it was democratic, inculcated by Western-oriented teachers using American-style textbooks to teach the entire post-Korean War generation; this ideology was in great tension with actual South Korean political practice. Authoritarian practice coincided with increasingly widespread democratic education and with dramatic increases in the size or cohesion of the principal democratically oriented opposition groups: labor, the intelligentsia, the middle class, and Christians. Moreover, while Park Chung Hee was able to professionalize the military and keep them out of domestic politics so long as he was in power (unlike, for instance, the situation in Indonesia), a severe military-civilian power struggle occurred after Park's assassination. And, despite a series of constitutional provisions for succession, there remains uncertainty regarding the viability of constitutionally mandated methods of succession. During the 1980s or early 1990s, the political question will probably have to be faced in much starker terms, given South Korea's social trends, than was the case under Park or in the early years under Chun.

The overall South Korean institutional system appears to have an unusual coherence by Third World standards. The economic institutions complement one another to achieve South Korea's goals and ameliorate conflicts among them. The open trading economy emphasizes exports of manufactured goods produced by labor-intensive means. Successful export of these goods raises the incomes of the poorest workers, thereby ameliorating the urban income distribution. These workers spend much of their additional income on food, thereby enhancing demand for agricultural products. Korea's farms, whose rising agricultural productivity would in other circumstances lead to gluts and disastrous declines in farm income, therefore face rising demand and rising prices. The good fortune of urban workers attracts the poorest rural people to the cities, thereby ameliorating the income distribution of the rural areas and offering improved conditions to the emigrants. Thus, agricultural income and urban income rise in tandem. Government works with business and with agriculture to ensure rapid technological progress and to minimize social disruption. Economic and social progress ameliorate, within limits, the political problems that represent the system's greatest vulnerability. Thus, while South Korea faces difficult problem of political development in the future, it addresses those problems with a base of institutional strength and competence that is almost unique in the Third World.

Social Coalition

Although the Park regime initially faced widespread opposition and possessed only a narrow base of support, its success in ensuring national security and in promoting economic growth and a good income distribution eventually broadened its supporting social coalition. By the early 1970s the Park regime was supported by the military (despite Park's insistence on a very low military budget), the civil service, the middle class (which had greatly benefited from growth), the industrial leadership, the farmers (whose income and social standing had greatly increased), and the minority of labor that served in high-technology industries. This was a very broad social base indeed.

The Opposition

Given the detail with which this chapter has analyzed the regime's organization, and given the ineffectiveness of the South Korean opposition to Park, it is appropriate to analyze the opposition in less detail.

The social base of the opposition consisted of academics and students (who have always opposed Korea's regime with great fervor regardless of its structure or policies), the Christians (who opposed Park's violations of human rights and who resented loss of their previous position as a dominant social elite), the majority of labor (which had been terribly oppressed politically, although wages rose very quickly), and an increasing proportion of the middle class (whose education had sensitized it to democratic values). The strength of these groups was greatly enhanced by economic development. Thus, the social base of the opposition was significant and growing, but not adequate during most of the Park years to mount a destabilizing challenge.

The opposition had few institutions. Efforts to create organizations were effectively suppressed by Park. He succeeded beause of his willingness to use whatever means were necessary, and because he had the support of broad elements of Korean society, many of whom did not like his political methods but were willing to accept them in return for security, growth, and equity. Moreover, Park successfully coopted virtually all of the most dynamic and well-trained potential leaders of the opposition into powerful positions in his government. Thus, only the students had a rudimentary, cell-structured revolutionary organization. The other elites were organized along lines of nascent democratic political parties, a form of organization utterly inappropriate for challenging a powerful and determined government. The Communist Party was small, discredited, and ineffectual. Thus, the opposition largely lacked institutions and was pursuing an organizational strategy inappropriate for overthrowing Park.

Finally, the top leadership of the opposition was drained by cooptation and relatively unskilled in economic and national security matters. It was deeply fragmented among several competing leaders who were unwilling to subordinate personal ambition to the requirements of unity.

Thus, the South Korean opposition had important trends on its side, namely the strengthening of its social base by modernization and the rise in popular concern for political dignity as fears of war and economic hardship diminished. But, as long as the military regime continued to enjoy economic and military success, and as long as the opposition could not unify its leadership, it had little early hope of success. Meanwhile, the military was modernizing its own leadership and organization at a far faster rate than the opposition civilians.

From this analysis it is quite clear why the widespread journalistic expectations that the South Korean regime would be toppled by public discontent did not materialize. In the end, it was possible to assassinate Park but not to destroy what he had created. These conditions could change, but only over a prolonged period.

THE SUCCESSION TO PARK CHUNG HEE

After a decade and a half of stability that defied the constant predictions by journalists of coming upheaval, Park's rule began to show signs of weakness. Park's economic decisions began to display a remarkable overconfidence. The country overinvested massively in heavy industry. Park raised workers' wages an average of 34% per year over a three-year period. Park's bodyguards increasingly isolated him from critical views and encouraged an increasingly rigid political attitude. Following the assassination of Park's wife, the president began going to parties with young singers. His speeches became longer and less disciplined. As a result, by mid-1979, the likelihood of an economic crunch and of a political confrontation was increasing. In the autumn, the chief of the Korean CIA, long an advocate of more democratic rule and a rival of Park's chief bodyguard, assassinated Park, plunging the economy and polity into a period of uncertainty.

The analyst looking at this period of uncertainty could not predict in detail what would happen. He had to explain the then-current situation clearly, then project alternative scenarios about what might occur. Organizational analysis could illuminate the strengths and weaknesses of contending parties, but could not predict in detail the outcome of a period of struggle.

The excellent pool of potential leaders, strong institutions, and relatively strong social base of the Park regime gave those who looked for continued stability and growth much on which to base their hopes On the other hand, South Korea's development had created some difficulties that were not overcome by institutional excellence and economic success. Economic growth bred strong, assertive pressure groups, such as business groups, labor movements, and the educational profession, which increasingly pressed for greater access to political power. Economic progress brought with it technological complexity and intricate social differentiation, making the economy and society far more difficult to control centrally from the presidential residence. Over the previous three decades, most of the population had been educated not only in literacy, but also in democratic values; this greatly heightened the tensions caused by the coexistence of authoritarian practices with democratic rhetoric. As fear of the military power of the North gradually receded, the popularly perceived tradeoff between security, which was the primary value, and democracy, which was the second value, weakened, and insistence on democracy became more thinkable.

Principal Scenarios

Under these circumstances there were two obvious, and one slightly less obvious, alternatives that would serve as the basis for scenarios. First, the forces pressing for democracy might succeed in establishing a second round (the first was in 1960–61) of democratic administration. Democratic forces were outspoken after the death of Park, and such civilian groups as students, intelligentsia, labor, and much of the middle class were joined by many leaders of the government in pledging commitment to new democratic institutions and to a fair, open election. The opposition party and the government drafted new constitutions, which were nearly identical, except that the opposition draft was somewhat more conservative. Government and opposition leaders publicly paid their respects to one another. Thus, there seemed to be a real possibility of democracy.

A second alternative was that military leaders, anxious to perpetuate the legacy of Park Chung Hee's success, fearful of a repetition of the disorder of 1960–61, and strongly opposed to the ascendancy to executive power of any of the three leading political party candidates, would seize power and institute military rule. This would stimulate an immediate, direct, and potentially very dangerous clash with the increasingly organized democratic forces.

A third major alternative was that progress toward democracy would be made, student and labor rioting would create a general sense of disorder, in consequence the economy would get into major difficulties, and the military would intervene to restore order and to revive the economy. In this event, most of the civilian population would probably support the military.

The principal potential surprise worth analyzing was the possibility that North Korea, encouraged by political uncertainty in the South and by U.S. President Jimmy Carter's ambivalence toward South Korea, would invade. While this scenario needed detailed analysis, such analysis revealed that, although invasion was not impossible, it was too unlikely to influence most business or government policy decisions.

A Democratic Scenario

To illustrate the process of scenario creation, it will be useful to develop one of the alternatives that did not happen, and to do so in a relatively detailed fashion. Let us suppose that the process of democratization had proceeded as originally planned by Korea's civilians, and examine the principal reasons why it might have succeeded, as well as the principal reasons for fears that it might have failed, in order to reach some conclusions about the likely development of the system.

The military and others feared that renewed democracy might revive the disorders of 1960–61. What if the nationwide student demonstrations of 1960–61 recurred? Would that risk the loss of all of the economic and social progress achieved through great sacrifices over the past two decades? Would social disorder and economic stagnation lead to desertion by the United States and to renewed risks from the North? These fears were not silly, after 1960–61, but times had changed in South Korea. The success of Park Chung Hee's administrative, social, and economic program not only brought the problems of complexity, pluralism, and democratic ferment, but they also created social and institutional conditions that were far more favorable to democracy.

First, as noted earlier, a widespread ideological consensus was created on crucial economic and social issues and on anticommunism. Second, South Korea changed from a largely uneducated society to an educated society. This education was necessary for voters to deal with issues rather than with personalities. While no education ever eliminates the danger of demogoguery, South Korea had reached a level of education that the classical philosophers of democracy would have regarded as appropriate for the establishment of democratic institutions. Moreover, South Korea's teachers and textbooks had inculcated democratic ideology.

Third, the objectively increased military security of South Korea, and the confidence accompanying it, provided an important prerequisite for democratic development. (Fear always undermines democracy.) Fourth, much of South Korea had experienced local democracy through the Saemaul programme, which had taught rural villagers to elect development leaders and to make decisions about development projects. Although the programs have seldom produced models of democratic achievement, the experience of issue-oriented electoral politics was auspicious.

Fifth, there had emerged a class of U.S.-trained technocrats who had firmly established a merit system within the government. No democratic administration was likely to factionalize or politicize these institutions to a dangerous extent. Nor was it likely that the technocrats would oppose democracy. The young, U.S.-trained technocrats who exercised the most important power condoned the system of Park Chung Hee, but they were mostly people who had absorbed democratic ideals. Sixth, South Korea's egalitarian income distribution facilitated democratic attitudes and removed class conflicts that undermine democracy elsewhere.

Seventh, and above all, South Korean society had the strong institutions outlined earlier. These provided an anchor for social order and a stabilizer for social and economic policies. Had the democratic administration of 1960–61 been able to implement its brilliant economic plans through such effective institutions, democracy might have been viable then.

Thus, the classic social and institutional prerequisites of democratic success were present in South Korea. However, the transition to democracy is difficult, as many nations have discovered. Moreover, political polarization caused by Park exacerbated the difficulties. There remained serious doubts about whether key social groups would cooperate in a peaceful democracy. Aside from the military, the principal issues concerned students, labor, and radical politicians.

In no Third World country do student activists support their government. But no student group elsewhere had established as strong a historical record of opposition as Korean students. Korean students promoted the colonization of the country by the Japanese in order to modernize the country, and then led the nationalist movement against the Japanese. Korean students deposed Syngman Rhee in the name of democracy, and then helped destroy democracy in pursuit of vengeance against Rhee's officials.

Although the students advocated democracy, they had never supported any government and would probably have turned against a democratic government. The issue of vengeance, fatal in 1961, was again important to radical students. On the other hand, conditions had changed. By 1980 students possessed a substantial stake in their society. In 1960 the primitive economy did not need sophisticated skills, and it was growing so slowly that unemployment was omnipresent. By 1980 most students had job offers long before they graduated, and a large majority might have proved unwilling to risk their futures for the sake of radical politics. Moreover, whereas in 1960 to be a student or professor in South Korea was to be a member of the small elite, by 1980 education was widespread, and the most talented people were in government service or in South Korea's rapidly growing corporations. Thus, students as a group carried less weight in Korean society.

Student activity now occurred in a very different social context. The supportive radical left hardly existed. Second, democratic groups now recognized that South Korea faced unique security problems, along with economic conditions that required a decisive, relatively centralized democracy rather than a decentralized checks and balances system. Finally, opposition political leaders were enthusiastic to be allowed by the military to achieve power and, to the extent that progress was made, encouraged students to moderate their positions.

While students were a lagging sector, workers were an emerging sector whose social power would rise for many years. In 1945 the whole of Korea had only 50,000 industrial workers. In 1961 South Korea had 350,000 industrial workers of low education and skills. In 1980 South Korea had 5 million workers of relatively high education and high skills. Behind these numbers was industrialization, which had employed vast numbers of workers who in earlier years lacked employment and often feared starvation. Vast numbers of people were pulled from extraordinary rural poverty into the beginnings of modern industry. As Korea's industry had risen from cheap textiles and shoes to more expensive textiles, radio and television sets, steel and petrochemicals, and 260,000-ton ships, hundreds of thousands of Korean workers had achieved steady salaries, skills, and responsibilities. (The average real wage increase until recent years was 8.5% per year.) Moreover, all of this was accomplished with a highly egalitarian income distribution.

On the other hand, there was a dark side to the Korean labor story. Early labor organization in Korea was primarily communist and sought to destroy all of the industrial facilities of the country. In response, Syngman Rhee organized company unions for all public utilities. Subsequently, unions were created by legislation and took government orders. After 1950, the labor unions were taken over by former Communists who had converted to right-wing positions. In 1951, during a famous strike at the Chosun Textile Company, the leader of the strike switched his loyalties to management and developed a unique, sexually abusive method of strike breaking against the young female workers who were the primary leaders. This man subsequently rose to become head of the textiles union and resigned only in February 1980. After 1963, an official of the Korean CIA became head of the Korean Federation of Trade Unions, and all union policies required the consent of the Korean CIA. And the National Security Act of 1971 restricted the right of bargaining—with the support of the trade union federation. All this ensured a legacy of antigovernment feeling among key workers' groups.

Because the living standards of Korean workers, although far better than in decades past, were still very low, any erosion of real living standards was very painful. Moreover, because expectations have been raised by two decades of progress, the disappointment of workers hurt by the anti-inflation policies required in 1980–81 was particularly great. The political implications were ambiguous. On the one hand, Korean workers could clearly manage under conditions far worse than those of 1980–81, and they were mostly patriots who responded to appeals for national unity. On the other hand, major economic disappointments could have caused political ferment. Given fair elections, however, potential student and labor dissidence might be minimized.

Finally, there was the fear of a radical being elected. Kim Dae Jung, the most popular political leader, was perceived as a radical because he strongly opposed Park Chung Hee. He had been supported by student and worker groups that frequently had radical ambitions, and he had campaigned strongly against what he characterized as a grossly unequal income distribution—despite the fact of the remarkably egalitarian income distribution. He was also a member of a communist front before the Korean War. In his frustration, Kim Dae Jung had made some extravagant statements. But to gauge whether he was really radical, it was important to look at his positions on the principal contemporary issues.

William Overholt interviewed Kim Dae Jung in 1979 and again in February 1980. Kim Dae Jung rejected the students' demands for vengeance against most of Park's officials, explaining that most of these officials would serve any government, that many were democratic, and that he would need their skills—except for the current ministers, vice-ministers, and a few others. Some followers of Kim Dae Jung who might have become ministers were demagogues who would have damaged, but not destroyed, Korea's institutions. Their goal was not institutional destruction, but the rise of power of people from traditionally excluded Kwangju,

Kim's home province. Kim Dae Jung believed in a market economy and supported a major role for the giant general trading companies. His desire to curb their special privileges (tax exemptions, interest subsidies, licensed oligopoly positions, and narrow ownership) coincided precisely with the views of Park's senior advisors. Kim favored close relations with the United States and Japan, had always vigorously opposed U.S. troop withdrawal, and had been wary of North Korean overtures He advocated a draft constitution giving the government special power to prevent strikes and control collective bargaining; his draft went beyond that of the government in this respect. He pressed in early 1980 for student-labor restraint. His party was South Korea'n traditional conservative party, descended from a conservative association of landlords. Kim Dae Jung was, in short, part of South Korea's conservative consensus.

While Kim Dae Jung's democratic predecessors had planned Korea's conservative economic program, Park Chung Hee had added radical egalitarian measures. Park imposed huge taxes on luxury goods. For instance, under Park, a four-cylinder automobile cost under $5,000, but government taxes raised the cost of a six-cylinder automobile to $26,000–$30,000. Although South Korea was one of the world's largest manufactures of color television sets and had enormous excess capacity, color television broadcasts were banned in South Korea because Park Chung Hee did not believe in creating social distinctions between those who could afford color television and those who could only afford black-and-white. When the achievement tests for admission to the university resulted in half the student body being drawn from five elite high schools, Park abolished all five schools in order to avoid the creation of a social elite.

Kim Dae Jung's predecessors knew that they were the conservatives and Park was the radical. In the 1963 election, former President Yun Po-Sun (currently regarded as a radical for his opposition to military government) had bitterly criticized Park Chung Hee's socialist economic ideals and former membership in a communist party front. Like Kim Dae Jung, Park Chung Hee was in fact a member of a communist front before the Korean War.

Thus, the critical issues in Korea's second attempt at democracy were not really radicalism, social underdevelopment, or fear of the North. The real issue was fear of economic stagnation brought on by political vacillation in the face of the manifest failure of Park's policies in his last years. Park's policies of 1977–79 had created an economic crisis whose solution required decisive action. And the risk of civilian dithering derived not from the early holding of an election that would bring radical, decisive leadership; it derived from the risk that the democratic political leaders whom Park had allowed to be active were too weak, too conservative, and too inexperienced to act. The risk was not Fidel Castro, but Jimmy Carter. In fact, had an election been held, Kim Dae Jung would almost certainly have been the victor, and many of his policies would have been weak and vacillating because his proposals always lacked concreteness and because so many of his supporters were moralizers rather than technocrats.

Finally, democracy would probably have received short shrift under Kim Dae Jung. Kim knew and loved democratic slogans, but during his short campaign his supporters made vigorous private efforts to get the United States to rig the election in his favor. In promoting this policy, Kim's supporters argued that the choice was between good and evil and that, faced with such a choice, the United States had no moral right to remain neutral.

Thus, the outcome of the "democracy" scenario would have been authoritarianism together with a great deal of economic inefficiency, without destroying the basic successes of the previous era. It would not have included radical threats to the existing economic order or to the roles of foreign firms. And, after a period of time, it would not even have been democracy.

In reality, the democratic scenario did not occur. Nor did the brutal, straightforward military takeover scenario which, because of the rising democratic forces mentioned above, would probably have brought prolonged civil conflict. Nor, strictly speaking, did the scenario of democracy, then leftist misbehavior, then military intervention. What happened was more subtle.

The military permitted plans for democratization to progress, but periodically stated loudly its opposition to Kim Dae Jung; key commanders occasionally denounced him as a communist. Meanwhile, young officers seized the leadership of the military and used the Defense Security Command, an agency that monitors the loyalty and efficiency of military units, to infiltrate all key civilian agencies. The civilian government watched these moves and vacillated—with little choice. Then, when it was gradually becoming clear that the democracy scenario was going to be short-circuited, a major uprising occurred in Kwangju, Kim Dae Jung's home province. The military allowed it to occur, then squashed it with considerable loss of life. The combination of civilian vacillation, economic decline, and violence at Kwangju so frightened the people of South Korea that they overwhelmingly accepted, at least for a time, the reemergence of military rule.

This result in South Korea could not have been predicted in detail. Nor was it likely to have been captured with any precision in a scenario. But the three scenarios originally chosen established the basic alternatives, and actual events were close to the third scenario. Someone who had mastered the details of argument behind the third scenario could have understood very early the implications of the emerging events. That is the central purpose of scenarios: not to predict, not to lay out all possible paths, but to describe the arena of uncertainty sufficiently to watch events and locate the kind of path being followed. In this case, a business or bank that had a vital interest in avoiding a situation of serious social disorder could have watched events with considerable confidence, ready to draw back in the event of crude military takeover, prepared to rest in neutral or move ahead in the event of democracy, and ready to move forward decisively in case of what actually happened. If it did move decisively with projects designed for the following few years, it would nonetheless bear in mind a few cautions that clearly followed from the scenario analysis. There were long-run social and economic trends that would eventually make difficult the indefinite perpetuation of Park's style of authoritarian rule. And there were aspects of the way President Chun ascended to power which, given any crucial errors by the new regime, could provide opponents with ammunition to challenge its legitimacy.

The Korean case study illustrates a number of the central methodological themes of this book. First, it shows that one can do systematic analysis without recourse to formal quantitative models. Second, it shows how an organizational framework, as proposed in the previous chapters, facilitates such analysis. Third, it shows how scenarios can be used to triangulate a situation where one cannot make definitive predictions. And, finally, it shows how such an analysis serves a heuristic, rather than strictly predictive, purpose, teaching the decision maker what the basic forces and options are so that the latter can infer the implications of an ongoing, unpredicted series of events.

NOTES

1. Sungjoo Han, *The Failure of Democracy in South Korea* (Berkeley, Calif.: University of California Press, 1974).
2. Irma Adelman and S. Robinson, *Income Distribution Policy in Developing Counties: A Case Study of Korea* (Stanford, Calif.: Stanford University Press, 1978), citing T. Kataka, *History of Korea* (New York: Clio Press, 1969), p. 126.
3. *Ibid*.
4. Shail Jain, *Size Distribution of Income: A Compilation of Data* (Washington, D.C.: Wold Bank, 1975).

Chapter 10
Mexico: A Case Study

This chapter outlines the considerations for undertaking a future-oriented political analysis of Mexico. It is not, for obvious reasons of space, the full analysis of the future of Mexico. Rather, it outlines the considerations that would go into designing the analysis. It also differs from the conventional case study in that it points out why certain approaches were rejected and demonstrates why certain avenues were pursued, rather than specifying detailed results.

Since the late 1970s, the political-economic future of Mexico has become a prominent focus of political forecasting. One of the world's biggest magnets for foreign investment, Mexico is nonetheless confronted by the problems of vast foreign debt, income inequality, and unemployment. Mexico is a focus of heightened interest because in certain ways the Mexican situation resembles Iran. It is in the middle of the troubled and changing Central American-Caribbean region. The specter of vast oil wealth and social change leading to revolution may not be regarded as the most likely scenario, but it is not a possibility to be ignored, least of all by the Mexican government. What kind of advice should be given to clients considering long-term, fixed investments?

In Mexico, 1982 was a presidential election year. The choice of president is of great importance owing to the enormous power of the Mexican presidency. Although the victor must operate within certain constraints, his general ideological orientation, leadership style, and stance on key issues—such as income distribution, foreign investment, oil policy, and political liberalization—are unquestionably important. To a certain degree, these aspects of attitudes and style can be summarized by the distinction between "populists" and "conservative-managerial" presidential types. Although populists have by no means been revolutionary in the sense of attempting to change the basic institutional structure of the political system, they have been more nationalistic in opposing closer ties with the United States, more antagonistic to big business in general, more committed (though ambivalently) to mass mobilization, and, at least rhetorically, more devoted to reversing the trend of the worsening overall income distribution. According to the values and the business interests of the forecaster's clients, these views may be regarded positively or negatively; in either case, the prediction of whether the next leader would indeed be a populist is important information, especially considering the rocky relations between business and the last populist president, Luis Echeverría.

This chapter addresses two major issues:

1. What are the long-term political-economic prospects for the country?

2. What are the short-term prospects of presidential succession? In particular, would the Partido Revolucionario Institucional (PRI) presidential nominee for the 1982 election—who, because of the PRI's political dominance, is virtually guaranteed to become the president—be a populist, a conservative, or something else? In this section, we present a case study from 1979 that can be compared with the actual 1982 results.

While these questions are important, and while most other political and policy issues depend on them, they would in most cases be the beginnings of a study rather than the end. For the U.S. government, the issues of stability and succession would need to be followed by an analysis of foreign policy positions—for instance, on trade, immigration, and Central America. For oil companies, the key issue would be how large Mexican oil production and exports will become. For banks, the central issues would be the politics of exchange rates and foreign debt rescheduling. Each of these issues can be addressed through the same methods used to analyze the succession issue: establishing the alternative dynamics that affect the decision, and then analyzing how the dynamics are triggered and weighted.

ASSESSING LONG-TERM STABILITY

A wide variety of approaches to assessing the long-term trends of stability come to mind, ranging from the highly quantitative to the completely journalistic. It is useful to explore where some of these approaches would lead, before embarking on our own preferred inquiry that links socioeconomic trends and organizational analysis.

Quantitative Approaches

What do the quantitative techniques have to offer? Or, more precisely, what can be gained by making quantitative projections of political trends per se, as opposed to using quantitative economic or social trends in the generation of political forecasts?

One possibility is to identify a measurable indicator of regime strength, and extrapolate it into the future. Organski offers one such effort.[1] He argues that, since governments generally seek to shape their environments, and since financial resources constitute one resource of governmental capability, it is reasonable to regard the "extractive capacity" of a government as a measure of its overall capability. He plots the ratio of actual taxes collected to "potential" tax revenues, the latter a function of per capita income. Essentially, he is comparing the actual volume of taxes to a theoretical expected volume based on the wealth of the country, on the grounds that more taxes can be extracted from a richer citizenry. In using this ratio as a reflection of governmental capacity, Organski dismisses the possibility that a government may not wish to collect the maximum possile revenues:[2]

> Willingness or unwillingness to use resources refers really to political constraints that cannot be surmounted. Regardless of the personal predilections of the leaders toward the gathering of added revenues, the administrative system may not be of the caliber necessary to collect the desired revenues, or it may prove impossible for the leadership to form a coalition of power necessary to exact support for increased taxation. The willingness of the leaders is not at issue here.

By this measure, the Mexican government turns out to be very weak. "The case of Mexico . . . offers the example of a country that has done worse than its economic base should have permitted it to do."[3] The graphs of actual and potential revenue levels for the 1950–74 period show an almost consistent actual tax ratio and a higher, upward-sloping "predicated" (potential) tax ratio, indicating that Mexico's governmental capability, as measured by its tax effort, started out low and has been declining steadily if only moderately over the 24-year period. In contrast, North Vietnam had a higher predicted than actual tax effort, while Syria had a rough equivalence of predicted and actual tax efforts.

This interpretation, for Mexico at least, borders on the absurd. One of the principal reasons for the Mexican government's remarkable record of longevity has been its ability to keep together a coalition of economic forces including big business, along with the capacity to coopt relatively small segments of marginal groups whenever they posed a challenge to the government. The system has been aptly described as a "government-business symbiosis."[4] This broad political-economic strategy explains how a "Revolutionary" government (founded in the Mexican Revolution and still drawing its legitimacy and rhetoric from it) could maintain a high level of economic growth: despite the so-called "populist" regimes, big business has been relatively unhampered and has responded with the greatest sustained economic expansion in Latin America, reflected in an average annual GNP growth rate of over 6% for the 40-year period 1935–75.

The unwillingness to tax business heavily may also explain—in part—the disparities in income and benefits between those who are out of the system because they lack political clout and economic status, and those who are "in." The disparities provide the government with the capacity to coopt additional elements into the system—by bestowing benefits of wealth and position—whenever it is politically convenient to defuse their opposition.

Thus, we see that the low tax effort, rather than reflecting weakness, has served two positive political functions for the government. It has created a positive business climate and high levels of economic growth, for which the government gets at least some of the credit. It has created enough distance between the haves and the have-nots to permit the government to use cooptation as a major political tool. Unlike so much of Latin America, no military coups against the Mexican government have been prodded by disgruntled business sectors; there have been no nationally organized revolutionary opposition movements that could count on highly competent, dedicated leaders. Many positions in the government and party administration are held by individuals who began as revolutionaries but were persuaded that it was better to be "inside."

If this particular measure of government capability makes little sense for Mexico, would the extrapolation of a straightforward measure of political instability or unrest serve instead? This requires, of course, that such quantitative information can be found. The difficulty is in measuring the phenomenon of instability or unrest in such a way that the instability of one period can be compared to the instability of another period with perhaps a very different way of manifesting instability (for example, military coup versus mass demonstrations). The considerable effort of trying to make time-series data comparable does not ensure that these problems have been overcome. One such effort was undertaken by Duff and McCamant.[5] Table 10.1 displays the scores for armed and unarmed violence they generated for Mexico from 1950–69. Naturally, if we were to use such figures for further extrapolation, we would require more up-to-date data, again requiring an enormous amount of work.

Is it worth it? We must ask whether the time series seems to be valid (if it measures what it purports to measure) in terms of other analyses of recent Mexican history. It is generally accepted that there was a severe confrontation between workers' groups and the government in 1958, entailing high levels of violence and repression, after which there was a decade of

Table 10.1   Mexican Armed and Unarmed Violence Scores, 1950–69

Year	Armed Violence Score	Unarmed Violence Score
1950	0	0
1951	4	3
1952	10	5
1953	—	0
1954	6	4
1955	6	3
1956	0	3
1957	0	2
1958	4	5
1959	5	2
1960	3	3
1961	6	5
1962	4	3
1963	4	4
1964	0	3
1965	6	2
1966	5	2
1967	5	4
1968	5	9
1969	2	3

Source: E. A. Duff and J. F. McCamant, Violence and Repression in Latin America: A Quantitative and Historical Analysis (New York: Free Press, 1976).

relative calm.[6] Yet the Duff and McCamant data score 1952, 1954, and 1961 as higher in violence; the levels for 1958 are not particularly noteworthy. On armed violence, 11 of the 18 other measured years show equal or higher scores; in terms of unarmed violence, three other years show equal or higher levels. It is hard to reconcile the measures with the historical assessment of the timing of the crisis.

At this point one might ask, "Why not use another data series?" The answer is that if one were found, its own differences with the Duff-McCamant series would have to be addressed; why should it be chosen over theirs? If the answer is that it conforms more to the conventional wisdom on how different periods should be scored in terms of levels of violence, then we must ask why "objective" measures, if they are accepted only when they fit our preconceptions, are useful at all.

Organizational Analysis

In our own preferred approach to the assessment of Mexico's long-term stability, we begin with an evaluation of the organizational structure of the regime and the PRI party upon which it based. These institutions must be examined with regard to their top leadership, their broad institutional structures, and their mass bases of support. At the same time, we must assess the organizational strengths and weaknesses of any potential "counterelites" who might challenge the supremacy of the PRI at some point in the future.

Top Leadership. The caliber of top leadership entails unity, commitment, competence, and honesty. There are two kinds of studies that help in assessing the caliber of top leadership in Mexico. There are direct studies of the backgrounds, recruitment patterns, and interactions of the leaders, such as Peter Smith's 1979 book, *Labyrinths of Power*.[7] Very briefly, these studies show that Mexico is capable of producing high-caliber leadership, partly by its well-known capacity to coopt the brightest of the potential opposition, partly by the stability of recruitment patterns that give emerging leaders long experience and weed out the inept, and partly by the institutional structure that gives the president so much power and prestige for his one term that his place in history as a competent leader must loom as his primary goal. These studies show the impressive capability of the Mexican recruitment system for instilling unity and for socializing (that is, passing on established values to newcomers), while still allowing for ideological diversity within to leadership. However, the top leaders rise up the government or party ranks without having to acquire or demonstrate the capacity to undertake bold new policy initiatives that crisis conditions may require.

Leadership caliber is also reflected by case studies of how Mexican leaders have responded to various predicaments that are common for developing countries: leadership succession, dealing with the industrial superpowers, disruption by those who challenge the legitimacy of the regime, allocating scarce resources, and so on. In these responses, too, Mexican leadership has shown itself to be rather competent and sober. Regular succession has been handled flawlessly in the past several decades. A crisis of legitimacy in the 1970s brought about liberalizing electoral reforms. Economic growth—until the mid-1970s—was maintained under diverse and difficult circumstances, and the population crisis brought a decisive response in government policy even though the same president (Echeverría) had to reverse his previous outspoken pronatalist position. The negotiations with the United States over oil, gas, and illegal migration have been competently handled by the Mexicans, by the large, except for the June 1981 impasse over the pricing of fuel exports to the United States.

Three problems do surface, all of significance not only for assessing Mexico's long-term stability but also for the day-to-day operations of the typical client of the political forecaster. First, Mexican leaders tend to overreact, through the use of the army and large-scale arrests, when confronted with antiregime challenges, an understandable response considering the utter chaos of the Mexican Revolution. In 1968 and 1971, student unrest brought about reactions that most outside observers considered excessive.[8] Second, the one-term limit on presidential tenure has sometimes pushed the president into grandstand gestures to mark his place in history or to promote his international standing. Third, the top leadership seems better at attending to the political ramifications of Mexico's socioeconomic problems than at solving them. Very high unemployment, maldistribution of income, and uncontrolled urbanization remain chronic problems even though the political turmoil that one might expect to emerge from these problems has been—so far—remarkably low.

Institutional Strength.   Moving from the top leadership to the middle levels of the government and the PRI, the evidence again consists of direct assessments of these institutions as well as case studies of how they perform their tasks. In general, their loyalty and coherence seem quite impressive, although there are significant problems of inefficiency and corruption. Overall economic policy making is carried out coherently, with close cooperation among the presidency, the finance ministry, the central bank, and the state development bank, linked in a system of mutual accommodation. However, other important government entities are not so well integrated into this system, most notably the state oil company PEMEX. The government can also rely on the considerable technical and policy-making expertise of formally private-sector think tanks, such as the Colegio de Mexico and certain technical institutes of the National Autonomous University of Mexico to augment its in-house capabilities.

Government personnel generally show solidarity and a strong sense of belonging to the "family." Although their inefficiency, as shown in the implementation of the PIDER rural development scheme and the administration of social services, is typical of public administration in developing countries, their loyalty to the regime makes it less likely that the public administration would deliberately undermine governmental programs (as was the case in Chile under progressive regimes).

In assessing the PRI, we must first dispense with our traditional notion of a political party. Given the size, dominance, and eclectic nature of the PRI, it is not simply a competitive party, but also (and perhaps more importantly) an arena of politics for those who are willing to abide by the rules of the game. The fact that the PRI has right and left wings, and can bring in organized groups of various kinds and individuals of widely differing ideological backgrounds, confirms this perspective. This distinction from the traditional notion of political party is very important for understanding the PRI's strength: the loyalty of its activists is to the political system and the broad rules of the game, rather than to an ideology or a particular leader (as is the case for many other Latin American parties).

In terms of the adaptability of the political institutions, it is noteworthy that the recent electoral reforms (which recognized a more diverse set of political parties and engineered greater congressional representation for non-PRI parties) were in fact just one more instance of adaptation of the institutional framework, though always within the parameters of one-party dominance. The PRI has changed its formal composition periodically in order to incorporate emerging organized groups, ranging from the Federation of Slum-Dwellers to peasant organizations.

The Military.   The political marginality of the military is another essential element of the soundness of Mexico's governmental structure. The military has played a consistently subservient political role (it had been one of the formal sectors of the PRI, but is no longer), and yet it responds competently when the government calls upon it to combat rural guerrillas or to stand down urban disruptions. In countering the sporadic guerrilla operations, the military has something important to do other than focusing on internal politics in the manner of so many Latin American militaries. The military is not starved for appropriations (a major cause of politicization of militaries in other Latin American countries), it has not been forced into playing the role of political moderator, and the top military officers seem to be happily ensconced within the PRI family. Therefore, the military is highly unlikely to be an initiating source of system change. Of course, if there were very serious unrest or fundamental change, then the views and actions of the military officer corps would become very important.

Mass Support.   This last point is also important in assessing the broad social base of support for the prevailing political system. Evaluating mass support and opposition has two components: the sentiments of various groups and their capabilities of acting upon those sentiments. Both depend on how well the system can adapt when it is necessary to accommodate to mobilized groups that otherwise might translate their dissatisfaction into open opposition.

The flow of benefits from Mexico's economic growth is a starting point for understanding where support and opposition can be expected—although, as we shall see, this is only a "first cut." Mexican growth has been characterized by great disparities between the haves and the have-nots, but the proportion of people who make it into the "have" category has been gradually but steadily increasing. The modern, dynamic industrial sector (where wages are relatively high) has been growing rapidly, the social security system covers an increasing proportion of the population, and rural development programs are finally reaching a substantial number of peasants. Opposition might be expected from the residue of those who have not yet entered into the stream of benefits provided by the impressive growth of the past 40 years. This residue, although declining in relative size, still constitutes an enormous number of people, encompassing the unemployed and severely underemployed, many elements of the urban traditional workforce (such as artisans, street vendors, and workers in factories too small to be unionized), and the landless peasants.[9]

Even so, studies conducted as late as the early 1960s showed that a high proportion of the population—considering how limited the economic benefits and the actual opportunities for meaningful political participation were—respected and admired the PRI. People voted conscientiously for the PRI, although its victory was virtually a foregone conclusion. This was, in a sense, a bonus of support, in that it did not have to be earned by directing scarce material resources to these groups.[10]

More recent studies show that the active and unqualified approval for the PRI as symbol of the Revolution and champion of land reform has declined, presumably because the Revolution is now more distant and because the government has not done very much to relieve the natural skepticism of the have-nots. Political observers and the PRI leadership have seen a crisis in legitimacy in the growing political apathy reflected by a decline in voter turnout. (This decline was at least temporarily reversed in 1982.) Yet this decline in "automatic legitimacy" has to be balanced by the extremely important fact that the established system has so far rather easily converted have-nots into haves when and if they became organized or showed signs of being mobilizable. *As long as the economy expands at a fast enough pace to permit the selective expansion of benefits to segments previously outside of the benefit system, entire segments of the population can be coopted. The key questions are whether the rising expectations triggered by the oil boom will no longer permit the government to satisfy economic demands selectively and whether the economy will continue to grow rapidly.*

Private Business.   The business community is at times distant from and at times irritated with the government, but overall the relationship between goverment and business has been constructive. Government economic planning has consistently favored a growth-oriented strategy of industrialization. And, despite the rhetoric of the populists such as Echeverría and the ill will they generated within the business community, the government has protected the domestic businesspeople by insisting on joint venture arrangements for foreign investors and multinational enterprises. Local businesses are in demand as partners for multinational enterprises. However, the business sector's support for, or acquiescence in, the PRI's political monopoly as been grounded on high rates of economic growth; whether this support would be withdrawn in the disappointment of stagnation remains to be seen.

Labor.   Organized labor is, paradoxically, closer to the PRI organizationally than is the business sector, but it is less favored than business in terms of economic policy. Organized labor constitutes one of the formal sectors of the PRI, and top labor leaders are very much within the "Revolutionary family." The absence of a radical labor threat has permitted the government to place the weight of austerity programs on wage restraint, most recently under López Portillo following the 1976 fiscal crisis. In the event of the continuation of a relatively conservative, managerial-style presidency, the labor movement may well become more restive. The fact remains, though, that in an economy of very high unemloyment and a large, low-paid informal economic sector, organized labor constitutes a labor aristocracy, beholden to the government for its special status (which could be changed, for example, through changes in official recognition of unions). Combined with the close ties between labor leadership and the PRI hierarchy, this fact minimizes the possibility of outright labor defiance.

Opposition.   When one turns from assessment of the prevailing structure to an evaluation of the potential challenges to the current Mexican system, the strength of the Mexican system shines through clearly. There simply is no nationally based, politically powerful counterelite. The success of the PRI's cooptation of potential opposition, along with military action against disruption, has prevented the rise of an opposition leadership with the organizational skills to go beyond local struggles over local issues such as land ownership. The nationally based political parties, ranging from the conservative PAN to the Communist Party, not only pose little threat to the PRI electorally, but also provide a modicum of prestige and patronage for their members so as to include them as insiders as well. Many observers regard the parties that play within the rules of the game as coopted every bit as much as the members of the PRI.

Outside the conventional political groupings of parties and formal movements, there are potential challenges from peasants, slum-dwellers, and the unemployed. The question, again, is not whether they are numerous, but rather whether they are likely to be organized into a real threat. Despite their periodic disruptions, none of these groups has had, nor is moving toward, organization on a national level independent of the PRI

The PRI itself has formal representation of peasants, and many previously unaffiliated peasant groups have found it convenient to join the PRI in order to gain modestly special favors and perquisites for their leaders. Although guerrilla movements are most typically generated by the frustration of forming new peasant organizations independent of the government and the PRI, which then fail to have any impact on agrarian policy while acting within normal channels, these peasant organizations tend either to disappear quickly or to realign themselves with the agrarian sector of the PRI. Thus, in 1974, most of the radical peasant organizations entered into the Pacto de Ocampo, an agreement whereby these organizations created a peasant union of the PRI's Confederación Nacional Campesina (the PRI's agrarian sector) in exchange for government commitments to spend more for agrarian reform, and, of course, greater access for the leaders of these formerly independent groups.[11] This pattern of absorbing once defiant groups leaves struggling guerrilla movements short of grass-roots support.

The unemployed and underemployed obviously have severe problems in organizing either to press for governmental action or to challenge the government's authority. Yet, when such groups do get organized, they are in a position to gain some recognition from the government, and hence to improve the lot of their limited membership. This explains the bizarre panorama of associations in Mexico, which includes an association of unemployed physicians. Slum-dwellers in the Federation of Low-Income Neighborhoods can also get special representation as a formal part of the PRI. In short, nearly every organized group has or can be provided with a vested interest in the maintenance of at least the broad outlines of the system.

Finally, there is the Intellectual Left, a diverse collection of professors, journalists, students, and political activists who are seen, even by the PRI itself, as espousing "the" alternative to the present system. The power of the intellectual Left has to be qualified by two considerations. First, although the Intellectual Left is undoubtedly a presence felt by the government, it does not command the electoral numbers or the potential to mobilize mass support to compete with the PRI. The Intellectual Left has more influence over the government's perceptions than concrete political power of its own. Second, the Intellectual Left in Mexico provides the system a degree of legitimacy in demonstrating, ironically, that vocal opposition is tolerated. The Left would, of course, protest this interpretation, pointing out that an efficient repressive system represses only when necessary; nevertheless, the highly visible presence of prominent left-wing critics castigating the PRI lends credence to the government's preferred image of the system as an open one in which its party happens to be more beloved and effective than the others.

In the course of examining the organizational status of these institutions, we have also discovered some of the central dynamics that explain Mexican political patterns thus far and are likely to be of predictive utility as well. The pattern of marginal groups first organizing, then challenging, and finally joining the PRI in exchange for significant but not enormous benefits is one such dynamic. Another dynamic is the tension between the PRI as a political arena in which ideological differences are manifested in largely behind-closed-doors confrontation and rhetoric, and the PRI as a single movement requiring conformity and solidarity. A third dynamic is the government's tendency to avoid improving the social welfare of population segments that are perceived as not constituting a potential threat. We would argue that conveying this understanding of "how Mexico works" is at least as important to the policy maker as are the specific forecasts we make along the way.

This evaluation of the dominant and competing institutions sets the stage for analyzing the impacts of the social, economic, and political trends that Mexico is likely to experience. We have assessed, in rather general ways, where the organizational strengths lie; now we must preview the particular challenges that the government is likely to face. Do these problems play on the government's strengths or weaknesses? Will government reactions exacerbate or reduce the problems?

The challenges are not difficult to identify. Some have already triggered crises that enable us to see how the government responds:[12]

> Mexico entered into a serious crisis during the seventies from which it has still not yet fully recovered. This crisis has manifested itself in a variety of forms: spiraling inflation, balance-of-payments problems, declining real wages, a growing external debt, inadequate food production, various forms of popular unrest, declining legitimacy of the political regime, capital flight, rising unemployment, declining private investment, etc. The high point of the crisis appears to have come at the end of 1976 . . . when the annual growth rate of the gross domestic product dropped to 1.7 percent (during the sixties it had been over 7 percent), the rate of private investment fell to below zero, the index of prices rose by 22.2 percent, the external debt increased to $19.6 billion (in 1971 it was only $4.5 billion), and the peso was drastically devalued under pressure from the International Monetary Fund.

In addition to these highly visible problems, the less visible, long-term demographic and income-distribution trends may well create additional challenges.

Several of the Mexican government's responses have been weak or counterproductive. First, the approaches to the overpopulation of urban areas have not been successful, although the overall population control program is showing impressive signs of success. The decentralization program, designed to halt the phenomenal growth of Mexico City, has failed to get the backing of the private sector, which still finds the infrastructure and markets of Mexico City more attractive than the "growth pole" alternatives. Rural improvement programs tend to encourage rather than discourage urban migration. There is also the agonizing problem of whether to upgrade the quality of life of the poorer sections of Mexico City, if that upgrading in turn makes urban migration even more attractive.

It is worth noting that analysis of the poplation and migration problems required a reexamination of the population problem, because published studies, even if only a few years old, could not capture the impact of recently introduced population-control measures.[13] These measures have been shown to be surprisingly effective in reducing urban fertility rates, but have as yet to prove themselves in reducing rural fertility. Moreover, it was discovered that by the year 2000 the population of Mexico City, even without additional migration, would exceed 20 million at only moderate internal rates of increase. This would strain some of the urban services (such as water and transportation) to the breaking point, even without the added burden of migrants.

Second, the problem of chronically high inflation, relatively new to Mexico (annual inflation was less than 2% during the 1950s, less than 3% during the 1960s), elicited a response in the 1970s (when the inflation rate reached a high of 32% in 1977) that strained the government-labor relationship.[14] The combination of devaluation and wage restraint, which allowed inflation to eat away at wages more than profits, is understandable given President José López Portillo's probusiness orientation and the perception that the antibusiness policies of his predecessor Luís Echeverría had to be reversed. Nonetheless, this response has become a favored recipe for handling inflation, which is likely to be persistent because the high foreign debt and the influx of oil dollars are both likely to have further inflationary effects.

The government's approach to resolving the decline in food production has emphasized agrobusiness instead of raising the agricultural productivity of the poorer segments of the rural population, and has been augmented with the importation of foodstuffs, which further discourages small-scale food production.

Most if not all of these reactions and difficulties relate to the built-in tendency to allow the high-aggregate-growth, capital-intensive development model to place the greatest burden on relatively poor segments of the population. Income distribution per se thus becomes an important problem; not because maldistribution is likely to ignite mass unrest and revolution, but rather because fears of the negative effects of maldistribution are likely to play an important role in molding policy.

Interpreting Income Distribution Trends.   This brings up one of the crucial distinctions in forecasting short-term and long-term political trends. For the long term (more than five years) the material conditions *per se* have a direct impact on resources, levels of satisfaction among the population, governmental strength, and so on. In the short term (two years or less), the major impacts of changes in material conditions will be mediated through elite perceptions of these changes and the opportunities and dangers they are perceived to present. Government policy is the product of the cognitions of policy makers, not an automatic response of "the system" to actual happenings.

This leaves room for two important discrepancies between actual material trends and what is believed to be happening. First, important material changes often go unnoticed for long periods of time because of inadequate information collection or the narrowness of the elite's frame of analysis, which may ignore or resist recognition of the importance of the trend. Often, the impoverishment of one sector of a population will be ignored for such reasons.

Second, perceptions tend to be more volatile than the actual long-term trends. This is because of the *attention cycle*. After being ignored, trends representing potential problems are discovered, receive high levels of attention that often exaggerate their importance, and then fade from attention as people become bored, institutionalized ways of addressed the problems are developed, or those involved simply presume something has been done about the problem. In each of these stages the *perceived* severity of the problem varies according to the stage of awareness and the actions taken, rather than to the material trends themselves.

In Mexico both of these patterns are relevant for understanding the government's reactions to the trends in income distribution. The rapid deterioration of income distribution in the 1950s and 1960s did not attract much attention. Yet, in the 1970s the attention level rose sharply. According to the available studies, income distribution had deteriorated from the beginning of the postwar period but stabilized by 1968. President Echeverría apparently tried to address the problem, but an important household budget survey undertaken in 1975 indicated another sharp drop in the income share of the bottom 40% of the population. According to this study, their share, at 10.3% in 1963 and 10.5% in 1968, dropped to only 8.1% in 1975. This was a major decline, a resumption of the income concentration that appeared to have been reversed in the mid-1960s. The fact that Echeverría had made an apparently vain effort to reverse this trend made the problem seem particularly intractable. Combined with the stagflation crisis of the mid-1970s, the perception of deterioration of economic crisis was looming.

Then, in 1977—but not reported until 1979—another survey was undertaken, which showed that the bottom 40% earned 10.9% of the national income. Various adjustments for presumed underreporting calculate the 1977 share as either slightly higher or slightly lower than the figures for 1963 and 1968, but nowhere near as low as the 1975 figures. The 1975 figures are clearly out of kilter. According to the figures for the other years, there has been no significant change in the income share of the bottom 40%, and the share of the top 20%, according to the 1977 survey, declined from its 1968 level whatever adjustment is applied.[15]

This may well mean that a false perception of income distribution trends was a significant factor in the outlooks of policy makers during the late 1970s. It is enlightening to see that the volatile shift in perceptions appears to have had more impact on policy perspectives than has the more gradual change in actual income distribution.

Despite the high level of attention focused on the potential repercussions of maldistribution during the 1970s, the Mexican government never enacted an employment program with any real prospect of greatly reducing the level of unemployment. Regardless of the preoccupation with income distribution, the Mexican administrations do not appear ready to change the top-heavy income distribution significantly, particularly if the López Portillo approach is continued. Rather than developing active policies to ameliorate income inequality, the Mexican government seems more likely to try to avoid certain policy options that might exacerbate the political problems stemming from maldistribution, but without encroaching on the privileges of the higher-income groups. This makes it more likely that risky behavior—such as boldly attacking socioeconomic problems with a flood of financial resources that could raise expectations very rapidly—will be avoided.[16]

Long-Term Economic Growth Patterns. The Mexican pattern of economic development is one of remarkable success at aggregate growth over two generations. Virtually uninterrupted rapid growth has been achieved by an economy tied to the growth of its larger northern neighbor, but protected by high tariffs and other devices from most direct competition from the United States. Mexico has created a strikingly large heavy industrial base, generated a growing number of jobs, and has acquired the funds necessary to maintain the existing patronage network of the PRI and to coopt newly organized social groups. In this way, the growth of the economy has provided a vital support of the sophisticated, PRI-dominated political regime.

However, the pattern of economic growth has other aspects, with possibly crucial political implications. Mexican growth, and PRI ties to business, have been achieved by protecting and heavily subsidizing Mexican industry; in consequence, most of that industry is hugely inefficient. Growth of employment, impressive though never sufficient to alleviate some of the world's worst unemployment and underemployment, has been accomplished in large part by expanding relatively unproductive civil service positions. There are natural limits on the expansion of such an economy. By the mid-1970s those limits appeared to be near. In 1976, Mexico encountered an economic and financial crisis and had to seek assistance from the International Monetary Fund (IMF) in return for agreement to implement a stringent austerity program.

However, the new Mexican president, López Portillo, saw an apparent escape from the limits of the old growth model and from most of the requirements of the austerity program: Mexico had vast oil reserves, and world oil prices had soared. Therefore, he ignored much of the austerity program, invested massively in oil production, and used Mexico's oil as a lever to secure foreign loans that created a foreign debt in excess of $80 billion. The old Mexican economic model was back on track. For most of López Portillo's term, the Mexican economy performed at its accustomed high rates of growth and continued to provide jobs and patronage.

By 1981, however, limits were reappearing. Even with oil prices that remained far higher than they were when López Portillo took office, and which remained within a few dollars of their historic peak, the Mexican budget was drastically out of balance, inflation was high, and the country's current account was experiencing severe deficits. High interest rates, world recession, and a slight decline in oil prices strained Mexico's financial capacities. Then three serious policy errors (discussed below) reduced Mexico's export revenue and stimulated a flight of capital. Suddenly Mexico was unable to pay its foreign debts and faced a period of severe austerity in order to regain solvency. The necessary austerity measures called into question the economic underpinnings of Mexico's political stability. If Mexico could not subsidize business, protect inefficient industry, and choose an overvalued exchange rate that gave the middle and upper classes access to cheap imported goods and luxurious foreign travel, could the PRI retain business and middle-class allegiance? If Mexico had to cut back civil service employment, would that hurt the public sector political base of the PRI? Above all, if Mexico had to severely reduce workers' wages, could the PRI count on the continued allegiance of the politically vital labor unions? Could it prevent a strike of the oil field workers, who were now able to shatter the economy for a long period of time by striking at a time of desperate need for foreign exhange that could only come from oil exports?

In short, the crisis of 1982 illuminated what most political scientists studying Mexico's sophisticated political system had failed to grasp: Mexico's two generations of political stability depended on continued rapid economic growth and the resultant availability of funds for patronage and cooptation. But limits on the Mexican economic model, which were already apparent by the mid-1970s, required major economic changes that went against the grain of Mexican political traditions.

Mexico's Revolutionary Ideological Legacy.   Aside from patronage, Mexico's PRI-dominated system is held together by the ideological legacy of the Mexican Revolution. The PRI presents itself as the inheritor of the Mexican Revolution and of the leftist ideology of that revolution. Inside Mexico, these PRI claims are widely accepted, for historical reasons. One indicator of public acceptance of the PRI as a leftist, nationalist force is the fact that protest votes accrue heavily to parties of the right, as occurred with Partido de Acción Nacional (PAN) gains in 1982. But, in fact, the PRI presides over a very right-wing society, with extraordinary income inequality and extraordinary unemployment. These structural features of Mexican society are promoted by policies that emphasize heavy industry (rather than labor-intensive light industry), neglect of agriculture, and emphasis within agriculture on agroindustrial development rather than on development of family holdings. Such right-wing, unrevolutionary policies serve the interests of the coalition of politicians, industrialists, and elite unions that constitutes the PRI at the expense of the rest of the population.

The nationalistic thrust of PRI ideology and policy supports the interest of this coalition by protecting its members against foreign competition, despite the long-term price the country pays for such policies. As in many Latin American countries, left-wing nationalistic slogans and policies actually serve as a cover to promote conservative domestic interests. There are dangers in such a coalition of conservative interests and nationalist ideology. Loss of long-term economic efficiency is a heavy price that is already being paid. There is also a striking tendency for nationalist rhetoric to replace sound decisions. Mexico's bankruptcy in 1982 was the direct consequence of three such decisions, each of which cost the country billions of dollars. First, when it was necessary to reduce the price of Mexican oil in order to avoid loss of Mexico's customers, President López Portillo replaced the minister who cut the price with another who restored the previous high price; as a result, Mexico's export revenues suffered major losses. Second, in early 1982 when devaluation of the currency was an obvious necessity, López Portillo adopted a posture of nationalism and machismo, saying, "I will not be a devalued president." The result was a massive flight of capital that cost the country much of its foreign exchange reserves. Third, later in 1982 when the same situation recurred, López Portillo made the same mistake again. He feared that devaluation, although an economic necessity, would do severe political damage by reducing the ability of the PRI's middle- and upper-class supporters to purchase imported luxuries at cheap prices and to vacation easily in the United States. The consequence this time was international bankruptcy.

López Portillo found his reputation as a technocrat ruined. He responded by trying to retrieve a favorable position in Mexican history with recourse once again to nationalistic policies: he nationalized the banks, winning acclaim from nationalists but postponing for his successor the difficult decisions needed to cope with the crisis.

Implications for the Future. Mexico's political system is extremely sophisticated as a mechanism for maintaining a coalition through patronage, maintaining national unity through ideology, managing mild discontents through democratic institutions, and suppressing or coopting major challenges to the system. This sophisticated system has yielded two generations of political stability and provides considerable undergirding for stability in the future. The system has talented leadership at the top, politically effective although corrupt and shortsighted institutions in the middle, and a reasonably broad base of public support.

However, this system depends on economic growth adequate to sustain its patronage and cooptation mechanisms, and the traditional PRI economic policies have been shortsighted. Sustaining the economic base for political stability will require drastic changes. Key parts of the PRI will be tempted to substitute rhetoric for economic reform. If such elements were to dominate, or if the crisis of 1982–83 were to prove so severe as to alienate key unions and large segments of the middle class from the system, then economic mismanagement and resultant economic decline could lead to gradual disintegration of the PRI coalition, emergence of serious and prolonged urban rioting, and the risk of anarchy and an eventual military coup.

Which outcome will happen is not firmly predictable. But it is clear that if stability is to occur it will require a more competitive and therefore more efficient economic system, a reorientation toward production rather than civil service as a source of employment, decisive establishment of priorities among subsidized state enterprises, and at least a gradual reorientation toward policies that would promote broad participation in the country's development at the cost of some of the short-term interests of the PRI elite coalition. Such changes will have to occur while the PRI manages to retain the allegiance of the elite unions—a delicate task. The decision maker who sees these scenario elements falling into place can be confident of future stability.

On the other hand, if the policy maker sees a second scenario emerging, there will be reason to fear for Mexico's future stability. In this scenario, key unions respond to austerity by beginning to withdraw from the PRI. Then, Mexican government leaders shrink from the painful economic decisions listed above and have recourse instead to traditional nationalist and leftist rhetoric, accompanied by purely symbolic gestures such as López Portillo's nationalization of the banks. The PRI then becomes caught in a no-win situation where it can choose the policies necessary for economic recovery only at the cost of disintegrating its coalition, and it can maintain the coalition only through policies that gradually destroy the economy. The likely outcome of such a scenario is the emergence of a period of prolonged urban rioting and immobilism, followed by the emergence of the Mexican army as the central political force of the country.

The policy maker could not know in 1982 which of these scenarios would transpire, although certainly the new president, Miguel de la Madrid, and his associates, like López Portillo at the beginning of his term, desired to follow the path of technocratic reform. But the policy maker could follow events in Mexico with the two scenarios firmly in mind and make decisions according to the dynamics that are occurring; the policy maker lacks a firm prediction but possesses a contextual understanding that can guide the decisions without blinding him or her to the real range of alternatives.

ANTICIPATING LOPEZ PORTILLO'S SUCCESSOR

Choosing an Approach

At first glance it might seem that predicting the type of candidate the PRI would nominate was a simple matter of extending the pattern that some observers claimed to see in the sequence of presidential succession over the past 40 years. They argued that there had been an alternation of conservative and populist presidents. Would this permit us to predict that López Portillo's successor would be a populist?

Not everyone even recognizes that this pattern has held in the past. First, there are some who have interpreted the alternation pattern differently, as entailing shifts among three positions: left, center, and right.

Second, many observers deny the alternation altogether, pointing to the continuity of an aggregate-growth-oriented economic policy, the endurance of the political formula of the PRI, and other persistent elements of Mexican politics and economics. Although the differences between an Echeverría and a López Portillo are certainly important to foreign investors or governments, there is clearly enough doubt raised by both these positions to reject the simplistic approach of presuming that the alternation pattern must recur.

In light of the precariousness of predicting alternation simply because it may have prevailed, the analytical design chosen for our study began with an inquiry into the dynamics responsible for the choices of presiden tial nominees within the arena of the PRI party. The strategy was to bypass speculation on the "macropattern" in favor of identifying "microlevel" dynamics (or developmental constructs). Once these dynamics were identified, it was possible to identify the trends that would enhance or reduce the possibility of each dynamic.

Four dynamics would bear on the selection of the PRI nominee, a behind-closed-doors process in which the outgoing president plays an important but not omnipotent role in the consultation and bargaining that culminates in the nomination. The first dynamic concerns the internal politics of the PRI itself. Since the party spans a broad range of ideological positions, alternation could relieve the pressure coming from whichever side was left unrepresented by the incumbent. This has historically prevented groups within the PRI from leaving the party, because opposition to presidential policies, though futile in the short run, may help to secure change in the next administration.

Shifting from one type of president to another was reinforced by the accumulation of resentment that usually grew as each president reached the end of his six-year term. Most of the resentment naturally came from the opposite side of the ideological spectrum, thus strengthening the case for this side to have greater weight in the choice of the incoming president. However, each new president, intending to redress the injuries done to his constituency during the previous administration, could only do so by antagonizing the party's other wings. Thus, it cannot be taken for granted that shifting necessarily reduces net dissatisfaction within the party.

Internal PRI bargaining is not the only determinant of presidential selection. Obviously, the decision also hinges on how the PRI leadership plans its ventures in the political world outside the party itself, and how the Mexican leadership defines the problems facing the country, assesses the severity of these problems, and decides how to attack them. Electoral calculations, growth strategies, and approaches to solving the country's major sociopolitical problems must also be considered.

The second dynamic comes into play simply because the PRI must run in and win elections. Even though the PRI is dominant in its electoral support, it cannot take its victories for granted. Reports that the PRI has had to resort to electoral fraud and other irregular tactics to secure some of its gubernatorial victories reinforce this point, since the PRI leadership would much rather win elections without having to resort to such legitimacy-threatening tactics. If and when an incumbent president wears out the political attractiveness of his particular ideological position, the PRI leadership may turn to a man of clearly different orientation to win back electoral support. This is, of course, contingent on the assumption that the PRI gives high priority to maximizing its electoral appeal—an assumption that does not appear to be borne out at this point.

The third dynamic is the preoccupation and highly institutionalized set of arrangements concerned with maintaining high levels of economic growth. Shifting from one type of president to another has been costly in terms of economic growth during the past two decades. It detracted from the certainty and continuity of economic policy, because several years were required for each administration to build up new programs to replace the plans of the previous administration that were discarded simply because of their association with the outgoing president.

Finally, the potential dangers of maldistribution have some bearing on the PRI deliberations over whether the next president ought to be a populist. In the past, populists revalidated the PRI's revolutionary credentials. If worsening income distribution fueled dissatisfaction, the switch to a "president for the poor" could perhaps defuse the potential for disruption. However, there is currently no agreement on whether a populist would do better because he could actually satisfy the potentially disruptive poor, or would fan the flames by raising aspirations that could not be met within the resource limits and political-economic structures of Mexico.

Therefore, knowing that the preoccupation with the problem of maldistribution would dominate the succession choice is not enough to predict the outcome. Additional questions must be raised to establish whether this preoccupation is likely to culminate in a strategy of attacking the distributional problem head-on or an attempt to suppress its political manifestations. How strong is the perception that a populist can indeed redress the imbalances in income? What theory prevails in the minds of the Mexican leadership about how improvements for the poor will interact with their expectations and their disruptive potential? A preoccupation with distributional problems would be likely to translate into the choice of a populist only if the Mexican elite is convinced that (1) the problem ought to be tackled, (2) a populist president would improve the position of the poor, and (3) this improvement would defuse rather than aggravate the political tensions. Note that for our immediate purpose the actual repercussions of populist policy are not really what we must predict. The issue is what the influentials of the PRI and other politically relevant groups believe the correct answer to be. The forecaster's task is to understand their diagnosis of the problems of poverty and political instability. This understanding can only be gained from reading and interviewing; no amount of "data" will resolve the issue. The trends we must monitor to analyze a near-term event such as the presidential succession have to do with perceptions rather than concrete realities.

To summarize, the selection hinges on the relative importance of several distinct dynamics:

1. Calculations over intraparty bargaining and balancing
2. Electoral calculations
3. Managing economic growth
4. Coping with maldistribution and its attendant problems

These dynamics are not mutually exclusive, yet they may lead to different predictions of the outcome of the nomination process. The question for our assessment thus becomes: "Under what circumstances would each of these dynamics dominate, and where would each lead if it did?" In identifying these circumstances, we can accomplish three related objectives. We can develop a more refined understanding of the populist-president and conservative-president scenarios. We can monitor the trends that are likely to trigger one dynamic or another for the longer-term future. Finally, we can develop an understanding of how the system works above and beyond the simple prediction of the type of president assuming office after the July 1982 election.

Enabling Trends

Party Balancing. Based on our analysis of the party-balancing logic of shifting from one type of president to another, four enabling trends for the dominance of the intraparty bargaining dynamic can be identified:

1. *Continuation of the relatively low perceived threat of massive disruption.* Insofar as the regime believes it is fighting for its survival, the internal accommodations within the PRI are likely to be regarded as only secondary considerations.

2. *Continuation of the high capacity of the president—regardless of his ideological position—to disconnect rhetoric from concrete economic policy.* This would make the costs of shifting to a populist tolerable to the business sector and to right-wing elements of the PRI.

3. *Continued perception that a leftist president could indeed satisfy the demands of the PRI Left.* If few believe that a switch to a populist president would solve the problems of unemployment, maldistribution, and the dissatisfaction of the PRI Left, there would be little incentive for undertaking this change in direction.

4. *Continued high level of prominence of the Intellectual Left.* Without this pressure from the Left, the need to compensate the PRI's own left wing would diminish significantly. The stature of the PRI's Left depends in part on the general standing of the Left in Mexico.

Electoral Calculation. The trends associated with the electoral-calculation dynamic are:

1. *Continued perception that the PRI will face electoral challenges.* If electoral strategy is given less importance, either because victory can be taken for granted or because the PRI begins to worry that lopsided victories will undermine the regime's legitimacy, the weight of electoral considerations would obviously diminish.

2. *Increased perception that the candidates' actual ideological stand can be discerned by the typical voter.* Since the PRI traditionally has been able to pass off conservatives as populists and vice versa, the nominee's actual ideological position is relevant only if it is believed by the PRI to be a factor in the election.

Growth management. Based on analysis of the economic challenges, one can identify the following enabling trends for the dominance of the growth-management dynamic:

1. *Acute short-term economic problems that would increase the perceived importance of this period as requiring a strong effort to safeguard the momentum of growth.*

2. *Perception of this period as critical for Mexico's long-term economic development.*

3. *Declining perception that a populist could redress the income distribution imbalances.* This would increase the likelihood that policy makers would focus on the growth possibilities, because the

income distribution problem would appear intractable through the direct populist approach.

4. *Decline in criticism from the Intellectual Left.*

Populist Income Distribution.   Finally, the likelihood that the nomination would primarily be an adjunct to coping with the problems of income distribution depends on the following enabling trends:

1. *Increasing perception of deteriorating income distribution and attendant problems.*   If distributional problems, appearing under such guises as unemployment and inflation, are seen as merely troublesome but politically manageable, then concern over the issue may not call for the populist risk. But if the problem is seen as no longer manageable politically but rather as requiring fundamental economic restructuring, then the distributional issue would be paramount in choosing the presidential successor.

2. *Continuing perception that a populist could redress the income distribution imbalances.*

3. *Declining perceived importance of this period as critical for Mexico's long-term economic development.*   As long as the current period is seen as pivotal for Mexico's capacity to turn the newfound oil wealth into sustained economic growth and modernization, the risks presented by a change in orientation to address maldistribution loom very large.

4. *Continued high level of criticism from the Intellectual Left.*

Weeding Out Dynamics

Several of the crucial underpinnings of the internal bargaining dynamic have eroded. This does not mean that the balancing of PRI factions will end completely, but rather that the rationale of balancing through shifting to a populist has declined. Perhaps the most important factor is disillusionment with the last populist. Echeverría incurred the costs of presenting himself as a populist—the economy suffered seriously—but the income distribution and unemployment situations did not improve. Therefore, the perception that a leftist president can satisfy the demands of the PRI Left is at a low point. Echeverría also demonstrated a dangerous inability to insulate the economic climate from the impact of his rhetoric. Although his economic policies were fundamentally in line with the modern-sector orientation of his predecessors, Echeverría managed to antagonize domestic and foreign business to such an extent that investment and growth suffered anyway.

Moreover, the perceived threat of disruption is high, despite the fairly low level of actual disruption in Mexico itself. Revolutions in Iran and Central America have raised fears in Mexican leadership circles that manifest themselves in various ways, such as the preoccupation with Guatemalan "provocateurs" crossing into southern Mexico.

Finally, contrasted with the situation during the system crisis that many believed Mexico was facing from the late 1960s through the 1970s, the attention given to the Intellectual Left has been overshadowed by other concerns. The criticism from the Left is still relevant; it simply has less relative weight compared to the preoccupations with managing growth, exploiting the oil, and avoiding an Iran-style loss of control.

The importance of the vote-maximizing dynamic also appears to have diminished when one examines the enabling trends. The concern over winning big in the election has been partially replaced by the worry over declining electoral turnout and the weakening of the appearance of truly competitive elections. Thus, the government's reforms of the legislative system in the late 1970s were motivated by a desire to give the other parties a greater voice. Consequently, it seems less compelling than before for the PRI to balance a conservative incumbent with a populist successor in order to court the left-leaning electorate. Indeed, it is unclear whether the PRI leadership would perceive an overtly populist president as more attractive electorally than a conservative one, or that they hold a high opinion of the electorate's capacity to distinguish a true populist from a posed populist.

The lower weight given to the challenge from the Intellectual Left, the disillusionment with the prospect of a populist being able to redress the distribution problem, and the increase in the perceived cruciality of the current period for Mexico's long-term economic growth all argue against the dynamic of decision making based on concern over maldistribution, and they all argue for the dynamic of preoccupation with overall growth. Regardless of whether equity or growth is indeed the more serious problem for Mexico at this time, the climate of opinion at the moment of the nomination process reflected greater concern over the economic growth problem. The problems are in fact inseparable, but insofar as different strategies are seen as requiring tradeoffs between the objectives of growth and equity, the preoccupation at the moment is more on the side of immediate problems of growth than of immediate opportunities to redress the distribution of income. There seems to be a complex attitude that the income distribution is not really deteriorating further, that little can now be done about it directly, and that the potential wealth of Mexico's vast oil reserves is too great an opportunity to entrust to a possibly unreliable populist president.

On the basis of these considerations, our study asserted that the PRI nominee would probably be a conservative, managerial type of the López Portillo mold. This assertion, made in late 1979, was borne out in the 1981 nomination of Miguel de la Madrid as the PRI candidate. Whether de la Madrid will be forced by political circumstances to adopt some of the characteristics of populism is the next question. Concessions to organized labor and the abandonment of wage-restraint approaches to inflation control were raised as strong possibilities. The possibility of the PRI's failure to hold onto its own left wing must also be raised and explored for its ramifications.

OVERVIEW

This chapter has illustrated once again the central themes of this book. Quantitative methods prove simplistic and lead the analyst into disregarding most of the context within which forecasted trends and events occur. Organizational analysis provides a systematic but nonquantitative way to assess the organizational strengths and weaknesses of a regime and the dynamics by which fundamental decisions are made. Organizational analysis of the contemporary situation, in order to generate understanding of the future, must be supplemented with analysis of the way fundamental social trends (such as income inequality, population, economic growth, employment, and structural change) alter the resources and strategic choices of the major political organizations. Firm prediction is seldom possible, but scenarios and analyses of organizational dynamics can provide the policy maker with a contextual understanding that conveys the real degree of uncertainty he faces, a sensitivity to the meaning of events, and a way of judging the central tendencies of complex events so that he can move decisively at appropriate moments.

NOTES

1. A. F. K. Organski, "Estimating Outcomes and Consequences of Interstate Wars," Final Technical Report, ARPA, Ann Arbor, Mich., 1977.
2. *Ibid.*, p. 21.
3. *Ibid.*, p. 21.
4. B. Gross, "Preface," in Robert J. Shafer, *Mexico: Mutual Adjustment Planning* (Syracuse, N.Y.: Syracuse University Press, 1966), p. xxiv.

5. E. A. Duff and J. F. McCamant, *Violence and Repression in Latin America: A Quantitative and Historical Assessment* (New York: Free Press, 1976).

6. E. Barkin and G. Esteva, "Social Conflict and Inflation in Mexico," *Latin American Perspectives* 9, 1 (1982): 55; R. E. Scott, *Mexican Government in Transition,* revised ed., (Urbana, Ill.: University of Illinois Press, 1965), p. 24.

7. Peter Smith, *Labyrinths of Power* (Princeton, N.J.: Princeton University Press, 1979).

8. It has been characterized as overreaction by both observers with a centrist viewpoint, such as R. D. Hansen, *The Politics of Mexican Development* (Baltimore: Johns Hopkins University Press, 1971), p. 229; and more leftist critics like K. F. Johnson, *Mexican Democracy: A Critical View* (Boston: Allyn and Bacon, 1971).

9. Joseph Hodara, *Los futuros de Mexico—un marco de referencia* (Mexico City: Fomento Cultural Banamex, 1978), pp. 50–58.

10. R. E. Scott, *Mexican Government.*

11. R. E. Montes de Oca, "The State and the Peasants," in *Authoritarianism in Mexico,* José Luis Reyna and Richard S. Weinert, eds. (Philadelphia, Pa.: ISHI, 1977).

12. R. L. Harris and D. Barkin, "The Political Economy of Mexico in the Eighties," *Latin American Perspectives* 9, 1 (1982): 8.

13. Lenero L. Otero, "Mexican Population Policies from a Sociocultural Perspective: Past, Present and Future," in *The Future of Mexico,* Lawrence E. Koslow, ed. (Albuquerque, New Mexico: University of New Mexico Press, 1977).

14. Barkin and Esteva, "Social Conflict," p. 52.

15. J. Bergsman, "Income Distribution and Poverty in Mexico," World Bank Staff Working Paper no. 395 (June 1980), p. 15. Bergsman summarizes the studies mentioned above.

16. Here a distinction must be made between what the analyst believes the "proper" Mexican response ought to be—perhaps exploiting the oil wealth rapidly in order to alleviate poverty and achieve a high enough level of growth to keep abreast of expectations—and what the policy-making style and preoccupations of the Mexican leadership are likely to produce.

Part 4
Bureaucratic Issues

Chapter 11

Institutional Arrangements of Forecasting and Planning Operations

The institutional arrangement of an analytical operation affects both the substance of forecasting and its reception. Each major institutional facet—the broad nature of the organization, its internal structure, and its relationship with policy makers—not only affects the accuracy and bias of analysis, but also influences its credibility, insofar as the conventional wisdom holds many (largely untested) rules of thumb about what sorts of forecasters and institutions are to be trusted.

Many strategies, involving every aspect of an analytical operation, can be developed to counter the pitfalls of forecasting and the tensions between policy makers and forecasters. The following discussion of institutional arrangements (as well as the review of presentation format in the next chapter) ought to be regarded as "selected tactics," designed to indicate how these problems can be approached, rather than as exhaustive survey.

NATURE OF INSTITUTIONS

Our rather extensive examination of U.S. forecasts indicates that, by and large, forecasting accuracy is not a function of the institutional source of the forecast. Governmental forecasters do as well as business forecasters, even if the government's contact with the phenomenon seems one more step removed. Research institutes, presidential commissions, business associations, and so on, are all roughly even in accuracy over the long haul. The reason is that the core assumptions establish the rough magnitude of the projected value of a particular trend, whether too high or too low, and common preconceptions of the future usually pervade most institutional sites at any point in time. These common perceptions generally yield uniformly optimistic or pessimistic forecasts regardless of the forecast source.

Biases do occur when an institution is so committed to a policy or outlook that its members cannot adapt their thinking to new realities. This is strikingly illustrated by the Federal Power Commission's forecasting record during the 1960s. In contrast to today's preoccupation with the adequacy of energy supply, the main preoccupation of many energy policy makers during the 1960s was the inefficiency resulting from unused capacity. Their preoccupation with low demand growth became a preconception of low demand growth, missing the effects of their own promotional campaign for all-electric homes. It is significant that the McGraw-Hill trade journal, *Electric World,* concerned more with the problem of keeping up with demand, forecasted higher demand levels. This demonstrates the importance to decision makers of obtaining relatively independent judgments.

STAFF-LINE RELATIONSHIPS

The Problem of Bias

This sort of finding confirms the very plausible premise that analysts are more likely to lose their objectivity when their own organizations are involved in the operations of controlling or regulating the phenomena under examination. Consequently, the traditional public administration distinction between line (operations) and staff positions is relevant in structuring analytical operations. Regardless of whether they are formally within the same institutional unit as the policy maker, analysts serving in the capacity of staff are more likely to avoid analytic bias, partly because they will not be biased by the need to defend their own decisions and partly because they will be more insulated from the pressures of self-justifying superiors. Furthermore, even if the biases of operating units did not in fact materialize, there is a strong expectation of such biases, so that the credibility as well as the impartiality of operations units is problematic.

The Problems of Cooptation and Isolation

A second danger results from having the analyst too close to line operations. Decision makers can be so voracious in their desire for information that would facilitate day-to-day decisions that the analyst gets nibbled to death by requests for small pieces of information. This has been the problem in the State Department's Bureau of Intelligence and Research.

Much of the value of a forecasting and analysis operation comes not from special knowledge and not from arcane methods, but from the leisure to focus attention on the big problems and the long-range issues. (The nibbling to death can easily occur from inside a forecasting unit, when managers fail to choose problems selectively, as well as from outside.)

While potential bias and the risk of wasting energy on minor issues rightly result in the relegation of forecasters and intelligence analysts to staff positions, there is an equal and opposite danger. Forecasting, analysis, and intelligence too frequently become isolated from decision making. The concerns of the long-range planner lack the immediacy of the crises decision makers face today. The patterns of thought employed by long-range planners differ from the patterns of daily decision making, and these patterns of thought and even the vocabulary easily appear academic and irrelevant to the busy decision maker. Even worse, the insights of the planner may give him perspectives that contradict the views of the decision maker without being very persuasive. Or they may simply irritate the decision maker's sense of bureaucratic prerogative. Every analyst has sometimes faced the view that, if the idea was "not invented here," it will be given short shrift. While the fate of the State Department's Policy Planning Staff after George Kennan's departure illustrates the problem of line executives subordinating the planners, the fate of much of the long-range planning in the Pentagon illustrates the opposite problem, that of being isolated and ignored. The solution is to maintain the forecasting and planning process as a staff function, but to conduct planning exercises that engage decision makers, to use decision makers part-time in staff planning functions, and to rotate analysts into line roles temporarily as appropriate. Without close, ongoing contact between analyst and operator, the planner or forecaster becomes a bureaucratic irrelevance.

If the analyst is regarded as a mere provider of data, or as an interloper in the decision process, then the true relationship between analysis and decision is obscured. But if the purpose of the analyst is understood as being primarily heuristic, as reommended earlier, then the necessity for constant communication between analyst and decision maker becomes self-evident. The analyst and the policy maker are not just exchanging information or contesting for power. They are intertwining habits of thought, exchanging experience, sharing patterns of judgment.

These observations have important implications for the evaluation of a planning process. Frequently, it is not specific plans or a specific series of actions that mark the success of a planning operation. More important in most cases are the sensitization of the policy maker to the broader and longer-term consequences of current decisions and the reorientation of the analyst toward the issues that are consequential for policy.

RESOURCE ALLOCATION

The Update Strategy

The first dilemma over how to allocate scarce resources for analysis revolves around the simultaneous needs for recency and for fundamental, intensive analysis capable of exploring and expressing basic assumptions. Where should the effort go if total resources are inadequate to support frequent *and* large studies? Spreading the resources over a large number of equally small projects would sacrifice the opportunity to do the fundamental analysis; infrequent all-out efforts would leave the policy maker with possibly obsolete analysis between studies.

The most reasonable compromise is to begin with an intensive initial study, in which the basic assumptions can be examined in detail, the context can be explored to identify factors that may have some future relevance, and a fundamental understanding of the dynamics of the system can be achieved. Thereafter, smaller update studies can be mounted to determine whether departures from the trends projected by the original study, or from the assumptions underlying that study, are significant enough to call the original conclusions into question.

In practice, such a procedure will tend to proceed somewhat opportunistically. Big studies that build intellectual capital will be possible when current problems focus attention on an issue. The years 1978 and 1979 · were good for geopolitical analysts to build intellectual capital on Mexico and China. Earlier, because of the Rhodesia/Zimbabwe crisis, there were good years for building intellectual capital about southern Africa, and, still earlier, about Southeast Asia because of the Vietnam War. To some extent, then, the cycle of crises supports a system of big studies and updates. But the natural cycles must be managed so that (1) a minimum capability is maintained even in the absence of current crises (note current U.S. lack of intellectual capital regarding South Asia), and (2) the advantages gained from crises are not dissipated (as has occurred with U.S. expertise regarding Southeast Asia).

Inevitably the crisis-oriented, large-scale studies will attract a different level of talent and originality from the more routine update studies. Seldom will the analysts doing the update studies have the same level of originality or the same confidence in challenging assumptions. The prestige and level of resources that the authors of large-scale policy-planning or analysis efforts can bring to bear will inevitably imbue their findings with an aura of authority that relatively junior analysts will hesitate to challenge. Large-scale quantitative models constructed under such circumstances may be so complex as to intimidate potential challengers, either because of intellectual complexity or because of the resources required for a successful challenge. To some extent such consequences follow inexorably from scarcity of talent, prestige, and resources. However, such consequences can also be dangerous and therefore must be ameliorated as far as possible.

Above all, in order to facilitate such amelioration, the major studies must fully display their basic assumptions and must fully elaborate the methods used to proceed from basic assumptions to conclusions. This is contrary to the strong tendency of analysts to obscure their most problematic assumptions. It is also helpful to preserve dissenting views and to articulate differing perspectives, even if not in the main document. Finally, updating analysts should be specifically directed to inquire whether the basic assumptions of the big study remain valid.

There is an equal but opposite pitfall to be avoided: the analysts engaged in updating must be urged to avoid the temptation of challenging the original study simply to establish their own originality or to convince funders that another big study is required. These temptations can be avoided to a large extent if at least some of the original analysts are included on the update teams (which would also relieve the first problem), along with some new analysts to keep the others from defending the original study too strongly.

The "Islands of Excellence" Strategy

Despite these efforts to keep analysis "fresh" between crises and between big studies, scarcity of top-level talent inevitably combines with bureaucratic pressures to ensure that, in any large and long-lived analysis operation, obsolescence will begin to affect many sections. The analysis groups will become too inbred and will accept too many preconceptions. Members of a China analysis group, for instance, may interact over many years and come to share common views to an excessive degree. Over time, pressures to conform to line managers' policies take their toll on innovative questioning. And group members may simply grow old and rigid together. Moreover, much analysis may be dull and routine rather than imaginative and insightful just because of the inevitable scarcity of talent. To the extent that the techniques mentioned above fail to alleviate such problems, it is often useful to design "islands of excellence," teams or informal groups of the most capable staff who protect each other, move with fewer bureaucratic impediments, possess highly generalized skills, and can move quickly to shake up or take over analysis operations that have become stale at a time when high-quality work is needed. Such teams develop of their own accord in most dynamic organizations but may benefit from managerial nurturing. The risk of demoralization if such groups are used excessively is balanced by the risk that managers will habitually ignore analysis if they cannot depend on the product.

ORGANIZATIONAL TECHNIQUES

Unity versus Diversity

Normal administrative procedure requires managers to press for unity and to eliminate redundancy. In line operations, and in most staff operations as well, redundancy simply adds cost. Similarly, in most administrative operations, disunity of views within an operating group slows down implementation of decisions and may even render decisions ineffective. However, in an analytical operation, and particularly in a forecasting operation that requires substantial exercise of judgment, organizational arrangements that would in other contexts constitute redundancy may be essential to successful operation.

Long-range forecasting, particularly in a heuristic mode, is an exploratory operation. In any mode, as indicated by earlier discussion, forecasting results are frequently not susceptible to rigorous testing or standard methodological criteria. This means that there is no basis for imposing conventional standards of unity and nonredundancy.

More generally, the inability of any particular method, discipline, or political perspective to capture the full richness and complexity of most situations requiring high-level executive decision implies that any forecasting or analysis effort confined to a single discipline or to a single political perspective usually will produce narrow or biased results. Thus, in analytic or forecasting operations there is an inherent requirement for diversity of disciplinary and political perspectives. Frequently there is even a need to mix different generations, because the experience of different generations heavily determines their perceptions of current and future events. (For instance, there is an identifiable generation of economists that worries primarily about depression and unemployment, and another that worries primarily about inflation; similarly, there is a cold-war generation of political analysts and a post-cold-war generation.)

On the other hand, the problems of getting the job done remain and are exacerbated greatly by the need for diversity in analysis. Lack of common assumptions and common vocabulary among different disciplines and conflicting political perspectives cause time-consuming, resource-diverting discussion. Bringing together a group of people who disagree with one another risks raising unpleasant and hypothetical issues, which to administrators will often appear to be a diversion. Issues that are normally finessed may be posed with excessive starkness. If members of the group represent important bureaucratic or political actors, they may seek to mobilize support outside the group and thereby provoke unnecessary conflict within the administration or within the society. Administrative morale may erode, public support may weaken, and the responses of participants in the debate may become increasingly rigid. Moreover, the search for diversity leads to another danger, namely the risk that an analysis group may simply become so large as to prove unwieldy.

The need to integrate diverse perspectives and the need to get the job done are both powerful imperatives. A forecasting effort can be vitiated either by a small group of right-minded, similarly inclined officials who proceed to produce analytic pap, or by a group of diverse academic prima donnas who proceed to produce more dissents and caveats than useful analysis. The organization of analysis teams must therefore avoid both Scylla and Charybdis. While there is no single channel the manager can follow to successfully avoid both risks, there are several basic techniques from among which the manager can choose.

First, there is the *A Team, B Team* approach. This is the method used by a university dean who suspects that the political science department has become ingrown and increasingly incompetent. The dean brings in a team of outside observers who criticize the work of the existing faculty and recommend administrative and personnel changes. It is also the technique used to challenge CIA estimates of Soviet intentions during Gerald Ford's administration. These two examples illustrate the most fundamental aspect of this approach: it is a technique used by administrators acting on the assumption that their analysts are wrong. The head-on approach of opposing one more or less coherent team to another, with the so-called *B Team* asked primarily to criticize the *A Team,* guarantees maximum resentment, maximum conflict over responses, and maximum rigidification of intellectual positions. The costs in time, intellectual rigidification, and reduced morale make this technique a last resort. Only where there is a presumed need for a severe shakeup is such a technique appropriate. Such situations do, of course, occur, perhaps more often than is recognized, so the technique should not be dismissed out of hand.

A second technique is encouragement or toleration of *competing analysis groups*. It is quite common for the Treasury, the CIA, the State Department, and others to prepare position papers that contain different perspectives, analyses, and forecasts. The differences reflect different administrative interests, different team compositions, and frequently even different ideologies. The resulting diversity of analyses reflects not only competing bureaucratic viewpoints but also the checking and balancing process of the American system of government. It has all the virtues and all the vices of that checking and balancing process. As long as there is a system for integrating the diverse perspectives or deciding among them, and as long as the diverse perspectives are perceived as legitimate and reasonable, this form of diversity constitutes not a form of redundancy, but a way of ensuring that all major vews are heard, while avoiding the severe clashes of the *A Team, B Team* arrangement. Problems arise with this competition when the individual perspectives are allowed to become too narrow and also when they are presented to decision makers sequentially rather than in a simultaneous or integrated fashion. Sequential presentation of differing positions, a frequent phenomenon in many industrial democracies today, can lead to changes in major policies every six weeks.

When different forecasting organizations attempt to *cooperate,* rather than to compete, there is a different result. For instance, when the experts of State, Agriculture, and Treasury attempt to create a unified forecast, the different perspectives are likely to get full play. Moreover, substantial advantages are gained from the interdepartmental communication that occurs in such a process. The danger is that the coordination will prove so expensive and time-consuming, and the departmental mobilization of political resources in support of its interest so stultifying, that the mutual communication does not result in a timely and useful analysis. The risks and benefits of such interorganizational efforts must therefore be carefully weighed in each case.

Finally, there is usually some necessity for *diversity* within a given forecasting team, except in those few cases where there is a single agreed-upon method that does not require the exercise of judgment. For the purposes of many decisions it is imperative to have on the team a military expert, an economist, a political scientist, a conservative, a liberal, a young person, and an old person, ideally for a total of three people. This hope is important, because diversity creates enough obstacles to getting the job done without complicating the problem by having to coordinate a large number of people. Assuming that the individuals selected for the team are individuals who can cope with complexity and disagreement (and most good analysts should be able to do this), and assuming that those analysts are free of large administrative stakes in the outcome of the analysis, diversity should not make production of an intelligent and useful document impossible. Diversity in such circumstances should ensure that uncertainties and disagreements surface rather than remain hidden. It should ensure some corrective to the almost universal tendency to overestimate the certainty of a forecast. It should also increase the likelihood that areas of consensus surface explicitly; for instance, it has been noted that despite the remarkable diversity of views about Soviet military intentions there is a surprising consensus among specialists of all perspectives that Soviet-American war would only arise indirectly or through Soviet miscalculation, not from a conscious, deliberately calculated Soviet plan to attack and conquer Western Europe. Such illumination of common ground can be invaluable.

Differing expert opinions can, of course, create problems for the credibility of an analysis. Nuclear arms strategists have been embarrassed by dissension over technical facts. Similarly, the reputations of petroleum geologists decline whenever two experts come out with different ultimate-reserve estimates. The U.S. Geological Survey has been wracked with conflict between those predicting high recovery rates and those predicting low rates. Such conflicts can be partially alleviated if the analysts can convey that (1) their analyses still have much in agreement, (2) attention is inevitably focused on the points where experts disagree because that is where the problematic decisions must be made, and (3) expert disagreement does not imply expert incompetence, since there will always be a frontier of knowledge for which consensus has not yet been reached.

Within both government and corporation, the conflict between the imperatives of unity and those of diversity frequently takes on a particularly delicate form. It is not uncommon for an analyst to produce a forecast that is acutely embarrassing to current policy and substantively or methodologically controversial. The government department or private firm may have no one else competent to assess the forecast, but may shy away from outside consultation because of fear of "embarrassing the Secretary," as the Washington phrase puts it. Traditionally this problem has been resolved by reliance on trusted outside individuals or on contract research centers where discretion has been assured through traditional or proprietary legal arrangements.

The Prospects for Interdisciplinary Analysis

As we saw in Chapter 3's review of forecasting approaches, interacting social, political, and economic contextual assumptions are critical for good analysis and prediction. The dependence of each forecasting task on several others is a severe dilemma for all forecasters, but especially for highly specialized ones. The imperative of diversity of perspectives conflicts with academic and bureaucratic trends toward specialization.

The specialization of most forecasters preoccupied with their technical problems is one reason why obsolete assumptions are often retained. A specialist in one forecasting area—say, energy demand—must rely implicitly or explicitly on forecasts in areas that are beyond his own expertise (for example, population forecasting). Since the forecaster's own knowledge of appropriate assumptions outside of his specialty is limited, he will not produce definitive forecasts in these other areas. More importantly, the specialist may not be able to appraise the validity of the older forecasts lying around so conveniently. Unless the resources are available to mount new studies in these supportive areas, forecasters will often rely on the older, existing studies whose assumptions are frozen at the times when they were produced. This is most commonly seen in the projections of materials and energy demands, based on inaccurate contextual assumptions of population and economic growth. For example, the underestimates of transportation demand after World War II reflected reliance on low projections of GNP expansion and the presumption that the low birth rates of the prewar period would continue.

In addition to the appraisal techniques suggested in Chapter 6, these considerations clearly call for interdisciplinary analytic efforts. Interdisciplinary teams can keep the contextual assumptions fresh. Since it has been shown that sociopolitical forecasting is generally the weak link in projecting a wide range of trends, interdisciplinary teams that include social scientists and practitioners of other disciplines can at least partially relieve this problem. Interdisciplinary teams are also less susceptible than experts from a single discipline to the methodological fads that usually rise and fall within single disciplines. Since different disciplines rarely experience the same fad at the same time, at least some members of an interdisciplinary team are likely to hold a healthy attitude of skepticism toward any given fad.

The call for interdisciplinary efforts has been made so often, and the term "interdisciplinary" has become such a buzz word, that it is only fair to ask whether the call for interdisciplinary analysis is superficial (maybe such analysis goes on all the time but has not been prominent simply because the presumed advantages have not materialized) or, if few interdisciplinary efforts have been mounted despite all the advice in favor of the approach, whether interdisciplinary analysis may not be feasible.

In view of the lack of empirical data on the magnitude and performance of interdisciplinary efforts, one can only guess about the obstacles to interdisciplinary success. However, it seems reasonable that many interdisciplinary initiatives are cut short when it is discovered that the theoretical frameworks of different fields (for example, economics and political science) do not easily mesh. Not only does the practitioner of a given discipline have trouble understanding the jargon of the other discipline, but, more importantly, he cannot integrate the considerations contributed by the other framework into his own analysis. Some analyses make oversimplified assumptions about conditions that are the principal foci of other disciplines. For example, many economic analyses assume that political constraints and governmental policies will not stand in the way of optimizing benefits under the presumption of competitive markets. Decision theorists may base their analyses on the presumption of the availability of information that economists would consider problematic.

This problem is particularly acute when the analyst is strongly oriented toward gaining recognition within his discipline. For the "technical" fields (economics, operations research, decision theory, and so on), additional considerations tend to be construed as fuzzy or extraneous, and the classic career advancement pattern within such disciplines has generally favored purist approaches over eclectic approaches.

The integration required for interdisciplinary efforts to be effective can be aided in the format of analysis, by treating the condition, events, or trends indicated by the analysis of one discipline as the scenarios or conditionals of the other, and vice versa, along with some indication of the likelihoods assigned to the scenarios or conditions. (See the discussions of conditional forecasting and scenarios in Chapter 12.) Short of using intricate models expressing mutual constraints and reciprocal causation, these simple format devices can provide a framework of contextuality within which each specialist can ply his trade.

Personnel selection itself can ameliorate the problems of having decided to employ an interdisciplinary team. Using at least some individuals with interdisciplinary training, either to conduct the analysis or to synthesize the analyses of others, can smooth over some of the clashes between the language and outlooks of different disciplines, though admittedly the jack-of-all-trades problem sometimes arises. In addition, although government and academia both tend to produce and reward narrow specialists, there are organizational sources of broader perspectives. Contract research centers often counteract academic tendencies toward overspecialization. Business management at high levels often forces individuals to diversify their experience. In summary, there are enough possibilities for increasing the feasibility of interdisciplinary analysis to reject the pessimistic suspicions that it is a dead end.

Functional versus Geographic Orientation

One of the ultimately unresolvable issues in any forecasting organization of extensive geographic range and functional scope is whether to emphasize a geographic or a functional orientation. Asking this question is a bit like asking whether businesses should be centralized or decentralized. There is no definitive, universal answer. Excessive geographic specialization risks inability to perceive important trends that cut across regions. It also risks the deveopment of an inbred perspective that sees every problem as a special case. Excessive functional orientation, on the other hand, risks loss of the rich contextual information that a regional specialist can bring to analysis. For very large forecasting organizations with global, multifunctional responsibilities, as in a corporate planning department, a think tank, or a government intelligence agency, the only answer is probably one that most businesses have discovered with respect to centralization and decentralization: do both, always maintaining both regional and functional expertise, and accept a cycle in which a period of emphasis on regional expertise is periodically corrected by a period of emphasis on functional expertise, and vice versa.

Analytic Routines

One of the greatest temptations in organizing analytical operations is to institutionalize the procedures so that standardized routines developed by the "star" analysts will be utilized by more "routine" personnel. The incentives are many. First, innovative analysts can derive tremendous personal satisfaction and considerable professional advancement from establishing a system or model for others to follow. Second, the top-level management of analysis operations yearns to guarantee competent, systematic analysis by imposing standardized methods. Third, the requirements for the most intensively trained and highly paid personnel may be perceived as eased—the genius of the rare innovators is captured in the routine while the innovators themselves go off to other tasks. Finally, formal routines look scientific.

Institutionalization can proceed in three directions. First, *procedural guidelines* can describe how the routine-following analyst should gather, categorize, and interpret information. The many how-to books and articles on forecasting and analysis offer this sort of advice, which in some organizations becomes dictum. In some analytical operations a home-grown brand of procedure is developed, and personnel are required to follow it more or less step by step.

Second, *quantitative evaluation routines* can even more strictly bind the analyst to precise algorithms that transform information into quantitative measures. Figures of merit or related composite scores of weighted indices are used to rate different situations or options in terms of their desirability, risk, or likelihood. These include the numerical ratings of credit worthiness or stock growth potential, the Dow Jones Industrial Average, and other familiar indices of the business world. In political-economic analysis, these can be ratings of political risk, overall military strength, composite measures of economic development, and so on. These quantitative indices are particularly popular because they can give inherently judgmental information a scientific, precise patina. Judgment comes in when deciding which preexisting quantitative data should be included to make an index meaningful (for instance, which stocks should be included in the Dow Jones average), or simply by converting judgments into numerical rankings (such as Russell Fitzgibbons's rating of how democratic Latin American nations are, based on responses of a panel of U.S.-based Latin Americanists).

Third, *complex computer models* represent the ultimate in institutionalized routines. While the modelers themselves are prone to tinker with their models continually, once the model is handed over to operators rather than modelers the results may be generated rather mechanically, especially if the operators do not feel competent (or lack the authority) to alter specifications or parameters.

In addition to the obvious benefits of institutionalized routines mentioned earlier, all three forms of standardized routines have an additional advantage and several serious drawbacks that are not so obvious.

The subtle advantage of institutionalized methods is that they permit the analysis to proceed with relatively little additional plausibility testing, beyond that which has been imparted in the original development of the routines or models. Consequently, routinized procedures forego the continual censorship of judgmental screening, which is an advantage if and only if there are counterintuitive surprises on the horizon and the routines are really good enough to anticipate them.

The first disadvantage stems from the same characteristic. When the routine or model is not appropriate for a particular situation, when it produces misleading or even nonsensical results, the routine-following analysts may lack the ability or authority to modify or disregard the routine. In other words, suspending plausibilty testing is a risky strategy.

The second disadvantage is that preset routines or models fail precisely when good analysis is most needed: when the basic structure of the situation is changing. Routines that work well when a constant set of factors is relevant in consistent ways fall apart when new conditions make additional considerations suddenly relevant or alter the relationships among the original factors. If assumption drag is the main villain in failures of forecasting, institutionalized routines have the severe liability of ossifying core assumptions that can be rendered obsolete by subsequent events. This is why all of the macroeconomic models failed so miserably immediately after the 1974 oil price increase. The models' structures were not equipped to trace the consequences of expensive energy as a growth-constraining factor.

The third disadvantage is that routines cannot guarantee insight, so that substituting institutions for top-level analysts may sacrifice the quality of judgment while maintaining the trappings of expertise. A prominent example of this problem was the Planning-Programming-Budgeting System (PPBS) invented at the Rand Corporation and first instituted by a contingent of "whiz kids" at the Department of Defense in the 1960s. When President Johnson saw the success of PPBS in the Defense Department, he ordered it to be used in most other federal executive agencies for preparing and evaluating budgets submitted to the Office of Management and the Budget (OMB). But without the expertise, dedication, and dynamism of the original team, the operation of PPBS as a hand-me-down routine in the other agencies was a fiasco, applied with so little finesse that OMB disregarded the PPBS reports almost completely.

Finally, routinized procedures suffer from the general lack of inside information and top-level contacts on the part of the subordinate personnel designated to follow the routines. Thus, even if these personnel have the authority and willingness to screen the results of the routines, they are in an inferior position to do so as compared with the high-level innovators. For example, the econometric modeling operations overseen by insiders like Otto Eckstein or Lawrence Klein generally produce at least reasonable results if only because Eckstein and Klein know as well as anyone what is happening in governmental and corporate circles. If technicians were running their models (which is increasingly so), such vital knowledge would not be available to correct an errant model.

Large government or business organizations cannot, of course, avoid institutionalized procedures. What they can do is to institutionalize procedures that ensure a certain degree of ferment. They can formally require the periodic review of major assumptions. They can insist upon the formation of forecasting teams that incorporate a certain degree of diversity, as discussed above. They can encourage frequent contact with outsiders (for instance, in the academic world), and reward efforts to acquire new techniques or substantive knowledge. Where intellectual incest has reached an unacceptable level, they can deploy a *B Team*. Perhaps, above all, they can systematically cultivate islands of excellence, where groups of more creative people can develop in an environment more protected from ordinary bureaucratic pressures, and then encourage those groups to develop broad skills that will enable them to intervene in many different substantive areas as necessary to shape up existing procedures or to meet immediate policy challenges.

Expert Consensus

Another popular resource-saving strategy is to rely upon expert consensus without undertaking new research. However, the strategy of establishing a consensus of experts by compiling existing forecasts ("passive consensus"), rather than eliciting current opinions from experts ("active consensus"), is risky. First, whereas the active approach permits the compiler to impose some uniformity on the specific definition of the trend to be projected, the passive compiler may end up with some obsolete forecasts or some forecasts of similar but not identical trends.

The other "quick and dirty" option is to establish an active consensus by eliciting the opinions of a panel of (usually outside) experts without undertaking a major project of research. Such expert-panel analysis is most prominently represented by the Delphi method, a multistep questionnaire technique that queries expert opinion on a given set of topics, provides the experts with feedback on the opinions of the other panelists, and then permits them to alter their prefeedback positons, usually resulting in a convergence to consensus positions. Many policy makers and analysts look askance at Delphi and other expert-panel techniques, on the grounds that they seem to be creating analysis out of nothing. In fact, however, expert-panel analysis works surprisingly well, largely because the experts are aware enough of recent developments to hold accurate core assumptions. Our findings show that Delphi studies and kindred techniques have an excellent record of forecasting computer capability advances, nuclear energy expansion, energy demand, and population growth. They offer a very inexpensive means of achieving interdisciplinary interaction. By requiring feedback on why each panelist took his position, expert-panel analysis can provide the reasoning behind the choices, thus enhancing its heuristic value. Finally, expert-panel analysis can have the additional advantage, if at least some of the panelists are from within the organization sponsoring or undertaking the study, of intensively educating these in-house analysts through contact with the rest of the panel.

PERSONNEL

The composition of analytic teams established within a given institution can vary widely, with the selection and training of analysts as the major discretionary aspects. The need for diversity has been discussed above.

Substance versus Method

What kind of expertise is desirable? There is no conclusive evidence as yet that training in any particular substantive discipline makes for more accurate and less biased forecasting. However, the relative unimportance of methods in establishing the accuracy of analysis naturally downgrades the relative importance of methodologists on analytical teams. The importance of accurate core assumptions calls for personnel selection that enhances familiarity with substantive trends and their broader context. Thus, if the choice is between an expert in a planning discipline (like operations research) and someone with an intimate knowledge of the phenomena under examination, our findings would give preference to the latter.

Experience

While our analysis downgrades the role of forecasting methodologists, it underlines the value of experience and talent for intellectual synthesis.

Experience is important because of the important role of judgments and because of all of the delicate balances required in producing useful forecasts. If there were a single rigid mathematical method that could be employed for most forecasts, then forecasting managers could be trained in school and proceed directly to the production of exceedingly useful material, in much the way that a good surveyor can move directly from school to job. The leader of a forecasting effort, however, must acquire over time a sensitivity to disciplines other than his own, a capacity for creating smooth working relationships among people with conflicting intellectual and political perspectives, and a talent for creatively employing the tension between the needs of decision makers and the needs of analysts. While these requirements may not be qualitatively different from the requirements of good managers of any kind, except for the overwhelming need to emphasize the values of diversity, the requirements for broad intellectual perspective and delicate personal relationships are far greater in analysis groups.

The Need for Synthesis

Above all, there is the need for an intellectual synthesizer. Having enhanced creativity and ensured the surfacing of disagreements and differing perspectives through the creation of an intellectually and politically diverse team, the team leader confronts immediately the danger of intellectual chaos. Western society has become increasingly a society of specialists, and neither academia nor bureaucracies cultivate large numbers of people with broad synthetic intellectual talents. As a consequence, in an academic, business, or government forecasting team, the time will come when the economist had done his job, the political scientist has done his job, the military specialist has delivered his opinions, and the liberal and the conservative have delivered opposing perspectives. The decision maker lacks the time and energy to read all of the separate papers and to integrate the views himself. Only a synthesizer of great skill can write an overview sufficiently unified to convey the dynamics of the situation but sufficiently complex to convey the richness and uncertainty of the situation. It is worth emphasizing this point by concluding with it. Most organizations that need to engage in forecasting will not find themselves short of specialized experts (as consultants if not as employees), nor will they find themselves short of ordinary management talents or exotic methodologies. Most, however, chronically find themselves short of minds that can cut across disciplines and political perspectives to convey a coherent rather than fragmented forecast.

Synthesis of diverse perspectives is, of course, radically different from imposing layers of review by people with different perspectives. The latter process, more common than successful synthesis, simply reduces a forecast to its lowest common denominator.

Chapter 12

Presentation of Forecasts

Like so many other aspects of analysis, the issues surrounding the format of presentation appear technical but really are not. The integrity of the analyst, his relationship with the policy maker, and the usefulness and credibility of the analysis itself depend on the format of the presentation. It is in the presentation of the analysis that the analyst must convey the uncertainty of the predictions and estimates, despite his own reluctance to appear fallible and despite the pressures for certainty often applied by the policy maker. The format of the presentation also constitutes the framework for conveying the various types of information that establish the relationship between analyst and policy maker. Presentational format may seem like a formality, or it may be regarded simply as the medium for conveying what the analyst wants to convey, but, in fact, once a particular format comes to be standard, it poses real constraints on what the analyst *can* convey.

OBJECTIVES OF PRESENTATION

To reiterate, the analyst's objectives to be maximized through proper presentation are (1) to make the analysis as convincing as it deserves, (2) to enhance the utility of the analysis to the policy maker, (3) to get the policy maker to pay attention to the analysis, and (4) to convey the uncertainty inherent in the analysis. In order to achieve these objectives, the presentation of the analysis ought to reduce the strains between policy makers and analysts, particularly those concerning demands for certainty beyond the level warranted by the analysis, and it ought to alleviate the policy maker's suspicions of being manipulated by the analyst.

In concrete terms, this means that the analyst is well advised to display openly his reasoning, assumptions, uncertainties, and qualms. It is ironic that the credibility of analysis is in greatest jeopardy when it is presented as too "pat." While policy makers often push for excessive certainty, they also often know how complex reality is and are consequently suspicious when the reasoning underlying the conclusions of analysis is presented as clearcut, when all the details seem to fall the right way, and when every consideration or datum examined fits neatly with the conclusions. This sort of presentation is easily interpreted as either superficial or biased advocacy. It is equally ironic that as long as the analyst can come to some reasonable conclusion, the more evidence he can provide showing the complexity of the situation, and the conflicting trends and considerations that make pure prediction uncertain, the greater the long-run credibility will be, since the analyst has shown the depth of his understanding and awareness of other arguments and considerations. The advantage of clearly indicating assumptions and uncertainties is further heightened by the benefits of structuring forecasting as *thinking* about the future rather than simply projecting trends into the future. Analysis as heuristics obviously requires that the assumptions be made explicit; it also helps when uncertainties (surely an integral part of understanding a situation) are also explicit. Finally, in order to use to best advantage the strategy of mounting a large original study followed by frequent small-scale updates, the assumptions underlying the original analysis must be prominently displayed so that the update efforts can readily identify and reexamine them.

DISTORTIONS IN PRESENTATION

While these concerns are relevant to all aspects of the task of analysis including the format of presentation, there are a few additional problems peculiar to presentation alone. These are related to how information tends to become distorted once it has been presented.

The first problem is *contraction,* the tendency of information to be received and retold in increasingly simplified ways, so that each new recipient of the message receives, in effect, less information. Contraction occurs for a host of reasons, including the sheer physical limitations of information transmittal (recall how the newspapers could not handle headlines with the phrase "Break-in at the Democratic National Headquarters at the Watergate Building," and consequently used the misleadingly simple term "Watergate"), lack of time to read or otherwise absorb information, and the difficulties of people other than the original analysts in condensing the information without losing important nuances or qualifications.

Because there are so many different causes of contraction, it is unlikely that the problem can be completely eliminated. However, its effects can be reduced by making sure that the original presentation is rich in detail and explicit in its underlying assumptions. Making explicit linkages of predictions or estimates with the premises and conditions required for their validity is the best way to convey the architecture of analysis and to ensure that this architecture is preserved in subsequent retelling.

Confronted with the loss of information caused by the contraction effect, the audience of a communication often compensates by reading into it many implications that are not manifest in the original. In the case of analysis, policy makers may perceive arguments and stances that they attribute to the analyst. This mechanism of *inference* also creates distortions, since the attributions of meaning do not necessarily correspond to the analyst's true intentions. For example, there are numerous cases in which analysts who argue against one prominent school of thought are automatically lumped into the contending school. Critics of the methodology of the *Limits to Growth* study have been labeled as "antiecology." The least mention of nuclear plant safety problems is often enough to have an entire analysis construed as antinuclear. Sometimes the use of particular terms or even numbers evokes entire arguments.

If unchecked, these mechanisms in combination can first erase the specification of assumptions—the intended architecture of the argument— and then replace it with another architecture that is more a projection of the policy maker's expectations of the analyst's opinions than of the analyst's true position. Similarly, factual information that is summarized through contraction may be incorrectly reconstituted as distorted information when the policy maker interprets and draws inferences from second-hand reports.

CONDITIONAL FORECASTS

The most fundamental decision concerning the format of forecasting is whether to project absolute or conditional forecasts. Absolute forecasts would seem to be more audacious, since they are of the form "X will happen," and thus imply that all the conditions and policies on which X depends can be predicted by the forecaster. Conditional forecasts, of the form "if one set of conditions or policies holds, then $X(1)$ will happen; if another set holds, then $X(2)$ will happen," are employed when the forecaster is unwilling or unable to project all aspects of the future. The conditionals are presented as possibilities but are not themselves predicted. Conditional forecasts are often submitted to policy makers when the conditional aspects are policy choices at least partly controllable by those policy makers. Under these circumstances, in which the forecaster does not presume to anticipate what the policy maker will do, different forecasts are generated for different policy scenarios. However, analysts may resort to conditional forecasting out of simple ignorance, not knowing what situations or policies will prevail, even if their immediate audience does not control these factors.

The use of conditional forecasts can overcome the problem of self-defeating prophecies, relegating these apparent paradoxes in the appraisal of analysis to their proper status as red herrings. It has been claimed that the accuracy of a prediction is not an appropriate criterion of evaluation because, if predictions of negative outcomes are heeded, policy makers will take actions to avoid those outcomes. Such forecasts should have been conditional in the first place, displaying different outcomes resulting from different policy choices. The absolute prediction of negative outcomes is certainly no more useful than the corresponding conditional prediction that such outcomes will result from inactivity, and the conditional form (assuming that the analysis is correct) avoids the inaccuracy of presuming that no action will be taken.

When conditional forecasts do avoid the presumptuousness of predicting all aspects of the future, conditional forecasting that employs a range of policy scenarios carries an often unrecognized audacity in presuming that this particular set of policies includes all viable policy options. In choosing a set of policy scenarios, the analyst focuses policy makers' attention on this set and implies that it covers the politically and technically feasible alternatives. This problem is exacerbated by the analyst who, believing that the policy makers can only digest a limited amount of analysis, restricts the policy scenarios to a very limited number of options. Thus, if the policy maker does not initially recognize that the analysis implies a narrowing of policy alternatives under consideration, the quality of decision is likely to suffer. If the policy maker does realize, before or after, that the analyst has taken up the task of narrowing the range of policy options, the analyst may be denounced as manipulative.

There are two ways of attacking this problem. The first is to demand that the policy maker specify the policy options under consideration, so that the analyst can then work from this range. Of course, the policy maker may very well be in the process of defining alternatives rather than choosing from a fixed set of options, and would therefore be unwilling to provide a range for the analyst.

The second is to define the policy conditionals in terms of changes in the parameters that are directly affected by policy and in turn determine the eventual outcomes. For example, in projecting conditional forecasts of energy supply and demand the analyst may define one of the conditional parameters in terms of the levels of electricity-generating capacity, on the grounds that many different combinations of governmental policy instruments (such as nuclear plant licensing, tax incentives for investment in utility expansion, and so on) could be employed to establish each partic-

ular level of generating capacity. This approach poses a formidable challenge for the analyst. In order to avoid restricting choice through the
neglect of some parameters potentially influenced by policy, the analysis
must devise a categorization of parameters that is both inclusive and
workable. If the dynamics of the phenomena under examination are complex,
it is difficult to isolate a sufficient set of parameters that are not influenced
as much by the trends to be projected as they are by the policy choices.
Mutual causation makes it difficult to classify anything but the conditional
policy choices as fixed parameters.

EXPRESSING UNCERTAINTY

Strictly verbal expositions of the pros and cons of various arguments and
conclusions have liabilities. There are difficulties in relying on verbal
terms such as "likely," "highly likely," "high estimate," "low estimate," "optimistic," and so on. These terms do not always convey the
same meanings to different people. A casual survey of how much probability ought to be encompassed by the "high estimate" trend line and the
"low estimate" trend line would yield a range running from 50% to 90%.
Such imprecise terms provide little meaning to the analysis of combinations of trends and events (as for the purposes of cross-impact analysis).
Because by convention many strong arguments are presented with hedges
and caveats, the presence of qualifiers does not consistently convey the
intended indication of uncertainty. Also, verbal qualifiers are often interpreted as wishy-washy evasions of responsibility. Consequently, they reduce
the credibility of the analyst and the analysis.

One way to avoid this problem might be to state explicit subjective
probabilities. Some theorists have claimed that subjective probabilities
have no empirical referent or meaning, because the frequency-of-occurrence notion of probability (the probability of heads for a fair coin flip is
0.5 because over the long run half of the flips will be heads) does not
apply to unique events. However, the analyst's subjective probability that
an event will occur does not—and is not supposed to—convey the proposition that the world has a mechanism that spews out different events with
different probabilities. Instead, as discussed in Chapter 3, it may convey
a more modest and straightforward notion that there is uncertainty in the
analysis of reality (akin to betting odds); it conveys the probability that
the analyst or the analysis is correct. Designating specific probabilities
would seem, therefore, to be the most straightforward way to convey
uncertainty. However, in assigning probabilities and probability-bounded
confidence intervals, there are several problems.

The first of these problems is that, whereas confidence intervals are easily applied to quantitative trends (for example, there is a 90% probability that Soviet GNP in some particular year will fall between $1.4 and $1.5 trillion), probabilities are less meaningful and more difficult to assign to qualitative trends because of the fuzzy boundaries of qualitative descriptions. (This does not imply, though, that arbitrary quantitative cutoff points are any more meaningful.) If, for example, an analyst must assign a probability to a particular scenario entailing a "major change in the government" or a "swing to the left," the probability would naturally vary according to how significant the change would have to be to qualify as fulfilling that scenario.

Second, the fact that scenarios are stories involving numerous points complicates the assignment of probabilities. To what extent is the likelihood of one scenario component dependent upon the likelihood of others? This complication is exacerbated by the fact that the number of events or conditions of a scenario, and the level of detail, are chosen arbitrarily, yet greater elaboration and finer detail increase the probability that the scenario will hold at least some incorrect elements.

Third, experimental evidence suggests that confidence levels are consistently overestimated; that is, the frequency with which outcomes actually do fall within a given range is generally lower than the probability assigned by the analyst.[1] These results pertaining to quantitative confidence intervals probably can be generalized to the assignment of probabilities to the occurrence of "most likely" scenarios or other qualitative predictions.

Finally, as a practical matter, the effort to assign explicit probabilities in most cases guarantees extraordinary organizational problems between members of the analysis group, and between different analysis groups. In practice, the difference between 62% and 65% can easily become a matter of intense bureaucratic struggle, especially when great stakes hang on the outcome of the analysis.

For most large analysis organizations, these objections to the effort to assign explicit probabilities are overwhelming. In Washington, assignment of numerical probabilities to a series of scenarios would be unmitigated bureaucratic disaster. However, the individual analyst, whose work is not subjected to intense review by competing interests prior to publication, may find it more useful and more precise to state probabilities explicitly— so long as he does not have to waste time and the reader's attention by providing intricate calculations of "nests" of probabilities applicable to multiple elements of diverse scenarios. The analysis organization will usually find it more helpful to establish a relatively rigorous use of probabilistic language for its presentations. There is ambiguity in all uses of language rather than numbers, but it need not be disproportionate to the ambiguity inherent in the situation.

PRESENTATION OF RECOMMENDATIONS

Since analysis in support of decision making almost invariably has policy choice implications (if only in providing information that implies the advantages of certain choices over others), the question arises of whether the recommendations implied by the analyst's conclusions should be made explicit. Should the analysis be even more ambitious, casting its conclusions in terms of what ought to be done? The analyst, whether concerned with enhancing his own role or simply improving the quality of decision making, would naturally want all of the valid implications of the analysis to emerge in its presentations. But what of the policy maker's own discretion?

Two findings based on several case studies on the impact of forecasting efforts provide insight into these questions. First, the acceptability of the forecast (or other technical information) is enhanced to the extent that it can be portrayed as "firm information." A comparison of the impact of two major comprehensive forecasting studies published after World War II, the Paley Commission's *Resources for Freedom* and the Twentieth Century Fund's *America's Needs and Resources,* reveals that the straight projections of the former study were more easily and willingly accepted by policy makers than were the more elaborate recommendations of the latter, which seemed to present the policy maker with a virtual fait accompli: "Accept the analysis, accept the recommendation." Similarly, the failure of explicit optimization techniques to gain wide acceptance in corporate and governmental planning reflects not only the policy makers' resistance to analysis as recommendation, but also the policy makers' ease in rejecting and ignoring these techniques. In contrast, the U.S. Census Bureau's demographic projections, which are deliberately presented as merely mechanical extensions of various sets of explicit assumptions on fertility and mortality rates, come very close to monopolizng population forecasting in the United States.

Second, although policy makers are naturally loath to jeopardize their power by relying on analyses that leave no flexibility of choice, analysis without a message cannot engage the policy maker's interest or distinguish itself from all of the other information impinging upon him or her. Another important advantage of the Paley Commission study over the Twentieth Century Fund analysis was that the Paley report had very clear implications for natural resource conservation, whereas the Twentieth Century Fund study was a mass of narrowly specific expenditure recommendations. The *Limits to Growth* study of the Club of Rome was prominent as much for the shock value of its message as for the credentials of its authors. It seems clear that analysis with obvious policy implications—which, however, does not force detailed policy choices—has the best chance for usefulness and impact. Yet the analyst must resist the temptation to be bold when it is not warranted. The strident criticism against the Club of Rome and the associated methods of Jay Forrester and Donella and Donald Meadows (see Chapter 4) provides an object lesson against analysis as show business.

SEPARATION OF METHOD AND SUBSTANCE

Because forecasting techniques evolve so quickly, and because new substantive issues constantly require new approaches, any serious forecasting team will be involved both in producing estimates for decision makers and in purely methodological experimentation. In consequence, presentations must explicitly and rigidly distinguish between results that are primarily methodological and results that are intended to be substantive forecasts. One does not send a primarily methodological result to the Secretary of Health and Human Services with a demand for immediate action, nor does one send it to the *New York Times Sunday Magazine* in a form designed to influence public opinion about important issues.

Stated abstractly, this point is an obvious ethical imperative. Yet, in practice, few organizations adequately maintain the distinction. A classic example of failing to observe the distinction was the presentation by some members of the Club of Rome of early results of an effort to model the development of world economic growth, resources, and pollution. The model was a very simple one, which assumed resources to be constant, ignored technological change, and assumed pollution to be a straightforward function of economic growth. The results showed that, if these assumptions were adequate, continued economic growth would very quickly produce a catastrophe in which much of the world's population would die. The results were announced with great fanfare as scientific evidence of the validity of the conclusions, and copies were mailed to key decision makers throughout the world. People like Elliot Richardson, then a Cabinet member, were urged to pursue policies that would avoid the catastrophe. Then, several scientific journals began to carry articles showing that the results were artifacts of the overly simple assumptions mentioned above and that the conclusions were, therefore, very dubious. The authors of the report and some of their modeling collaborators responded to such criticism by arguing that the results were just preliminary methodological efforts and that one could not expect scientifically valid conclusions from such a preliminary effort. Later, other members of the Club of Rome published another book with quite different results based upon a more sophisticated model. The episode was damaging to the reputation of the Club of Rome and a source of severe controversy within the organization, many of whose members were distinguished scientists who clearly understood the distinction between method and substance and the contradiction between demanding action and insisting that critics wait for future results. Such episodes and such consequences are unfortunately not rare in the forecasting world. A forecaster can often obtain widespread publicity and acclaim by publishing preliminary, experimental results as if they were scientifically validated substantive forecasts, but his long-run credibility will—and should—suffer.

QUANTITATIVE PRESENTATION

The use of quantitative indicators in the presentation of analysis, as distinct from the use of quantitative methods of analysis, carries both advantages and dangers. Quantitative indicators provide a compact way of encoding information that sometimes can protect the information from contraction. A table or graph that can be reproduced in full is less likely than a verbal description to be condensed and run the risk of being distorted. The precision of quantitative information—if it is legitimate—is less open to inappropriate interpretation than is verbal discourse. In the analyst's struggle to avoid having to present simplistic or unduly certain analysis, irreducible quantitative presentations, such as the display of multiple scenarios or conditional projections in a "take it or leave it" chart, can fend off selective condensation.

The direct dangers of quantitative presentation stem from unwarranted inference. First, quantitative indices are quite prone to misinterpretation. An index that summarizes a wide range of phenomena under a single term (which ostensibly captures the element common to those phenomena) may measure, in any particular instance, one sort of occurrence, but then be interpreted as reflecting another class of occurrences. There is, for example, a great variety of quantitative measures of violence that include political demonstrations and strikes as well as assassinations and insurrections, summed according to a particular (and necessarily somewhat arbitrary) weighting procedure. A country receiving a high violence score because of numerous demonstrations may be misinterpreted as being politically violent in a fundamentally different way, with very different implications for future developments in that country. One could argue that a quantitative measure encompassing such disparate phenomena is simply a bad measure, but it must be recognized that quantification, and more specifically the development of indices, necessarily entails disregarding some distinctions so that different cases can be placed in the same standard category. In other words, part of the contextual meaning of specific occurrences is sacrificed in order to categorize, and it is worthwhile if and only if the disregarded dimensions are theoretically unimportant while the defining dimensions are salient. An obvious corollary is that the use of ready-made indices, developed (in all likelihood) for other uses and within a different theoretical framework, can result in quite misleading presentation and worse analysis.

The second danger is that the policy maker may infer that the superficial appearance of data says more about the analyst's true choices than the analyst actually intended. Numbers are often construed as more precise than the analysis warrants, regardless of explicit caveats. The middle numerical projection may be incorrectly presumed to be what the analyst really believes is the most likely projection, while the higher and lower trend lines may be interpreted as simply the analyst's attempt to hedge his or her bets.

Finally, an indirect danger of quantitative presentation is the common presumption that, it if is indeed preferable, it requires that the method of analysis also be quantitative. Therefore, quantitative methods may be adopted, not because of whatever advantages they hold in particular cases, and not weighed against their drawbacks (summarized in Chapter 3), but rather for this superficial reason. In fact, the results of quantitative analysis can be conveyed verbally, and judgmental analysis or other nonquantitative approaches can, of course, produce numerical results that can be displayed as such.

Thus, quantitative presentations, including specific facts, carefully designed indicators, and various judgmentally derived characterizations, can be quite useful, but only if they avoid the above pitfalls.

THE CONTENT OF PRESENTATION

Even in a highly condensed presentation for a high-level policy maker, the presentation should consist of a tightly woven logical argument. The conclusion should read, "While U.S. reliance on renewable energy resources is widely viewed as highly desirable, 19 out of 20 proposed conservation programs use more energy than they save, technological problems with solar energy make it cost four times as much as a nonrenewable alternatives, and startup problems make biomass unavailable on a sufficient scale for many years." The conclusion should never read, "Our cliometric, technological and econometric models demonstrate conclusively that conservation and renewable resoures are not adequate answers to the energy problem." The first conveys analysis; the second just conveys conclusions. The first permits reasoned response; the second uses the computer to short-circuit debate. Although the conclusions may have emerged partly through use of a model, it is always possible—and obligatory—to explain the reasons why the model generated such conclusions; there is no such thing as a model or a problem so complex that the reasons for a result cannot be clearly explained. The model belongs—at most—in a footnote.

THE NEED FOR INFORMAL PRESENTATIONS

Every analyst dealing with important issues will eventually find that a forecast completely contradicts current policy and is potentially threatening to powerful policy makers. On such occasions; normal direct presentation may lead to suppression of the forecast, to the firing of the analyst, or to a political row of uncertain outcome. Sometimes such consequences are unavoidable. However, in many such situations a forecaster who has confidence in his or her own position and in the integrity of the policy maker can avoid an unfortunate situation by initially presenting the findings, with a careful discussion of associated ambiguities and controversies, informally and respectfully to the policy maker. The quiet lunch whose tone is set by the comment, "There's a problem that has arisen which we want you to be the first to know about," has defused many potentially explosive situations. Such a lunch does not, of course, relieve the forecaster of an obligation to the public or to responsible officials for ultimately providing a formal report. And, it must be admitted, the luncheon gambit does not always relieve the analyst of the choice between maintaining his integrity and keeping his job.

TIMING A PRESENTATION

Timing is often the key to the success or failure of a forecast presentation. If the decision must be made today, the forecaster will have to provide an answer today, even if the presentation is incomplete or unpolished. The forecaster has the right to note that the results were prepared under excessively rigorous deadlines or with ambiguous data, but he or she usually does not have the right to abdicate. Similarly, the forecaster who has uncovered important issues may not be able to get a hearing until an appropriate crisis arises. Many specialists on energy issues could not get a hearing on U.S. energy policy until the gasoline shortage of 1979—even though the problems had been around for at least six years. The proper policy response to the gasoline shortage addressed long-range problems, not just the shortage. Given the competition among analysts for policy-level attention, such a phenomenon is inevitable. The forecaster who wishes to be effective must exploit cycles of attention and take advantage of crises. Any conscientious forecaster has a positive obligation to exploit crises in order to surface important issues that have been ignored.

CONCLUSIONS

A carefully considered presentation can improve the quality of decision making and enhance the position of the analyst in many ways. Details that are important include the labeling of scenarios and projections, capsule descriptions of what indices actually represent, graphics that resist distorting condensation, careful timing, and political sense regarding the manner of presentation. The common practice of foisting off the responsibility for presenting analysis to lower-level personnel out of touch with the analyst can be unacceptably costly. The analyst must keep in mind that, for the policy-making process, analysis is not what goes on in his mind but rather what is conveyed to the policy maker. The soundest advice on presentations not surprisingly mirrors the soundest advice on methods. Convey the logic of the situation, uncluttered with jargon and spurious quantification. As much as possible, define the full context of the decision. Never allow method to dominate substance. Acknowledge complexity and uncertainty, employing scenarios and conditional forecasts where necessary. Focus on findings with policy implications, but respect the experience of the decision maker, his need to bring additional judgments to bear, and his ultimate authority to decide.

NOTES

1. J. Scott Armstrong, *Long-Range Forecasting: From Crystal Ball to Computer* (New York: Wiley, 1978), pp. 129–30.

Political-Risk Theory and Strategic Planning

This is a selected bibliography on strategic planning, the theory of social prediction, and the use of expert input in large organizations. Because the prediction of political risk depends on political analysis in general, an exhaustive bibliography would literally include every work in the social sciences. This bibliography, in contrast, is intended to guide the reader through the morass of literature by identifying a little more than 100 of the most useful sources on the conduct of political analysis and its role in policy making. This includes some of the "old classics," which are essential reading despite their age, and some much newer works that may or may not be of enduring value. The emphasis on old works is an effort to refocus attention onto basic sociopolitical theory, which we believe has been neglected in the past few decades because of the infatuation with technique.

This bibliography does not include all of the technical sources cited in the text of the book. Much more extensive bibliographies on forecasting per se can be found in J. Scott Armstrong, *Long-Range Forecasting: From Crystal Ball to Computer* (New York: John Wiley Inter-Science, 1978); Albert Somit, *Political Science and the Study of the Future* (Hinsdale, Ill.: Dryden Press, 1974) and Bettina J. Huber, "Studies of the Future: A Selected and Annotated Bibliography," in *The Sociology of the Future*, Wendell Bell and James Mau, eds. (New York: Russell Sage Foundation, 1971), pp. 339–454.

Some authors have summarized their longer works in shorter articles. To aid the harried or lazy reader, some of these summary articles are included and are indicated as such by indentation.

GENERAL WORKS ON STRATEGIC PLANNING AND DECISION MAKING

Ackoff, Russell A. *A Concept of Corporate Planning*. New York: Wiley, 1970.

Ackoff, Russel L. *The Art of Problem Solving: Accompanied by Ackoff's Fables*. New York: Wiley, 1978.

Black, Guy. *The Application of Systems Analysis to Government Operations*. New York: Praeger, 1968.

Braybrooke, David, and Charles E. Lindblom. *A Strategy of Decision*. New York: Free Press, 1963.

Lindblom, Charles. "The Science of 'Muddling Through.' " *Public Administration Review* 19 (1959): 79–88.

Crozier, Michel. *The Bureaucratic Phenomenon*. London: Tavistock, 1964.

Downs, Anthony. *Inside Bureaucracy*. Boston: Little Brown, 1967.

Dror, Yehezkel. *Design for Policy Sciences* New York: American Elsevier, 1971.

Drucker, Peter F. *Managing in Turbulent Times*. New York: Harper and Row, 1980.

Quade, Edward S. *Analysis for Public Decisions*. New York: Elsevier, 1975.

Rhenman, Eric. *Organization Theory of Long-Range Planning*. London: Tavistock, 1973.

Rivlin, Alice M. *Systematic Thinking for Social Action*. Washington, D.C.: Brookings Institution, 1971.

Schwendiman, John S. *Strategic and Long-Range Planning for the Multinational Corporation*. New York: Praeger, 1973.

Stinchcombe, Arthur L. *Creating Efficient Industrial Administration*. New York: Academic Press, 1974.

Vickers, Geoffrey. *The Art of Judgment: A Study of Policy-Making*. New York: Basic Books, 1965.

Vickers Geoffrey. "Planning and Policy-Making," *Political Quarterly* 38 (July 1967): 253–65.

WORKS ON PSYCHOLOGICAL AND INFORMATION-PROCESSING LIMITATIONS ON THE USE OF EXPERT ANALYSIS

Janis, Irving. *Victims of Groupthink*. Boston: Houghton Mifflin, 1972.

Janis, Irving, and Leon Mann. *Decision Making: A Psychological Analysis of Conflict, Choice, and Commitment*. New York: Free Press, 1977.

March, James G., and Johan P. Olsen. *Ambiguity and Choice in Organizations*. Oslo: Universitetsforlaget, 1976.

Miller, George A. *The Psychology of Communications*. New York: Free Press, 1967.

Miller, George A. "The Magical Number Seven, Plus or Minus Two: Some Limits on Our Capacity for Processing Information." *Pychological Review* 63 (1956): 81–97.

Simon, Herbert A. *Administrative Behavior.* New York: Macmillan, 1957.

WORKS ON FACTORS IN THE USE OF EXPERT ANALYSIS

Allison, Graham T. *The Essence of Decision.* Boston: Little Brown, 1971.

Allison, Graham T. "Conceptual Models and the Cuban Missile Crisis." *American Political Science Review* 63, no. 3 (September 1969): 689–718.

Argyris, Chris, and Donald A. Schon. *Organization Learning: A Theory of Action Perspective.* Reading, Mass.: Addison-Wesley, 1978.

Bauer, Raymond A., and Kenneth Gergen, eds. *The Study of Policy Formation.* New York: Free Press, 1968.

Benveniste, Guy. *The Politics of Expertise.* Berkeley, Calif.: Glendessary Press, 1972.

Cyert, Richard M., and James G. March. *A Behavioral Theory of the Firm.* Englewood Cliffs, N.J.: Prentice-Hall, 1963.

Dahl, Robert A., and Charles E. Lindblom. *Politics, Economics, and Welfare.* New York: Harper and Bros., 1953.

Flash, Edward S. *Economic Advice and Presidential Leadership: The Council of Economic Advisors.* New York: Columbia University Press, 1965.

Halperin, Morton, et al. *Bureaucratic Politics and Foreign Policy,* Washington, D.C.: Brookings Institution, 1974.

Lindblom, Charles E., and D. K. Cohen. *Usable Knowledge: Social Science and Social Problem Solving.* New Haven: Yale University Press, 1979.

Wildavsky, Aaron. *Speaking Truth to Power.* Boston: Little Brown, 1979.

Wilensky, Harold L. *Organizational Intelligence.* New York: Basic Books, 1967.

WORKS ON THE USE OF ANALYSIS, MODELING, AND FORECASTING IN ORGANIZATIONS

Blank, Stephen. *Assessing the Political Environment: An Emerging Function in International Companies.* New York: Conference Board, 1980.

Brewer Garry. *Politicians, Bureaucrats, and the Consultant*. New York: Basic Books, 1973.

Greenberger, Martin, Matthew Crenson, and Brian Crissey. *Models in the Policy Process*. New York: Russell Sage, 1976.

Jantsch, Erich. *Technological Forecasting in Perspective*. Paris: Organization for Economic Cooperation and Development, 1967.

Meltsner, Arnold J. *Policy Analysts in the Bureaucracy*. Berkeley, Calif.: University of California Press, 1966.

Naylor, Thomas, and Horst Schauland. "A Survey of Users of Corporate Planning Models. *Management Science* 22, no. 9 (May 1976): 927–37.

Tugwell, Franklin, ed. *Search for Alternatives: Public Policy and the Study of the Future*. Cambridge, Mass.: Winthrop Publishers, 1973.

WORKS ON THE GENERAL THEORY OF SOCIAL ANALYSIS

Aristotle. *The Politics*, trans. Ernest Barker. London: Oxford University Press, 1946.

Brunner, Ronald D., and Garry D. Brewer. *Organizational Complexity: Empirical Theories of Political Development:* New York: Free Press, 1971.

Forrester, Jay. *Principles of Systems*. Cambridge, Mass.: Wright-Allen Press, 1968.

Hempel, Carl G. *Aspects of Scientific Explanation and Other Essays in the Philosophy of Science*. New York: Free Press, 1965.

Kaplan, Abraham. *The Conduct of Inquiry*. San Francisco: Chandler, 1964.

Lasswell, Harold D. *Politics—Who Gets What, When, How*. New York: McGraw-Hill, 1936.

Lasswell, Harold D. *World Politics and Personal Insecurity*. New York: McGraw-Hill, 1935.

Lasswell, Harold D., and Abraham Kaplan. *Power and Society*. New Haven: Yale University Press, 1950.

Lipset, Seymour M. *Political Man: The Social Bases of Politics*. Garden City, N.Y.: Doubleday, 1960.

Machiavelli, Nicolo. *The Prince*. London: Oxford University Press, 1935.

Merton, Robert K. *Social Theory and Social Structure*. rev. ed. Glencoe, Ill.: Free Press, 1957.

Moore, Wilbert E. *Social Change*. Englewood Cliffs, N.J.: Prentice-Hall, 1963.

Moore, Wilbert E. "Predicting Discontinuities in Social Change." *American Sociological Review* 29 (June 1964), pp. 331–338.

Ogburn, William F. *Social Change*. New York: Viking, 1922.

Schumpeter, Joseph A. *Business Cycles*. McGraw-Hill, 1939.

Schumpeter, Joseph A. *Capitalism, Socialism and Democracy,* 3rd ed. New York: Harper and Row: 1950.

Sorokin, Pitirim A. *Social and Cultural Dynamics, Vol. 3: Fluctuation of Social Relationships, War, and Revolution*. New York: American Book, 1937.

Weber, Max. *Theory of Social and Economic Organization*. Glencoe, Ill.: Free Press, 1947.

WORKS ON POLITICAL STABILITY AND INSTABILITY

Brinton, Crane. *The Anatomy of Revolution*. New York: Vintage Books, 1960.

Dahrendorf, Ralf. *Class and Class Conflict in Industrial Society*. Stanford: Stanford University Press, 1959.

Dahrendorf, Ralf. "Toward a Theory of Social Conflict." *Journal of Conflict Resolution* 2 (June 1958): 170–83.

Gurr, Ted R., ed. *Handbook of Political Conflict*. New York: Free Press, 1980.

Gurr, Ted R. *Why Men Rebel*. Princeton, N.J.: Princeton University Press, 1970.

Gurr, Ted R. "A Causal Model of Civil Strife: A Comparative Analysis Using New Indices." *American Political Science Review* 62 (December 1968): 1104–24.

Huntington, Samuel P. *Political Order in Changing Societies*. New Haven: Yale University Press, 1968.

Huntington, Samuel P. "Political Development and Political Decay." *World Politics* 17 (1965): 386–430.

Johnson, Chalmers. *Revolutionary Change*. Boston: Little Brown, 1966.

Linz, Juan J., and Alfred Stepan, eds. *The Breakdown of Democratic Regimes*. Baltimore: Johns Hopkins University Press, 1978.

Skocpol, Theda. *States and Social Revolutions*. Cambridge: Cambridge University Press, 1979.

Skocpol, Theda. "Explaining Revolutions: In Quest of a Social-Structural Approach." In Lewis Coser and Otto N. Larsen, eds. *The Uses of Controversy in Sociology.* New York: Free Press, 1976, pp. 155–75.

Tilly, Charles. *From Mobilization to Revolution.* Reading, Mass.: Addison-Wesley, 1978.

WORKS ON THE STRENGTH AND COMPETENCE OF GOVERNMENTAL INSTITUTIONS

Deutsch, Karl. *The Nerves of Government.* New York: Free Press, 1966.

Fiedler, Fred E. *A Theory of Leadership Effectiveness* New York: McGraw Hill, 1967.

Gouldner, Alvin W. *The Future of Intellectuals and the Rise of the New Class.* New York: Seabury Press, 1979.

Hirschman, Albert O. *Journeys toward Progress.* New York: Twentieth Century Fund, 1963.

LaPalombara, Joseph, Ed. *Bureaucracy and Political Development.* Princeton, N.J. Princeton University Press, 1963.

McGregor, Douglas. *Leadership and Motivation.* Cambridge, Mass.: MIT Press, 1966.

Riggs, Fred W. *Administration in Developing Countries.* Boston: Houghton Mifflin, 1964.

Riggs, Fred. "Bureaucrats and Political Development A Paradoxical View." In Joseph LaPalombara, ed. *Bureaucracy and Political Development.* Princeton, N.J.: Princeton University Press, 1963, pp. 120–67.

Selznick, Philip. *Leadership in Administration: A Sociological Interpretation.* New York: Row Peterson, 1957.

WORKS ON THE THEORY AND METHODOLOGY OF FORECASTNG

Armstrong, J. Scott. *Long-Range Forecasting: From Crystal Ball to Computer.* New York: Wiley, 1978.

Ascher, William. *Forecasting: An Appraisal for Policymakers and Planners.* Baltimore: Johns Hopkins University Press, 1978.

Butler, William F., and Robert A. Kavish. *How Business Economists Forecast,* rev. ed. Englewood Cliffs, N.J.: Prentice-Hall, 1974.

Choucri, Nazli, and Thomas W. Robinson, eds. *Forecasting in Interna-*

tional Relations: Theory, Methods, Problems, Prospects. San Francisco: W. H. Freeman, 1978.

Duncan, Otis D. "Social Forecasting: The State of the Art." *The Public Interest,* no. 17 (Fall 1969): 88–118.

Kahn, Herman. "On Studying the Future." In Fred Greenstein and Nelson Polsby, eds. *Handbook of Political Science: Volume 7, Strategies of Inquiry.* Reading, Mass.: Addison-Wesley, 1975, pp. 405–42.

Klein, Lawrence. *An Essay on the Theory of Economic Prediction.* Helsinki: Jahnsson Lectures, 1968.

Klein, Lawrence, and Richard M. Young. *An Introduction to Econometric Forecasting and Forecasting Models.* Lexington, Mass.: D. C. Heath, 1980.

Kobrin, Stephen J. *Managing Political Risk Assessment: Strategic Response to Environmental Change* (Berkeley, Calif.: University of California Press, 1982).

Kobrin, Stephen J. "Political Risk: A Review and Reconsideration." *Journal of International Business Studies* (Spring 1979): 67–80.

Linstone, Harold A., and Murray Turoff, eds. *The Delphi Method: Techniques and Applications.* Reading, Mass.: Addison-Wesley, 1975.

Martino, Joseph. *Technological Forecasting for Decisionmaking.* New York: American Elsevier, 1972.

Overholt, William H. *Political Risk.* London: Euromoney Press, 1982.

WORKS OF APPLIED POLITICAL FORECASTING AND POLITICAL RISK ASSESSMENT

Bell, Daniel. *The Coming of Post-Industrial Society: A Venture in Social Forecasting* New York: Basic Books, 1973.

Bell, Daniel. *The Cultural Contradictions of Capitalism.* New York: Basic Books, 1976.

Bhagwati, Jagdish N., ed. *Economics and World Order: From the 1970s to the 1990s.* London: Macmillan, 1972.

Brown, Harrison. *The Challenge of Man's Future.* New York: Viking, 1954.

Brown, Harrison, James Bonner, and John Weir. *The Next Hundred Years.* New York: Viking, 1957.

Brzezinski, Zbigniew. *Between Two Ages: America's Role in the Technetronic Era.* New York: Viking Press, 1970.

De Jouvenal, Bertrand. *The Art of Conjecture*. New York: Basic Books, 1967.

Ewald, William, ed. *Environment and Policy: The Next 50 Years*. Bloomington, Ind.: Indiana University Press, 1968.

Falk, Richard A. *A Study of Future Worlds*. New York: Free Press, 1975.

Hellman, Donald, et al. *Forecast for Japan: Security in the 1970s*. Princeton, N.J.: Princeton University Press, 1972.

Hudson Institute. *1973 Synoptic Context on the Corporate Environment: 1975–1985,* five vols. Croton-on-Hudson, N.Y.: Hudson Institute, 1973.

Huntington, Samuel P, ed. *Changing Patterns of Military Politics*. Glencoe, Ill.: Free Press, 1962.

Jungk, Robert, and Johan Galtung, eds. *Mankind 2000*. London: Allen and Unwin, 1969.

Kahn, Herman. *The Emerging Japanese Superstate*. Englewood Cliffs, N.J.: Prentice-Hall, 1970.

Kahn, Herman. *On Thermonuclear War*. Princeton, N.J.: Princeton University Press, 1960.

Kahn, Herman. *World Economic Development: 1979 and Beyond*. New York: William Morrow, 1979.

Kahn, Herman, and Anthony Weiner, eds. *The Year 2000*. New York: Macmillan, 1967.

Koslow, Lawrence E., ed. *The Future of Mexico*. Tempe, Ariz.: Center for Latin Amercan Studies, 1977.

Lasswell, Harold D. "The Garrison State." *American Journal of Sociology* 46 (January 1941): 455–69.

Leontief, Wassily W., A. P. Carter, and P. Petri. *The Future of the World Economy: A United Nations Study,* New York: Oxford University Press, 1977.

McDougal, Myres, Harold Lasswell, and Ivan Vlasic. *Law and Public Order in Space*. New Haven: Yale University Press, 1963.

Meadows, Donnella, et al. *The Limits to Growth*. New York: Universe Books, 1972.

Mendlovitz, Saul H., ed. *On the Creation of a Just World Order: Preferred Worlds for the 1990s*. New York: Free Press, 1975.

Overholt, William H., ed. *Asia's Nuclear Future*. Boulder, Colo.: Westview Press, 1977.

Overholt, William H., ed. *The Future of Brazil*. Boulder, Colo.: Westview Press, 1978.

Perloff, Harvey, ed. *The Future of the U.S. Government: Toward the Year 2000*. New York: George Braziller, 1971.

The World Oil Market in the Years Ahead. Washington, D.C.: U.S. Central Intelligence Agency, National Foreign Assessment Center, 1979.

Index